Audio Error Codes

Beep Pattern	Device at Fault
No beep	Power supply
Unremitting beep	Power supply
Short, repetitive beeps	Power supply
Long beep, short beep	Motherboard
Long beep, two short beeps	Video
Long beep, three short beeps	Video
Two short beeps	Video
Short beep, long beep	Video
No beep	Speaker

D1277671

Technical Data for the Four Floppy-Disk Formats

	360K	720K	1.2Mb	1.4Mb
Disk Size	5¼″	3½″	5¼″	3½″
Tracks	80	160	160	160
Sectors	9	9	15	18
Tracks per Inch	48	135	96	135
Sides	2	2	2	2
Cylinders	40	80	80	80
Density	Double	Double	High	High
Total Bytes	368,640	737,280	1,228,800	1,474,560

Recommended Minimum Specifications for Maximum Performance

	PC/XT	PC/AT	386
RAM	640K	1Mb	1Mb
Memory Access Time	120 nanoseconds	100 nanoseconds	80 nanoseconds
Hard-Drive Capacity	20Mb	40Mb	40Mb
Hard-Disk Access Time	65 milliseconds	40 milliseconds	28 milliseconds
Power Supply	150 watts	200 watts	200 watts

The ABC's of Upgrading Your PC

The ABC's of Upgrading Your PC

Dan Gookin

San Francisco ■ Paris ■ Düsseldorf ■ Soest

Acquisitions Editor: Dianne King
Editors: Richard Mills, Vince Leone
Technical Editor: Michael Gross
Word Processors: Winnie Kelly, Scott Campbell, Lisa Mitchell, and Deborah Maizels
Book Designer: Suzanne Albertson
Chapter Art and Layout: Suzanne Albertson
Illustrations: Rick van Genderen
Technical Art: Delia Brown
Typesetter: Elizabeth Newman
Proofreader: M.D. Barrera
Indexer: Nancy Anderman Guenther
Cover Designer: Thomas Ingalls + Associates
Cover Photographer: Mark Johann

Library of Congress Card Number: 90-70567
ISBN: 0-89588-626-X
Manufactured in the United States of America
10 9 8 7 6 5 4 3 2

# *Acknowledgments*

BOOKS JUST DON'T HAPPEN OVERNIGHT. ALWAYS THERE, assisting in the effort to complete this tome, were the following folk: Dianne King, Vince Leone, and Richard Mills at Sybex; Art Grockmeister, who supplied his technical expertise; and Tina Berke, whom I still need to take out to lunch someday. Finally, thanks go to Waterside Productions and Bill Gladstone—*the* computer book agent.

Dan Gookin
July 1990

Contents
at a Glance

Table
of Contents

3   Getting to Know Your PC   27

13 Making Your PC Faster and More Efficient 263

 **Introduction**

THE PERSONAL COMPUTER IS THE MOST WONDERFUL tool ever invented, enabling you to express your creativity in ways never before possible. Whether you are using a word processor to write a letter or a spreadsheet to analyze the company budget, your PC's hardware and software work together to help meet your computing needs.

The pace of technology is relentless, and it's easy to get left behind. Most people are comfortable with upgrading their software: They read about a new program or a new version of a program they already own, buy the software, and install it. Maybe they also read a few books on how to use it and pick up a few tips from coworkers or a users' group.

Hardware, however, is a different story. Most people fear the inside of their computer. But they fail to realize how much more computing power and efficiency they can achieve by upgrading their hardware.

You can expand your system to add more memory, another hard drive, a larger-capacity floppy drive, a new monitor, or an internal modem. You can give your system a new microprocessor or add an accelerator card to turn your XT into an AT or a 286. The variety of upgrading options is almost endless. I know of no user who can sit down and say, "Well, there's nothing more I can add to my computer. It's perfect!"

The purpose of this book is to help you get comfortable with the idea of getting inside your computer's case and making changes. Along the way, you'll pick up a lot of useful information about how your computer works and what you can do to make it work better. You'll also have a lot of fun—and you don't have to have a PhD in electrical engineering to do it!

*W*ho You Are

This book was written for the average PC owner. You don't need a degree in computer science, nor do you have to understand Ohm's Law or know how to use a soldering gun. There are no technical readouts, data sheets, or lists of numbers comparing circuitry in different PCs. All you need to follow the upgrading procedures in this book are a few basic tools, patience, and the desire to do it yourself.

You should have a PC if you want to get the most out of this book. This includes any IBM or IBM-compatible computer system, from the original PC-1 through the latest, most expensive PC compatibles. This book does not cover other systems, such as the Apple Macintosh.

Your PC does not have to be broken for you to benefit from the information here. The subject is *upgrading,* not repair. Though troubleshooting and replacement of parts are covered, the emphasis is on improving your PC.

You should know the basics of DOS (this book will refer to specific versions when appropriate) and be comfortable with operating your computer. You should know, for example, how to use Control-Alt-Delete to reset your system and how to insert a disk in a drive and call up a directory. Nothing advanced. Just basic stuff.

*A*bout Your Hardware

There is no single, definitive type of PC. Though all PCs are based on IBM's original design for the PC/XT and later the AT, each computer is different. To deal with these differences, this book approaches the task of describing computer hardware by using the AT as a generic example. The components inside an AT are in the same general locations as they are in other computers. I describe variations in systems when appropriate.

This book assumes that you do not have a laptop PC, most of which are difficult to upgrade anyway. It also assumes that your system unit lies flat on your desk. If you have a tower model PC (which stands upright on the floor), you can use this book, but the location of components will be slightly different. I cover the configuration of tower PCs in Chapter 4.

Finally, you should know what kind of microprocessor your PC has. The microprocessor (sometimes called the CPU, for *central processing unit*) is your computer's brain and is commonly referred to by number: 8086, 8088, 80286, and so on. PCs are differentiated by the microprocessor they have:

PC/XT	Original IBM PC, PC/XT, or any system with an 8088, 8086, or equivalent microprocessor
PC/AT	Original IBM PC/AT or any system with an 80286 or equivalent microprocessor
386	Any IBM-compatible 80386 system
486	Any IBM-compatible 80486 system

Note that a 386 is not an AT and should never be treated as one (though they come in similar cases). In this book, the terms *clone, compatible,* and *PC* are all used interchangeably. Any computer that is compatible with IBM and uses DOS is considered a PC.

How This Book Is Structured

You should read the first four chapters of this book before you begin upgrading your PC. Chapter 1 gives you reasons for doing upgrades yourself, and Chapter 2 tells you the tools and equipment you'll need to get started. In Chapters 3 and 4, you learn everything you need to know about the components of your PC—what they do and where they are located.

Chapters 5 and 6 cover one of the most useful upgrades you can do, adding memory to give your PC more RAM. Chapter 5 talks about the subject from a software perspective, while Chapter 6 plunges into the actual physical installation of chips.

In Chapters 7 and 8, you learn how to upgrade your floppy-disk and hard-disk drives, to give your PC more storage capacity and to increase your computing speed.

Chapter 9 covers the removal and installation of expansion cards, an upgrade that enables you to add all sorts of options to your PC, including a modem and a mouse.

Chapter 10 covers the replacement of the power supply and includes some basic information on electricity.

Chapters 11 and 12 take you outside the system unit and discuss the different kinds of monitors and printers that are available.

Chapter 13 covers specific upgrades you can do to make your PC faster and more efficient, and Chapter 14 gives you some troubleshooting and maintenance tips.

Generally speaking, the material in this book doesn't need to be read from cover to cover. Only Chapters 1–4 should be read right away. Then feel free to refer to those chapters covering the upgrades you want to do. The bottom line is getting to know your PC's hardware better. Even if you plan on never opening your computer's case, you'll know more about your hardware by reading this book, and from that knowledge, you'll be a better PC user.

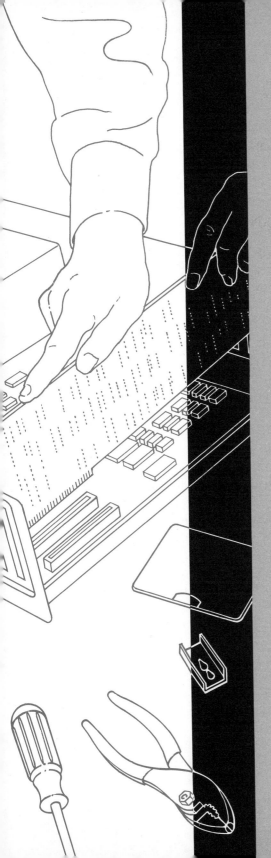

1

Do It
Yourself

A SMALL NUMBER OF PC OWNERS NATURALLY WANT TO mess with the guts of their PCs—they don't need to be persuaded. But most people need a reason to open up a computer, add a component, or make an upgrade.

This chapter's purpose is to give you reasons for upgrading your PC by yourself. It includes some comforting words and careful explanations of what's required to work on computer hardware.

I'd be kidding you if I said this is child's play—we're dealing with a complex piece of hardware. But upgrades can be done by just about anyone. There's nothing hard about it at all. "Be careful" is about the only rule you need to remember.

Why You Should Upgrade by Yourself

Why upgrade by yourself? Because you can.

Millions of people monkey with their cars every day. They have no degree in Automobilology, no years of apprenticeship, no authority from Detroit (more likely Japan) to do so. So why do they mess with their cars? Because they can.

Your computer can be monkeyed with in the same manner as a car. Sure, with any electronic appliance, your natural tendency is not to mess with it. Electricity is scary! But hey, cars are loud and smell bad. And consider this: You won't get greasy working on a computer.

As in working on a car, you save yourself time and money by working on a computer. Suppose your power supply blows up. Don't worry—it's built so it won't take the rest of the machine with it. You just yank out the old one and replace it with one that works. If you know how to do it, it costs you maybe $75 and only an hour of downtime. Compare that with three days in the shop plus labor.

And computers are easier to work on than cars. There's nothing heavy, no jacks or special tools are required, and most of the PC's parts are cheap and widely available. There is nothing preventing you from opening up your PC and upgrading it yourself. You don't need specialized tools, and the case isn't sealed with epoxy. The whole computer is designed to be a user-serviceable unit.

Hardware parts are generally sold off the shelf. Instructions are even available, which sometimes describe the installation in very simple terms. Manufacturers wouldn't provide instructions if you couldn't upgrade the PC yourself.

Here are some reasons for upgrading your computer by yourself:

You Overcome Your Fears

Being scared of the computer is a common phobia. But PCs aren't intimidating. Certainly, the technology inside the PC is as advanced as technology gets. But it isn't forbidden knowledge, and it isn't anything dangerous to you as long as you're careful and take precautions.

The fear of electricity or that you'll screw something up is probably the biggest fear you have when you consider upgrading by yourself. But this is easily overcome by practice. Keep in mind that even the experts screw up occasionally. And the PC is robust—it takes some deliberate action to really foul up the hardware.

You Get to Know More About Your PC

Quite a lot of people are fluent in DOS. They're even experts with certain pieces of software. They know all the commands and tricks to get work done effortlessly. That's the payoff for knowing PC software. But what about the hardware? If you know the potential of your PC hardware, then you are better able to match that potential with the software to exploit it.

Getting to know your PC involves getting some hardware knowledge. Fortunately, it doesn't involve knowing circuitry, ports, or technical data. It does involve knowing whether a problem is located in a RAM chip or a disk drive and the consequences of adding memory to your system. And it's about being able to upgrade your system without taking your computer into the shop. Hardware knowledge helps make you a better PC owner and user. It will also make you a more valued employee, which is something to think of come raise time.

Your PC Is Modular in Nature

The original PC was designed using mostly off-the-shelf parts. One component snaps onto or plugs, slides, or screws into another.

There may be a few connectors to check, but other than that, all the innards of a PC are parts you can install, remove, or replace with relative ease.

The PC is not one integrated unit; it is built with modular parts. This allows you to plug in or swap certain items without putting your entire system at risk. And your mechanical skills can be limited to simple Tinker Toy or Erector Set skills.

No Change You Make Is Permanent

Because you aren't soldering or threading wires, any change you make to your PC can be undone. In fact, that's the basic idea underlying the PC's modular design: Create your own system. If you don't like your changes, you can change back. In fact, in the end you'll probably have a closet full of old drives and hardware—almost enough to build another computer.

So breathe easy. I once installed a memory board in my first PC that proved to be incompatible. I just unplugged it and took it back for a full refund.

You Save Money and Time

When you decide to upgrade your PC, you have two choices: You can do it yourself, or you can have someone else do it.

When you have someone else work on your PC, there are two negatives. First, they do it on their time. They come over to fix it at your home or office when it's convenient for them. Until that happens, your computer sits there and does nothing but waste your time. If you take it to a shop, this wastes even more time, because a shop will take from one to several days to work on your computer, and you have to figure in your own transportation costs and time as well.

The second drawback to having someone else upgrade your system is that it costs money. Sure, sometimes you can have a knowledgeable friend install your new floppy drive for free. But most of the time, repair people are going to charge you. At the shop, they'll charge you labor plus a hiked-up price on the floppy drive. Why should you pay someone else to install it when the skills required to install it yourself aren't anything great?

It doesn't take a magic potion to understand how to upgrade your system. This book gives you all you need: friendly, step-by-step instructions. Sometimes even the manual will tell you how. But it's not really worth paying someone else to do it, while losing productivity in the meantime.

Reasons You May Have for Not Doing It Yourself

Along with all the nice, comforting reasons why it's beneficial to upgrade a computer yourself, there are reasons you may have for not wanting to do it yourself. Your computer is a scary thing. You rely on it. It costs a lot of money. So why bother when professionals will do the upgrade for you, with no risk to your personal safety and little risk to your computer? Here are some fears you may have and why they're unfounded.

You Might Get Hurt

Rest assured, you're insulated fairly well from anything dangerous when you're working inside your PC. And this book shows you how to venture inside that territory with little risk to life and limb. As long as you take the necessary precautions, you should never have any problems.

Of course, if your fears are too great, then maybe upgrading by yourself is not for you. I'm not trying to sell computer equipment or tools. However, if you have the desire to do it yourself, there's no sense in not moving ahead.

You Might Mess Something Up

There's really little you can do to physically damage your computer. The PC's modular design means that most of the pieces inside your computer box function independently of one another. They rely on each other, but if one part is missing, that won't cause other parts to blow up.

For example, suppose you forget to plug in your hard drive after you install it. The rest of the computer will probably work—you just won't have access to the hard drive. Or suppose a new hard drive slides off the table into your lap. Chances are pretty good it will survive. (But being careful to prevent these types of accidents is the best policy.)

Computer components are quite delicate. The electronic information in a computer chip is highly susceptible to static electricity. If you've ever been shocked by touching a doorknob or by shaking hands with someone after crossing a carpeted room, you should know that static can instantly kill a chip.

And remember, if you ever do mess something up, you can always take your computer to your local repair outlet. But chances are you'll never need to.

Your Computer Is Still Under Warranty

Most computers are sold with a 90-day warranty. This means that if the computer or any of its parts fail within that period, you can send it back to the shop for repairs—for free.

Electronic components do fail sometimes. When they do, chances are they will fail sometime within the first 48 hours of use. Other components (particularly mechanical ones, such as your disk drives) will usually fail within the first two weeks of use. After that, most components will probably run happily for two to six years, depending on how much you use your computer.

So if you really want to test the warranty, leave your system turned on for the first two weeks you own it. Turn the computer off and on once a day to test the power supply. Also, turn off the monitor when you're not using it (this helps prevent phosphor burn-in). After two weeks, you'll know whether the PC is likely to fail.

The 90-day warranty shouldn't prevent you from opening the case and installing your own components. But if you're concerned about the warranty, wait it out and do your upgrades after the warranty has expired.

Also, you may feel more comfortable with a dealer-installed upgrade because of the dealer's installation warranty. But this is really a feeble excuse. Most hardware add-ons come with warranties of their own, which are sometimes good for up to five years. There's no reason not to install a new component yourself and take advantage of the manufacturer's warranty by sending in your hardware registration card.

You Think You Can't Do It

This is the biggest, and most unsubstantial, reason for not doing upgrades yourself: You just can't do it.

The belief some people have that they can't do it themselves comes from a lack of knowledge—not about hardware matters but about how absolutely easy and painless upgrading your PC can be. Others may reason that God and Thomas Edison just don't want plain folk thumbing around inside a PC's case. If that were really true, the thing would be sealed with rivets instead of common screws. And spare parts and upgrades wouldn't be sold off the rack or through the mail. The PC would have been designed as an integral unit, without slots or snaps for easily replacing individual items.

Things to Look Out For

Upgrading your PC's hardware is easy and fun. This subject can be discussed lightly (and it should be, because it's not that hard), but it also has some serious aspects.

Before you get all gung ho and ready to go and before you ever pick up a screwdriver, keep the following items in mind:

Unplug Everything Before You Start

If you touch something "live" while working on your computer, you can get hurt. Or you can hurt the system by doing so. Or you could kill yourself.

Fortunately, you are well protected from most of the dangerous stuff. The biggest threat comes from your PC's power supply, which is encased in a sealed unit. Your monitor also carries a lot of voltage, but this book doesn't require you to take apart your monitor.

The best way to avoid getting shocked is to unplug your system before you work on it. Because the plug on a PC can be removed from both the computer and the wall, I recommend you unplug it from both ends before you start. (Also, you should turn off the computer before you unplug it.)

Note that you can run your PC with the cover off, and at times I will recommend you do so. But don't work on it with the cover off and the power on. In fact, doing so will damage your system.

Beware of Static!

The second half of the electrical enemy is static. Although your system could jolt you if you're not careful, you can jolt the system if you build up static electricity and touch something you're not supposed to. This especially applies to RAM chips. If you're plugging in a RAM chip and build up some static, ZAP!, there goes the RAM chip.

But you can prevent the buildup of static. As long as you hold still (especially your feet), touch some metal to keep grounded, or wear a grounded wrist-strap, you don't need to worry about static.

Watch Out for Really Cheap Stuff

Once you get going, you may find that the urge to add new goodies to your computer is irresistible. Especially with the proliferation of mail-order warehouses, you may want to send away for cheap and powerful equipment to install in your PC. But caveat emptor.

Most mail-order outfits will suit you fine: They offer reliable products, speedy delivery, and low prices—perfect for a hardware upgrade. But some "deals" may turn out to be rotten.

Look out especially for a large quantity of seemingly bargain stuff being sold at an electronics swap meet. The bozos selling this stuff usually pick up the dead inventory from original equipment manufacturers. It's typically second-rate or used crap that doesn't come with a warranty—and you can bet the guy who sold it to you won't be there next week if he did offer you some type of "warranty."

If It Works, Don't Fix It

A few self-made hardware upgraders get the fix-everything disease. Once they conquer the interior of the PC, they're always in there. One guy I know even keeps the case off his PC so he can switch monitor cards more easily.

The rule "If it ain't broke, don't fix it" applies to all computer hardware. If you need a bigger hard drive, add one. If you want a 3 1/2-inch disk drive that is compatible with your laptop, add one. But some other kinds of upgrades may only complicate life for you. If you don't need it, don't buy it.

And avoid the urge to tinker. Keep the case on the PC, where it belongs. If you want to see the insides, read a book that tells you how to make a plexiglass case for your PC.

Keep a Rein on Yourself

Don't go nuts! Since the PC is modular in design, this stuff is all going to be quite easy for you. After a while, you won't give a second thought to opening up your PC's case. But be serious when you do so. This stuff is money!

Never smoke around a PC. Minute particles of smoke can eventually make their way into the sealed environment of the hard drive and cause a lot of damage.

While not as bad as smoking, computing and drinking can also be hazardous. (Drinking any liquid beverage, by the way.) As I write this, I have a bottle of sparkling mineral water by my keyboard. A swipe of the hand to answer the phone could send it tumbling, glup, glup, glupping into the keyboard.

Putting a beverage by your keyboard is OK if you're careful. If it spills, shut down the computer and wait for the keyboard to dry out. As long as the drink isn't sugary-sticky, the computer and keyboard should work again in a few hours. But worse than that is drinking while working *inside* the computer. Under no circumstances should you have liquid or food next to an open PC.

◢◣ Summary

The primary reason for doing a hardware upgrade yourself is because you can. The PC is modular in design, so upgrading it is a snap. But beyond that, you need to convince yourself that doing it is worthwhile and will save you time and money.

There are also some good reasons for not doing an upgrade yourself. The most important is that you really don't know how. This book will help you learn how to do it and conquer any fears you may have about venturing into the hardware of your PC.

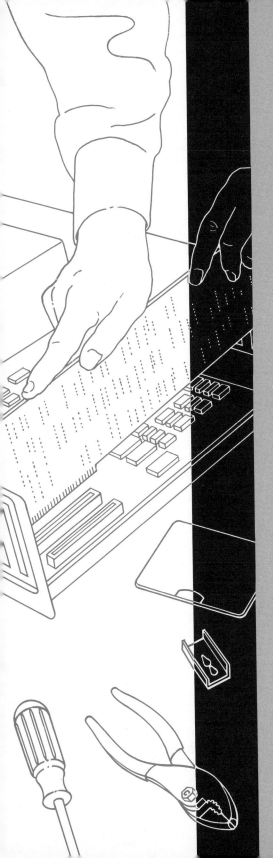

2

Handling Tools and Equipment

COMPUTERS USE A VERY SIMPLE ASSEMBLY TECHNOLOGY. It can be compared to an Erector Set, but it's really not even that complex—it's more like Tinker Toys. Most parts slide or snap into place, anchored by tiny screws. It's all part of the PC's modular design, and it allows common people like you and me to easily upgrade our systems. There are no secrets; everything's fairly straightforward.

This chapter deals with two subjects: the tools you need to work on your PC and the supplies you'll use for your upgrades. You need the tools to open your case and assist in your minor PC surgery. The supplies give you the reason for needing the tools; they're the things you're going to install into your PC. These two subjects are handled in six sections:

- Tools to buy
- Tools to avoid
- Working tips
- Locating equipment
- Handling computer components
- Helpful advice

You may already have most of the tools mentioned in this chapter. Only a few of the more esoteric ones will you need to rush out and buy, and then only if you want to increase the weight of your tool chest.

 ## Tools to Buy

When you buy a new car, you often get a little package of tools. You get a screwdriver plus a wrenchlike thing and maybe a cheap set of pliers. If you look in the trunk, you may also find some kind of flimsy jack and a lug wrench.

Computers are usually put together with screws. That's about it. All the major components can be taken apart piece by piece. They're built this way to make them easy to assemble, repair, and upgrade. But you don't get any tools with the computer. Why not?

With the early Apple II, you didn't need any tools. The lid just popped off. You could add expansion cards, remove the power supply, or unhook the keyboard without unscrewing anything.

The Radio Shack TRS-80 didn't have any upgradeable parts inside—but that didn't stop third parties from making those parts or people from opening the computer's sealed case. Tandy even put a warranty sticker over a key screw hole. If you ripped off the sticker, you voided your Radio Shack warranty.

But there were lots of upgrade options for the old TRS-80. I added my own serial port, saving fifty bucks off Radio Shack's version. Once I realized it wasn't any big deal, I also upgraded memory and changed the monitor.

But the PC was made to be messed with. You just need the will to do it yourself—plus some tools.

There are several categories of tools you can draw from. The basic category includes "must-have" tools. But beyond these, you can add tools and supplies to build up your own private tool pouch—or you can even buy a premade tool pouch from companies that offer them.

Must-Have Tools

The basic tool you need to work on your PC is a screwdriver. They come in various makes, models, and sizes. The two models you need for your PC are a Phillips-head screwdriver and a flathead screwdriver, each in two sizes. (These screwdrivers are shown in Figure 2.1.)

A Tiny Flathead Screwdriver   A tiny flathead screwdriver (with a blade between $1/8''$ and $3/16''$ wide) is excellent for those tiny screws that anchor computer cables.

A Small Phillips Screwdriver   A small Phillips screwdriver will probably be your weapon of choice when you work on your PC. Most of the internal screws are of the Phillips variety, too small for the medium-size screwdriver.

A Medium-Size Phillips Screwdriver   A good 90 percent of computer cases are sealed with Phillips-type screws. So if you ever expect to get in the case, you're going to need a good medium-size Phillips screwdriver.

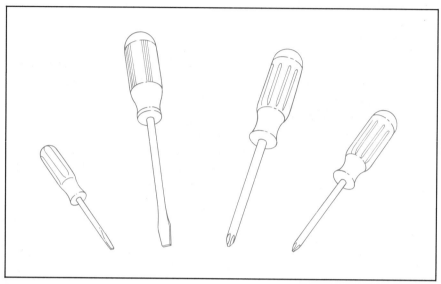

Figure 2.1: The essential tools

A Medium-Size Flathead Screwdriver

This is one of those "just in case" tools. It's a good idea to keep a medium-size flathead screwdriver around should you encounter any medium-size flathead screws.

That rounds out the basic tool set. If you're lucky, you may find your PC uses only one type of screw and you can get by with one screwdriver. But having enough of the proper tools around can never be a problem. And if you have to buy one or more of these screwdrivers, do yourself a favor and get some top-quality tools. Sears's Craftsman line is about the best you can buy.

Tools That Are Good to Have

There are tools that you may need for special occasions. None of these are really required to upgrade your PC, but they're invaluable to have around for general purposes.

A Tiny Phillips Screwdriver

Once in a blue moon you may encounter some peripheral or installable item that has a tiny Phillips screw in it. Or maybe your small-size Phillips screwdriver is just too big for the screw.

A Medium Phillips Screwdriver with a Long Handle   Occasionally you may find a Phillips screw residing in some deep cavern inside your PC. The early Tandy 1000s had a screw way inside the disk-drive bays. The only way to get at it was through the side of the computer, about ten inches into the center of things. Only a long-handled Phillips screwdriver could do the job.

Needle-Nose Pliers   You may find yourself using needle-nose pliers a lot in the PC. Because computer components are small and human fingers are relatively fat and awkward, you may need some needle-nose pliers to get down into places where no finger has gone before.

Needle-nose pliers also come in handy for changing jumpers, as well as for rescuing screws that fall down into the electronic under-growth on your motherboard.

A Bent Paper Clip   This may seem like a silly "tool," but the bent paper clip is in just about every PC hardware hacker's tool kit. It comes in handy for setting DIP switches, which are often too tiny to set with a finger or screwdriver.

Other Tools

Finally, there are other tools you may want to collect, some really specific to certain tasks, but nonetheless useful when you upgrade your PC. (See Figure 2.2.) Take your pick of what you feel you need. You're better off with them in the long run. They make the upgrading life more bearable. But if you're short on funds or live thousands of miles from the nearest Electronics Hut, then you're still in good shape.

Chip Puller   A chip puller is a specialized set of pliers designed to reach around the ends of a computer chip. It enables you to safely lift the chip out of its socket without bending any of its little legs. (Some enterprising hackers use a screwdriver to wedge the chip out. Ugh.)

There are some expensive chip pullers on the market; you'll usually get a cheap set when you buy chips to install yourself. But if you're going to be doing a lot of chip yanking, it's a wise idea to buy a good chip puller.

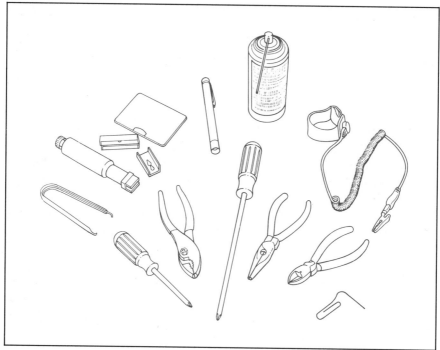

Figure 2.2: Optional tools

Chip Inserter   The opposite of the chip puller is the chip inserter. Most people insert chips simply by lining up the chip's legs with the socket's holes and then pressing firmly with their fingers. But specialized chip inserters are available to make the job easier.

Computer chips are similar to Lego blocks in the way they plug into sockets. It's possible to do it by hand (and most people do), but it isn't foolproof. A chip inserter almost guarantees the chip will be installed without any bent or broken legs.

Penlight   There's a lot of empty space in some PCs, but others are crammed full of add-in parts and tangled cables. Sometimes it's really hard to see the bottom of the case—which you'll have to examine if you're setting DIP switches or reading the serial number. A penlight comes in very handy to illuminate those deep, dark crevasses.

Small Mirror   A companion to the penlight is the small, hand-held mirror. Sometimes serial numbers and tiny toggle switches are hidden behind printers and PCs. The only way to see them (without rearranging the office) is to use a small mirror.

Can of O₂ O_2 is oxygen, and several companies make a living selling cans of compressed air. You use the air to clean dust and debris that accumulate inside your computer—and especially in your printer. (It's much safer than blowing; the can doesn't run out of air so quickly and there's no spit intermixed.)

Grounding Wrist-Strap   The purpose of a grounding strap is to absolutely guarantee that you won't produce any static electricity while working on your computer. There are other ways to avoid static, but the wrist-strap is virtually foolproof. One end of the wrist-strap goes around your wrist. The other end is anchored to the grounding plug on a wall socket or some other electrically grounded object.

Sticky Labels   Finally, you may want to have a sheet of sticky labels handy while you work on the PC. You can use them as you're disassembling the computer to label any cables you disconnect. On one end of a cable you can put a sticky label ''A.'' On the cable's socket you can put another ''A.'' On another cable and socket you can put a ''B'' label, and so on.

The sticky labels help some people to remember which cables are plugged into which sockets. This book is specific about where and how cables are plugged in, so sticky labels aren't required. But if you think you may need them, then buy a sheet just in case.

The Most Important Tool

The most important tool you can have, which is almost invaluable when you work on a PC, is patience. Don't be in a hurry. Don't rush things. Relax. Give yourself plenty of time to do the upgrade. Patience is a valuable tool when working on anything, but it really comes in handy when you upgrade your PC.

Some people may naturally take to the hardware. Others may find it confusing and become quickly frustrated. The best way to prevent that is to have patience.

Tools You Should Avoid

There are some tools you definitely won't need to work on your PC. A lot of tool kits will include some of these weird tools, and some salespeople may try to sell you some. Anything aside from the tools I've already mentioned should be looked upon with some question. But there are two tools you should definitely avoid:

A Magnetized Screwdriver   The magnetized screwdriver is really a boon to mankind. Its magnetized head will hold a screw in place as you line up screwdriver, screw, and hole. And if you're clumsy and drop the screw, you can touch it with the magnetized screwdriver to quickly pick it up.

So why should you avoid them?

Although it's perfectly safe to use a magnetized screwdriver on a PC, the magnetic field generated by the screwdriver—no matter how slight—could affect your floppy disks. Do you have a floppy disk lying around by your computer? All you have to do is set the magnetic screwdriver on it and—poof!—the data are gone.

Head-Cleaning Disks   Some people just love to play computer doctor. One way they do so is by purchasing a head-cleaning disk, squirting it with cleaning fluid, and then shoving it into an innocent disk drive.

Head-cleaning disks remove iron oxide from your drive heads. In a few cases, a cleaning will bring a dead drive right back to life. But most of the time people use these disks like voodoo, expecting that they will cure any number of disk-drive ills, none of which are related to magnetic oxide buildup on the drive head.

Head-cleaning disks are abrasive. The best advice I can give is not to use them or to use them no more than once a year. If you're having serious drive problems, the way to fix the drive is not to keep jamming a head-cleaning disk in there; use discretion.

Working Tips

It would be really silly for me to explain how to use a screwdriver, though I'm sure a small portion of first-time hardware upgraders may benefit. Just remember these rules:

- To tighten a screw, turn it clockwise.
- To loosen a screw, turn it counterclockwise.

You should also follow these two rules:

- Work in a well-lit area.
- Give yourself lots of desk space.

Most people compute in caves. They dim the lights, or turn them off, and close the windows—assuming they have windows. This is not the type of environment you want to be in when you work on your PC. Even a penlight isn't going to help you if it's too dark to see.

You need about three times the amount of desk space your computer occupies to successfully work on it. No matter how big a table you have for your computer, you'll never find room. There will always be stacks of papers, open books, magazines, and disks lying around. If you're going to work on your PC, you're going to have to clean things up first. Once you get the lid off and set a few things aside, you'll quickly be out of room. And never work on a PC on the floor.

Locating Equipment

Once you have the tools in hand, you need something on which to use them. You have your PC, and you could go ahead and take it all apart and put it back together. But that isn't upgrading. So eventually you're going to have to hunt down those parts you want to add to your PC.

Where to Find Equipment

There are lots of places to find the equipment necessary to upgrade your computer. Before going hunting, though, you should know what it is you're hunting for. Although this section does cover the different options you have for locating equipment, you really need to know what it is you need before you set out to buy it.

Once you do know what equipment you want, you can get it from the original equipment manufacturer or a local dealer, order it through the mail, or buy used parts. There are advantages and disadvantages to each of these options. After you've done a few upgrades, you will probably develop your own preference.

Original Equipment Manufacturers

The original equipment manufacturer, or OEM, is the original source of whatever upgrade part you're buying. After all, your computer dealer doesn't make his own hard drives; he buys them from Seagate or Maynard or any of a number of manufacturers who build the equipment themselves.

There are many advantages when you buy parts from an OEM. Since the OEM makes the equipment, you avoid any dealer markup. But they usually sell at a volume discount only to dealers, so the price issue is moot. But you do get the real thing when you buy from an OEM. You get their warranty and often their direct support.

OEMs don't usually sell items to individual users. (OK, if you buy 100 pieces of equipment, then they may sell to you. But for one power supply or one memory board, forget it.)

Local Dealers

Local dealers are often the most reliable source of computer parts. Some dealers are part of national computer-store chains, some are locally owned and operated outfits, and others are electronics warehouses.

The primary advantage of going to a local dealer is that the dealer is local. The store's right in town, close enough to drive to or to call without running up a phone bill. Also, if you are fortunate enough to live in a town with a lot of local dealers, you can hunt for bargains. Competition can be fierce in some markets, allowing you to make some nice deals on equipment. And if you're just starting out, a local dealer is there to hold your hand and help you if needed.

There are only two disadvantages to a local dealer as your computer equipment source. First, it's not the cheapest option. The dealer has to pay employees, local taxes, and overhead to keep the store open. This cost is added to your hardware upgrade (but it's often returned in the form of personal service and support). Second, dealers, especially those that are part of national chains, would much rather install the equipment themselves. In fact, some chains include the installation cost in the purchase price. When that happens, you might as well have them do it because you're already paying them to.

Mail Order

Ordering through the mail used to be the creepy, seedy way to get computer parts. But recently, mail order has become a sophisticated business, often offering speedy overnight delivery of computer software and hardware. The companies are, for the most part, reliable. They usually have knowledgeable sales staffs and support lines if you need technical help. (One outfit will even reimburse you for DOA equipment, refunding your cost for shipping the equipment.)

The main advantage of mail order is that it's the cheapest way to buy computer equipment. Because there's no showroom overhead, the cost and savings are passed on to you. Many mail-order houses offer full warranties on what they sell; some even add their own warranty extensions. And you get a full refund (maybe minus a restocking fee) if you're dissatisfied. Mail order is the best way to go if you know exactly what you want.

There are few disadvantages to mail order, if you know exactly what you want before ordering. You can't, however, pick up, examine, or test equipment, or read the labels on something in a catalog. So if you're unsure about what you need, try a local dealer.

Another disadvantage of mail order is that you have to rely on the mail system, which can be slow and sloppy. Also, the distance involved makes shipping things back for repair a nightmare (when you compare it to throwing a dead part in your trunk and driving across town to get another one). Also, keep in mind that the mail-order warehouse's service and support is long-distance. The ordering line may be toll-free, but support usually will cost you. (Usually only mail-order companies that make the parts they sell offer technical support.)

Used Parts

One option that may be tempting, especially if you're a beginner, is buying used equipment, or worse, going to an electronics swap meet. These are the worst ways to get started with upgrading your PC's hardware. It's just too risky.

The advantage of buying used equipment is that it's cheap. You may be able to pick up a used or refurbished piece of hardware for less than a tenth of what it costs new. And remember that older equipment, though still fully functional, is often discarded by major businesses and OEMs just so they can buy new stuff. There are some real bargains out there.

But the disadvantages of buying used or questionable equipment outweigh the advantages. You have no idea where the part came from, you don't know if it's compatible with your system, and you get no warranty. Even if Electric Earl seems like a nice guy and says you can return the hard drive at next week's swap meet, don't count on it. There are a lot of vultures who prey upon unsuspecting PC owners.

Types of Equipment to Look For

There are subtle differences between the makes and models of PCs. You should be aware of these differences when hunting down parts for your PC.

The major difference is between the design of the original IBM PC/XT and the AT. When buying hardware, you must know which type you have and which type of hardware you need for it.

For example, PC/XTs and ATs use different types of hard drives. (In the past this was very common, but recently many hard drives are compatible with both systems.) If you buy a hard drive, make sure you get the right one for your system.

The PC/XT also has an 8-bit expansion slot. The AT and 386 systems use a 16-bit expansion slot. Although you can plug an 8-bit card into a 16-bit slot, most 16-bit cards will not plug into the PC/XT's 8-bit slots. The exceptions are some memory boards and all video adapters. But be careful: Only get the type of expansion card that goes with your system.

Handling Computer Components

Aside from the physical aspect of what plugs into what, there are certain precautions you should take when you handle computer components, especially those that are electronic, such as circuitry boards and expansion cards. Most of the parts are fairly robust and well made, but if you've never done this sort of thing before, it helps to keep the following points in mind when you handle computer components.

Handle Circuitry by the Edge   When you pick up an expansion card or any type of circuitry, handle it by the edge. You never hold circuitry like a sandwich; it's just too risky. You might snap or break something or, if you generate any static, short something out.

Don't Force Anything   Don't force anything into the computer. Everything should fit snug and tight without any extra effort on your part. Computer equipment can take a surprising amount of punishment—but always be gentle and careful.

Ground Yourself   To prevent discharging any static onto computer components, you should ground yourself. You do this by keeping still and occasionally touching metal while you're working. You can also purchase and wear a wrist-strap to be absolutely safe. If you don't have one, you can reach over and touch the power supply to drain any static you may have acquired. Some computer peripherals, keyboards, mouse pads, and power units also have a "Touch Me" grounding button on them. Touching that occasionally or keeping one finger on it most of the time should suffice.

"No User-Serviceable Parts Inside" Means What It Says   Avoid the temptation to open up and fix something you weren't meant to open up and fix. The most dangerous components inside a PC are in the power supply—and that's in a sealed metal case. Don't try to open it.

Computer monitors also store a lot of voltage, sometimes up to 10,000 volts, which can enter your body through your thumbnail. Monitors are for professionals to fix. For your personal hardware upgrading, you can buy a monitor and install its graphic adapter card in your PC, but you don't need to venture inside the monitor.

Finally, though they're not as dangerous as the innards of your power supply or monitor, all hard disks come in a sealed hard-drive unit. There is nothing you can do inside there, so there is no reason to open it up.

◢ *Helpful Advice*

Here are some general words of advice to help you use your tools and parts to successfully upgrade your computer.

Know What You're Going to Do Before You Do It   Just setting out to install a memory board isn't enough. You need to know what type of memory your PC requires, how much memory your software needs to function, where you're going to put the memory board, where you're going to buy it, and how you're going to install it.

Do Only One Upgrade at a Time   You should develop a strategy. For example, install your memory first. Then, without putting on the case, start the computer and make sure everything works. Once you're certain the memory upgrade was successful, turn off and unplug the machine to proceed with the hard-drive upgrade.

Keep a Bookshelf   You should have a computer bookshelf near your PC. In the office, you should have a separate computer library or file cabinet. In it you can store all the manuals and documents for your computer and peripherals. Keep everything organized for reference purposes.

I know, some users like to call their manuals "useless." But they've never upgraded hardware before. Even if the manual is a word-for-word translation of Taiwanese, it still contains useful information you probably can't get anywhere else. (Ever try calling Taiwan?)

Keep All Your Old Boxes   If you ever have a problem with your hardware, send it back to the supplier in the original box. Dealers and OEMs like that. And it's a good way to store the equipment if you ever remove it or upgrade to something else. And if you move, using the boxes is the best way to pack the computer and all its components.

Have Fun!   It's the bottom line. While upgrading will save you time and money and help you to learn more about your computer system, you'll also be having fun. So set out with that in mind. Relax and enjoy yourself!

◣ Summary

This chapter covered the tools and supplies you'll need to begin upgrading your PC. Probably the only tool you'll need to work on your PC is a Phillips screwdriver. But beyond that, there's a whole chest full of helpful tools you can buy to make upgrading and repairing your PC easier.

There are a few places you can locate supplies. The best is a mail-order warehouse, though that's usually a better option if you've been doing upgrades for a while and know exactly what you want. Better still are the original equipment manufacturers themselves—if you can get them to sell you their stuff.

Finally, this chapter closed with advice on handling computer components and some general tips. Now you have no reason to feel intimidated by the process of upgrading your computer.

3

Getting
to Know
Your PC

BEFORE YOU GET TO WORK UPGRADING YOUR PC, IT WILL be helpful to know a little about its history, its basic components, and how it works.

The PC's History

During the early '70s, when the microprocessor was invented, the microcomputer was a curiosity in computer science classes, a cure for specific engineering problems, a source of projects for college students, and a pastime for thousands of hobbyists.

Slowly, more and more businesses began to use microcomputers, especially computers that used an operating system called CP/M. These systems used software that appealed to small businesses: word processing, accounting and finance, and databases for managing inventory and customer lists.

The Apple II computer, also available at the time, was the favorite among computer hobbyists. Although it lacked the business software base of the CP/M microcomputers, it had a lot of potential, thanks to its internal *expansion slots.* Into these slots the user could plug a variety of interesting devices—including a CP/M computer option, allowing use of CP/M business software.

The Apple II's capability to be expanded via expansion slots is called *open architecture.* It had a modular, upgradeable design. Users could configure the machines according to their personal preferences by plugging special options into the expansion slots. Apple also published a wealth of information about the Apple II, enabling third-party hardware manufacturers to come up with a plethora of expansion cards and adapters. Open architecture made the Apple II a flexible and potentially powerful computer system.

Eventually, a spreadsheet program called VisiCalc came out for the Apple II (VisiCalc stands for ''visible calculator''). When VisiCalc appeared, small businesses began to notice the advantage of the microcomputer—the spreadsheet offered everyone access to the microcomputer's computational power. This excited a lot of business owners, who could now automate lots of their business without paying a lot or making a major investment in minicomputer hardware.

This was about the time IBM started to notice the personal computer. IBM imagined a future where businesses didn't have one central computer with the three letters I-B-M on it. They saw a future where each person in the office would have a small microcomputer on their desk. To ensure that those microcomputers would have the letters I-B-M on them, IBM set out to make their own microcomputer.

IBM played it really smart. Rather than develop their microcomputer in-house, with all the bureaucracy and paperwork, they set up a small, semi-entrepreneurial group of engineers and team leaders in Boca Raton, Florida. The group was ordered to come up with a personal computer in less than a year.

In the new design, IBM borrowed open architecture from the Apple II. IBM created the PC with more or less off-the-shelf parts, adopting a a modular design (which is why we can upgrade our PCs ourselves today). IBM also published lots of documentation about the new PC. Hardware specs were made available to allow third parties to design expansion cards for the PC's Apple II-like expansion slots. And software specs were published, allowing software to be written for the new machine.

It was all that technical documentation that eventually led to the production of PC clones and compatibles. Although the makers of those clones that were direct rip-offs of IBM's original equipment were legally squashed, other clones and compatibles became work-a-likes without infringing upon IBM's copyrights.

◪ *An Introduction to Internal PC Hardware*

I'll be talking about these parts of the PC's hardware:

- The microprocessor
- ROM and the BIOS
- Temporary storage
- Permanent storage
- Support hardware

In Chapter 4, you'll learn where all these components are located.

The Microprocessor

The *microprocessor,* or CPU, is your computer's brain. It's basically a very fast calculator and a storage device. But its storage is limited, so it must have additional storage for the information it manipulates.

By itself, the microprocessor is a rather stupid device. It must be told exactly what to do, but it diligently carries out those instructions to the letter. The instructions are known as *software.*

ROM

ROM stands for read-only memory—the data on a ROM chip is defined by the manufacturing process and cannot be altered. The ROM chip contains the *BIOS,* which stands for Basic Input/Output System. It is software that has been encoded on a computer memory chip.

The information in your PC's BIOS plays several roles. The BIOS is primarily responsible for the Power-On Self-Test, bootstrapping, low-level interfaces, and the BASIC programming language.

The Power-On Self-Test

The BIOS's first duty, when the PC is initially turned on, is to perform a system checkout known as the *Power-On Self-Test*, or *POST*. The POST does an inventory of the various parts inside the PC, counting the number of disk drives, serial ports, parallel ports, and eventually counting and checking the memory. The POST's job is to make sure the PC's house is in order before the computer officially starts. (You'll learn more about the POST later in the chapter.)

Bootstrapping

The next responsibility of the BIOS, after checking out the system by means of the POST, is to load an operating system from the disk drives. This is known as *bootstrapping* because the computer is ''pulling itself up by its bootstraps.'' It's also where the phrase ''booting the computer'' comes from.

Low-Level Interfaces

The BIOS also provides communication links between your keyboard, video display, and serial and printer ports for the microprocessor. Each BIOS is customized by the PC's manufacturer to work with all the different components inside the computer.

The BASIC Language

Some PCs (only those made by IBM) come with a version of the BASIC programming language in ROM. This is because BASIC was usually the "operating system" of the computers of the early '80s. IBM continues to include BASIC in ROM though few people use BASIC.

Temporary Storage—RAM

The third major part of your PC's hardware is *temporary storage*—your computer's *RAM,* or random access memory.

The microprocessor itself can store information, but it only has a limited amount of space for it. Your computer has RAM chips that provide temporary storage for the information the microprocessor manipulates. Temporary storage is the microprocessor's work space.

This memory is temporary because RAM chips need electricity to stay alive. Without the constant flow of electricity, the information stored in memory is lost. This is why you lose everything when the power goes out. To make the computer really useful, you need to save information in permanent storage.

Permanent Storage

Memory in permanent storage doesn't disappear when you turn off the power. *Permanent storage* is another term for your disks or any other storage device you may have hooked up to the PC (though floppy and hard disks are the most common). You can transfer information from temporary storage to permanent storage. Then you can turn off the PC, knowing that your programs and data have been saved.

Other Hardware

Finally, your computer contains a lot of support hardware that isn't directly related to manipulating information or dealing with the microprocessor, including support circuitry, expansion cards, and the power supply.

Support Circuitry

Support circuitry is made up of chips, resistors, and other doo-dads in your computer. This circuitry supports the microprocessor, BIOS, RAM, and disk drives, making sure everything works together.

Expansion Cards

An *expansion card* is a plug-in option that becomes part of your total computer system. It plugs into another hardware item known as the *bus.*

The Bus

The bus is a direct line of communication between the micro-processor and the expansion cards.

The Power Supply

The power supply draws electricity from the wall, conditioning it for use inside the PC and dividing it up between the various parts.

PC/XT, PC/AT, and 386 Class Differences

Although we all like to think of any computer that runs DOS as a "PC," from this book's point of view there are really three different types of machines:

- The original IBM PC and PC/XT classes, which use the 8088 or 8086 CPU

■ The PC/AT class, which uses the 80286 CPU

■ The 386 class, which uses the 80386 or 80486 CPU

The discussion here concentrates on the differences between the PC/XT class and the AT class. The differences between the 386 and PC/AT classes aren't as great, but there are a few.

*P*C/AT and 386 Class Systems Have 16-Bit Slots

The original IBM PC and PC/XT had 8-bit expansion slots into which various option cards and expansion boards could be plugged. When the PC/AT was introduced, it had a 16-bit microprocessor. So to take advantage of the situation, IBM added a small extension to the end of the old 8-bit expansion slot. The extension created the 16-bit expansion slot.

The 16-bit expansion slot is fully compatible with the 8-bit expansion card. You can plug an 8-bit card right into the slot and everything works fine. On the other hand, you may have problems if you accidentally buy a 16-bit card and have a PC/XT with only 8-bit slots.

*3*86 Systems Have 32-Bit Slots

Most 386 systems have their own memory expansion system, different from the 16-bit expansion slots used in PC/AT systems. Why? Because to get the most from memory, the 386 uses full 32-bit mode. To make this happen, most 386 developers install their own, proprietary 32-bit memory slot.

*P*C/AT Class Systems Have Battery-Backed-Up RAM

Some basic parts of the PC/XT's configuration are determined by setting a tiny row of switches inside the computer. These DIP (dual in-line package) switches tell the PC about its memory configuration, video display, and so on.

The AT's setup information is stored by means of special battery-backed-up RAM, often called *CMOS* (complementary metal oxide semiconductor). This special area of memory keeps track of the AT's configuration, and it can be changed via a setup program that comes with the system; sometimes it is built into the AT's ROM BIOS.

Because of this arrangement, AT and 386 class systems have an internal battery and no hidden DIP switches. (Some older ATs have an internal switch to determine the video mode.) They also can keep track of the time even when the system's power is off. PC/XT class systems have a special clock adapter that has its own battery.

Basically, All PCs Are the Same

Keep in mind that, though the AT class systems have extended memory, 16-bit expansion slots, and battery-backed-up RAM (and 386 systems have their own, proprietary memory slot), all PCs are basically the same inside. There are only a few subtle differences between different models. Going from working on one model to another model doesn't involve any special training. This book will point out the differences when they are important.

About the PS/2 Line

The IBM PS/2 is notable for its Micro Channel Architecture and VGA graphics.

Micro Channel Architecture

With the PS/2, IBM introduced the Micro Channel Architecture, or MCA, type of expansion slot. This slot is "smart" compared to the older expansion slots.

There are lots of expansion cards for the PS/2's MCA. They are totally incompatible with the cards used in other PCs, but better in some respects. It's important to note that IBM's MCA isn't widely used in other computers. In fact, several PC makers have gotten together and developed a rival standard to compete with MCA, known as the EISA.

*V*GA Graphics

Although the MCA expansion bus bombed with the PC community, nearly everyone took up and noticed IBM's splashy new graphics standard, the VGA (Video Graphics Array). It's quite established outside of the PS/2 line.

The VGA graphics standard is built into nearly all the PS/2s (some low-end models lack the full VGA standard), but you can buy VGA cards to plug into your PC.

*W*hat Your PC Does When You Turn It On

Knowing what your PC does when you turn it on helps you understand how hardware and software interact. The material in this section looks at basic PC operations from the point of view of upgrading your hardware and will help you troubleshoot problems.

*T*he Hardware Side

DOS and the BIOS control communications between your software and the microprocessor. The microprocessor accesses RAM (temporary storage) directly, and DOS provides the interface between the microprocessor and permanent storage.

What's important to the topic at hand is how the PC gets itself up in the morning. You can use this process to assist you in troubleshooting problems with your PC—problems that may occur after you install or upgrade some hardware item.

When you flip the PC's power switch, it sends a surge of electricity through the computer. All the parts are powered up, the hard drive starts to spin, and the power supply's fan begins to whir. The PC comes to life.

When the microprocessor first receives some juice, it begins executing instructions found in ROM BIOS. It does this automatically, primarily to start everything working in the computer. Otherwise, the microprocessor would just sit there and you'd have no way to tell it to start working.

The instructions the microprocessor first starts to run are located in your computer's BIOS. And the first instructions it runs are known as the Power-On Self-Test, or POST.

The Power-On Self-Test

The Power-On Self-Test (POST) is run each time you turn on your PC before the PC is booted up. It consists of any messages you see displayed, any beeping that occurs, and the memory count most PCs show when they warm up. Nearly everything that happens before your disk drives fire up and load DOS is the POST working.

The POST does two things:

- It checks and verifies the configuration of your PC.

- It tests for any errors and alerts you to them.

On a PC/XT, the POST compares the actual configuration of your system with the way you have your system's DIP switches set. (Setting DIP switches manually is your own way of telling the PC what components are installed.) On AT and 386 class systems, the POST compares your battery-backed-up CMOS information with what it finds in the computer. If everything goes well, and the system checks out, then the POST passes control to the program in the BIOS that boots the PC.

It's when the POST detects an error that you're most likely to get feedback from it. The error is displayed as a number or an audible beep. This feedback comes in handy when you are testing and troubleshooting new equipment. POST errors, however, are rare.

About the most visible sign you'll see from the POST is the number show it gives when it tests your PC's memory. All memory locations are checked twice by the POST.

The first thing your PC does—even before the POST—is to get power. If you throw the switch and nothing happens, there's no need to run a POST. You know what's wrong! The computer isn't getting any juice, so it won't start.

If the system won't start, then you know it's either unplugged or there's a problem with your power supply. But beyond that, the POST takes over by checking out the following items in order:

The System Test The basic elements of your computer system are tested. This includes an extensive test of the microprocessor and the

POST itself. (The error-checking program must be free of errors.) The system unit is also checked to make sure all parts of the PC are getting enough power and communicating with one another, and internal memory locations are established for your serial and printer ports.

The Extended System Test   The POST tests the computer's timer chip, as well as other parts of the extended system. These parts include the BIOSs and control programs of special controllers and adapters that may have their own individual POST programs.

The Display Test   The POST checks your display adapter and sometimes just passes control to a secondary POST. For example, the EGA and VGA controllers have their own POST to check the video subsystem. If everything there checks out, control is returned to the main POST for more tests.

At this point, the POST may display a message on the screen, listing the BIOS manufacturer. Some computers just show a flashing cursor at this stage. That's fine; it means everything's OK.

The Memory Test   Most BIOSs use a POST that checks memory twice. On some computers, there's no memory display—a long pause (the longest part of the POST) occurs during the memory test.

The Keyboard Test   In this stage, the POST checks the keyboard and makes certain everything's OK. In case you didn't know, your PC's keyboard contains its own microprocessor. If you ever neglect to plug in your keyboard when you turn on your PC, the POST error you see (typically **301**) means you need to plug in your keyboard.

The Disk-Drive Test   In this test, the POST checks to see whether floppy drives are present. In the original IBM PC, the POST loaded the BASIC program in ROM, allowing you to program in BASIC and use the cassette tape to save and load your programs.

Since that time, the disk-drive test has also included a knock on the door of the hard-disk controller, causing the hard drive to warm up. The POST is finished—your system beeps once, signaling that all components passed the test. Your computer is fully functional and ready to run.

At this point, the BIOS's bootstrap loader program takes over. It first tries to load information from a disk in your A drive. If none is found, the bootstrap loader attempts to load information from your hard drive. Then, DOS and your PC software take over.

*T*he Software Side

Once the POST and your BIOS are finished, the bootstrap loader attempts to boot the rest of your system. Once it locates a disk in drive A or drive C, it loads the first sector, or *boot sector,* from that disk. That sector is transferred into memory, and the microprocessor starts executing its instructions.

Normally the boot sector directs the loading of additional information from disk, specifically from the file IBMBIO.COM (for PC-DOS) or IO.SYS (for MS-DOS). (This section will refer to IBMBIO.COM, but all references to it also apply to IO.SYS.) If you have a nonbootable disk in your drive, the program simply displays a message like this:

Non-System disk or disk error
Replace and strike any key when ready

IBMBIO.COM is the main program that communicates instructions to the computer's BIOS or directly to the microprocessor. Once it has set itself up, IBMBIO.COM loads a special start-up program called SYSINIT. It's SYSINIT's job to load the rest of DOS into your system.

SYSINIT first loads the second basic DOS file, IBMDOS.COM (or MSDOS.SYS) into memory. This is the DOS *kernel*, the main cluster of DOS routines and functions. It includes DOS's basic systems for file management, memory management, character input and output, support for the time and date, and the system environment and configuration.

Next, SYSINIT looks for a CONFIG.SYS file in the root directory of your boot disk. If SYSINIT finds it, SYSINIT executes any instructions found there, configuring the system according to your CONFIG.SYS commands or loading any specified device drivers or initialization programs.

The CONFIG.SYS stage is of particular importance when you add hardware to your PC. Computer mice, extra memory, and other special software typically come with software drivers that you must load into CONFIG.SYS. Until you do that, and until you've installed both the hardware and its driver in CONFIG.SYS, the upgrade or add-on will not function.

After finding CONFIG.SYS, SYSINIT looks for a COMMAND-.COM file and loads it. COMMAND.COM is DOS's command interpreter. It's what contains the prompt at which you enter DOS commands or run your own applications. Note that COMMAND-.COM is loaded *after* CONFIG.SYS. This is because CONFIG.SYS allows you to specify a location for COMMAND.COM other than the root directory—or a completely different command interpreter (something other than COMMAND.COM).

Finally, if COMMAND.COM is run, it will look for a special file called AUTOEXEC.BAT and run it as well. AUTOEXEC.BAT is a batch text file that may contain various DOS commands and special DOS batch file commands.

 ## When Something Goes Wrong

This is the normal procedure for booting your PC:

<u>1</u> Turn on the PC.

<u>2</u> A BIOS/start-up message appears (or you see the flashing cursor).

<u>3</u> The POST system checkout occurs (there is no indicator on your screen).

<u>4</u> The memory test indicators fly by (or you see the flashing cursor).

<u>5</u> The floppy disk starts up.

<u>6</u> The POST sounds a single beep, indicating everything's OK.

<u>7</u> DOS boots.

You may see other messages. For example, some device drivers in CONFIG.SYS will display messages like this:

Microsoft (R) Mouse Driver Version 7.00
Copyright (C) Microsoft Corp. 1983-1989. All rights reserved.

If you have an AUTOEXEC.BAT file, it may display messages as well, eventually returning you at the DOS prompt—though some AUTO-EXEC.BAT files end with a special menu program or load immediately a software application you have set up to start automatically.

That's what happens normally. When there's trouble in PC city, you'll know about it because you'll get a POST error.

POST *Errors*

There are two types of POST errors. First, there's the audible error message, when the computer beeps. Second, there's the visual error message, which is usually displayed in the form of a cryptic number.

If your screen doesn't work, then the only way the computer has to let you know something is wrong is by means of the speaker. Audio errors occur during the Power-On Self-Tests that are done before the monitor is checked out. There are numerous patterns to the number of beeps, timings, and all that. Table 3.1 describes some of the more common beep patterns.

Beeping is usually a sign of trouble, and you can use the descriptions in Table 3.1 to narrow down the problem. But not every PC is consistent with its beeping pattern; some AT systems play really bizarre tunes to clue you into what's wrong.

What is important with the beep codes is being able to recognize video failure. If the video is working and the machine still beeps, then you probably have some type of disk-drive failure. And if you never hear a beep at all, then the speaker is busted. But remember that a solitary beep after the memory count is to be expected.

After the video checks out, you may see one of the POST's visual error messages. These messages usually contain seemingly random numbers, yet if you have the proper tables you can look up the codes and see what they represent.

Table 3.2 describes the basic error codes produced by the POST. These codes tell you in which area the error occurred during the

Table 3.1: Audio POST Error Codes

BEEP PATTERN	MEANING
No beep	Power supply or motherboard bad
Unremitting beep	Power supply bad
Short, repetitive beeps	Power supply bad
Long beep, short beep	Motherboard bad
Long beep, two short beeps	Video bad
Long beep, three short beeps	Video bad
Two short beeps	Video bad (an error code may be displayed)
Short beep	Video, disk drive, controller, cable bad
No beep	Speaker bad or missing
Short beep	Everything's OK

initial tests. The *xx*'s represent numbers, which help narrow the error possibilities.

The most common error codes you might see are as follows:

201

A **201** indicates memory failure. This could happen right after you install memory in a PC, because you plugged in a dead chip, you plugged the chip in wrong, or you didn't set a DIP switch correctly.

***xx* 201**

Sometimes the **201** will be preceded by a value, represented by *xx* above. This gives you an approximate location of the malfunctioning chip.

301

You usually see a **301** error when you forget to plug in your keyboard when you start the PC. Sometimes other **3xx** errors occur if something is resting on the keyboard and is pressing a key. These errors usually

Table 3.2: Visual POST Error Codes

CODE, VALUE	DEVICE THAT FAILED THE POST
2x	Power supply
1xx	Motherboard
2xx	Memory (specific location also listed)
3xx	Keyboard (specific key may also be listed)
4xx	Monochrome video or adapter
5xx	Color video or adapter
6xx	Floppy drive or adapter
7xx	Math coprocessor
8xx	Not currently used
9xx	Printer adapter card
10xx	Secondary-printer adapter card
11xx	Serial (RS-232) adapter card
12xx	Secondary serial adapter card
13xx	Game, A/D, controller card
14xx	IBM Graphics printer
15xx	SDLC communications
16xx	Not currently used
17xx	Hard drive or controller
18xx	Expansion unit
19xx	Not currently used
20xx	Binary synchronous communications adapter
21xx	Alternate binary synchronous communications adapter

aren't fatal; just plug in the keyboard or make sure you're not pressing any keys and reset the computer.

1701

A **1701** is a common hard-drive error. It generally means something is wrong, though what could be wrong really isn't specific. Sometimes, just plugging in the cables a second time will rid you of the **1701** error. Other times you really need to troubleshoot to track down the problem.

Troubleshooting a Problem

When something does go wrong, you have a number of options to try to remedy the situation.

First, you can check installation of the hardware. If the error message indicates some piece of hardware isn't functioning—and you just installed it—then you should check the job you've done. (These errors may not be limited to the POST, by the way. For example, you may install a modem and, although it passes the POST, your communications software may not be able to find it.)

Second, you can run a self-diagnostics test on the upgradeable item. Some modems come with built-in diagnostic programs. Hercules graphics cards have a diagnostic program you can run from the DOS prompt. Try these out to make sure everything is functioning— even if you never see an error message.

Third, some computers come with a special, self-booting diagnostics disk. Others may have special diagnostic software you run from DOS. Still other machines may have a diagnostic ROM program you can call up when the computer first starts by pressing a special key combination. These diagnostic programs can be run to examine your memory and system configuration in more detail than the POST does.

Fourth, you can try any of the following general strategies to make sure everything is working properly:

- Turn off the system, wait a few moments, then turn it on again. Sometimes this will do the trick. (Be sure to wait at least 15 seconds before turning it on again.)

- Check or change your system configuration, including any DIP switches or jumpers on the motherboard, expansion cards, disk drives, and an AT's or 386's setup program.

- Check all cables and connectors, both inside and outside the PC.

- Check the disk drives. Disk drives are the only moving parts (besides the fan in the power supply) in your PC; they usually break before anything else.

- Check the display. If you don't see anything, maybe the monitor isn't plugged in or is turned off. Or maybe the brightness knob is turned all the way down.

- Check expansion card connections. Especially after moving a PC, some cards may wiggle loose.

- Check internal chips. Sometimes chips become unsettled. Press them back in firmly but carefully if you find any suspect chips. (Dealing with chips is covered in Chapter 6. Refer there before doing this.)

Additional Items to Check

In addition to the above troubleshooting strategies, here's a checklist of some items you may want to look over. Check out each of these before you become totally frustrated or give up:

- Is the computer plugged in? Is the power switch on? A lot of consultants make a quick $50 by showing up at a client's office and embarrassing them by plugging in a "broken" computer.

- Are there any missing pieces? Look for missing cables; loose cables; a printer without any paper, a ribbon, or toner; a modem not plugged into the phone system (wall jack); or anything that is not there that should be.

- Are any internal cables loose? Some computers have a tangle of cables internally. When you shut the lid too fast, the cables may be pulled from their sockets. All internal cables should be properly connected, and the lid should be carefully closed.

- Is the PC running too hot? Sometimes a computer doesn't get proper ventilation. If it's butting against a wall, or if something is blocking the front vent, the system can heat up and become nonfunctional in less than an hour.

- Is the operator the problem? Sometimes a user, after seeing the message "press any key," looks for the "any key." Sometimes a manual says to press the ↑ key, but the user finds numerous arrows on the keyboard, several of which are pointing up. And which key is the Control key? It doesn't say "Control" on any of them. Be patient if you're troubleshooting for someone else. Though this may all be second nature to you, a lot of people are intimidated and easily frustrated by computers.

- Is the software the problem? Remember that software instead of hardware sometimes causes the system to crash. There are thousands of variations in equipment in what we generally refer to as a "PC." Not every configuration is tested by the software developer, so you may have a genuine bug.

Switches and Setup Programs

There's been a lot of talk so far about DIP switches and the AT's setup program. What are these? Why are they important?

Both DIP switches and setup programs are used by the PC/XT and AT computer, as well as by certain expansion cards and peripherals, for hardware configuration. They help you set certain options to prepare and configure the computer for operation. When you upgrade your computer, you may have to set a DIP switch or run your setup program to configure the computer for the new hardware.

DIP Switches

DIP (dual in-line package) switches are a row of tiny slide or rocker switches. They're usually numbered 1 through 8 (or higher) on the *switch block*. An indicator on one side of the switch block shows which position is On—you can assume the other position is Off if it's not marked. Figure 3.1 shows a typical DIP switch block. The switches are numbered 1 through 8, and the On position is indicated by the ↑. The 1, 2, 3, 4, 5, 6, and 8 switches are off. Switch 7 is on.

You set a switch by sliding it to the On or Off position. You can slide it with a pen or pencil, but as a hardware-upgrading professional, you'll probably want to use your bent paper clip. (DIP switches are quite small, usually no more than an inch long.)

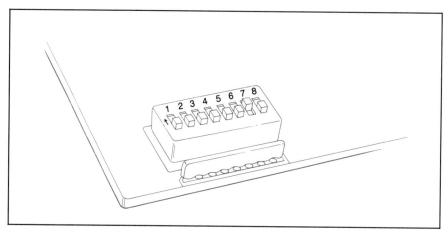

Figure 3.1: A typical DIP switch block

You set the switches according to your hardware configuration. This was the way things were done on the original IBM PC/XT and are still done today on most PC/XT clones and on memory cards and video cards. Your computer's manual lists the switch positions for various hardware add-ons in your system; you set the switches according to what you have.

The following list shows the items most often set by DIP switches in a PC/XT. For specifics, refer to your own PC/XT's manual.

- Number of floppy drives installed
- Presence of a math coprocessor
- Amount of memory installed
- Type of monitor display (monochrome or color)

Some expansion cards have DIP switches on them for configuration purposes. Printers also have DIP switches. If your printer is malfunctioning in some way, it probably means you have set one of its DIP switches improperly.

Some AT class systems have a small set of DIP switches to determine the type of video adapter installed. Normally, AT class systems use a setup program in the BIOS to set the video adapter, but this isn't always the case.

*J*umpers

Jumpers are found on various motherboards and also on some expansion cards. Like DIP switches, they let the hardware know about its internal configuration.

A *jumper* is a small black box, no bigger than a dime. It sits over two little metal poles sticking out of the motherboard or jutting out from an expansion card.

To set a jumper, you locate the two pins you want to place the jumper over. The pins are usually labeled, with something like *J1* or *J9*. You position the black box over the pins and press down. Figure 3.2 shows a typical jumper setup. There are four pins in a row, labeled *J1* and *J2*. The jumper is the black box over J2. It's considered to be set to position J2.

You can also remove jumpers. Because they're so tiny, you usually pull them off with a set of needle-nose pliers, but your fingers can do the job. You simply put the jumper over one of the pins instead of both, as shown in Figure 3.3—this doesn't set anything, but it helps prevent losing the jumper.

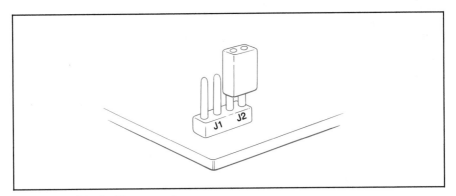

Figure 3.2: A typical jumper setup

Setup Programs

Instead of DIP switches, most computers in the AT class (which includes all 386 systems) have what's known as *CMOS memory,* which is constantly saved in the computer by a battery. (It's also called your battery-backed-up RAM.) CMOS stores all the basic information

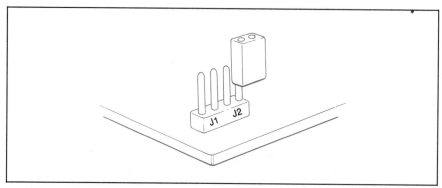

Figure 3.3: A jumper turned off

about an AT's configuration—the stuff normally set by DIP switches on a PC/XT's motherboard.

In addition to keeping track of the basic system configuration, the AT's CMOS memory also keeps track of the time and date. You have to manually enter these on a PC/XT or buy a clock card that has its own battery.

To change or to examine the contents of CMOS memory, you must run a special setup program. Sometimes this program is on disk, though that's only the case with some of the cheaper AT clones. Most of the time, this program is internal, part of your system's BIOS. You access it at boot time by pressing certain keys or when you normally run the PC by pressing a special key combination. (The key combination differs from PC to PC, though Ctrl-Alt-Enter is common. See your documentation.)

Once the setup program has run, you can change or modify the configuration of your system. The items controlled or specified from setup include the following:

- The system date and time
- The number and types of disk drives (both hard and floppy)
- The system memory, both main motherboard memory and extended memory
- The type of display
- The system's speed

- The presence of a math coprocessor

- Other system optimization options

You will want to run the setup program whenever you change anything in your computer. However, normally after you add a component, the POST detects the change and automatically brings up the setup program or prompts you to do so. When this happens, you simply locate the misinformation and correct it, then reboot. Some systems will even tell you which item is wrong and list the correct configuration.

Because the setup program and its contents are so important, you should print a copy of it. Check your manual on how to bring it up. Once it's on the screen, press the Print Screen key to get a hard copy of it. Keep that hard copy with your system's manuals. You should do this for three reasons:

- If you ever upgrade again, you'll have a copy of the original from which to take notes. Then, if you make any modifications, be sure to create another hard copy of the setup program's screen for the next time you change something.

- If anything ever happens to the CMOS RAM, you should have a copy of your original setup program so you can reset its values.

- Batteries don't last forever. At some point in the future, your AT's battery will die and your computer won't boot. At that point in time, you should buy a new battery and then use your setup hard copy to reset the values.

◣ *Summary*

This chapter was about getting to know your PC, specifically how the hardware works.

Central to the PC is the microprocessor, the computer's brain. It's responsible for your PC's computational and memory storage abilities. To help the microprocessor communicate with the rest of the computer, your PC's BIOS is used. And to help the computer communicate with you and your software, DOS is used.

Also covered in this chapter was a detailed description of what happens when your PC starts up. The PC's first duty is to perform the Power-On Self-Test, or POST, which tests each part of your system and makes sure everything's working properly. It also takes an inventory of what components you have.

The next step in knowing your PC is being able to recognize and locate all its hardware parts, both internal and external. This is covered in the following chapter, which also gives you the basic instructions required to upgrade your PC.

4

Locating Components: A Hardware Overview

THIS CHAPTER TELLS YOU WHERE EVERYTHING IS ON THE outside and inside of your computer, so you'll be prepared when it's time to take off the lid and do an upgrade. There are drawings to help illustrate the elements of the hardware, but what's important is that you personally take the plunge and look inside your own PC. But before you pop the lid off your case, read the first two parts of this chapter to get an overview of all the internal and external parts of your computer. When you have this background, you'll be ready to open the computer. This is actually the easiest part.

Before starting, note that nothing you will be asked to do in this chapter is dangerous or difficult. As long as you follow the instructions, set up everything properly, use the recommended tools, and stay patient, everything will come out fine and you'll have a lot of fun. So let's get going!

 ## The Outside of the PC

All PCs are different; there are thousands of variations. Trying to document them all in this book would be ludicrous. Figure 4.1 shows what I call the "generic PC." It has the three basic parts of all PCs: the monitor, the system unit, and the keyboard. I'll use this PC as the general model. It's up to you to locate items specific to your own computer. This book will tell you where to look and then what terms to apply to those options when you find them. Once you know this, you'll be better able to work through the hands-on examples later in this chapter and throughout this book.

After reading this chapter, you'll know your way around just about any PC. Since there are hundreds of outfits who make PCs, there are many variations. But the competition means we pay low prices for computers and have a variety of options to choose from.

All PCs look similar on the outside, because most clones and compatibles follow IBM's original PC or PC/AT design. There are, however, some external differences in cases.

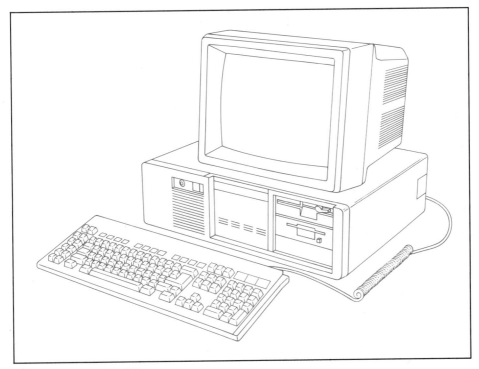

Figure 4.1: A generic PC

XT and AT Case Differences

There are two classes of PC case designs, the PC/XT-style and the AT-style. The most popular at present is the AT-style, but there are still plenty of PC/XT-style models.

Figure 4.2 shows a typical PC/XT-style case. This case has two full-height disk drives sitting side by side on the right side of the machine. The case is generally not as tall or as wide as the AT-style case.

Figure 4.3 shows a typical PC/AT-style case. Since disk-drive technology allows for smaller-size drives than existed when the original PC came out, the AT-style case makes the best use of ''half-height'' drives, disk drives that are half as tall as the drives that are on the original IBM PC. There is even additional room for a third drive, plus internal space for more drives. (Disk-drive height and internal arrangement is covered later in this chapter.)

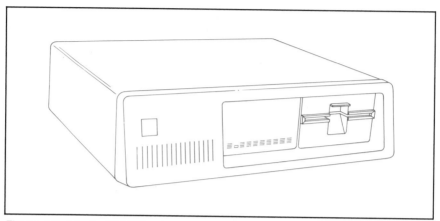

Figure 4.2: A typical PC/XT-style case

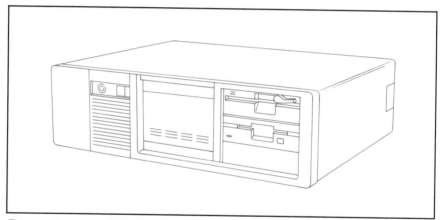

Figure 4.3: A typical PC/AT-style case

Keep in mind that an AT-style case can have an 8086-, 286-, or 386-based system inside. This case has just proven to be more flexible and useful as the standard PC case. Even though smaller versions exist, and there are variations, the AT-style case is currently the most popular PC case. (The Macintosh uses a similar arrangement.)

The most important difference between the two main PC case styles is in the arrangement of the disk drives. But note that in both styles, the drives are on the right side of the computer.

The other differences lie mostly in the front panel of the AT-style cases. (PC/XT-style cases usually don't have a front panel.)

There are lots of variations in the AT-style case's front panel. It's located on the left side of the case, toward the top. And it usually has some combination of the following items:

- A key and lock
- A power light
- A hard-disk activity light
- A turbo mode light
- A reset button
- A turbo shift switch

The key and lock are part of the PC/AT's original design. By using the key, you can lock up your PC, which freezes the keyboard and prevents others from using the computer. You can't even open the case on some PCs when the key is locked. Most people simply leave their keys dangling in the lock. But if you are security conscious, you should lock up your PC to prevent unauthorized access.

The first PC had no power light. You could turn off the monitor, and except for the hum of the fan, you had no way to tell whether the computer was on or off. If there is a power light on your computer's front panel, you can always tell when the machine is running.

Both hard and floppy drives have an activity light on their front panel that flashes when a drive is being accessed by the computer. With the AT-style case, most hard drives are kept inside, behind the system unit's front plate.

The turbo mode light is used by some dual-speed PCs to let you know when the system is running in the fast mode. Most PC microprocessors have two speeds: a fast speed (turbo) and a slower, compatibility speed. Most PC software can handle the faster speed of today's microprocessors. But some software, particularly for games, must time itself according to the slower, compatibility speed. So unless you're playing a game, you'll probably be using your PC in the turbo mode.

All IBM systems and many compatibles lack a reset switch. (You're more likely to find a reset switch on a newer computer.) If your software crashes or for some reason your system dies, and Ctrl-Alt-Delete doesn't reset the computer, then a reset switch is a great panic button. It saves you the trouble of having to turn off the PC, wait the required 15 seconds, and then turn it on again.

The turbo shift switch is also found on the front panel of many PCs. It's the control for changing your microprocessor's speed from compatible (slow) to turbo (fast). Some switches may have more than one position. And note that some PCs use key combinations as switches rather than a front panel device.

Figure 4.4 shows some typical arrangements of the PC's front panel. The main difference between panels A and B is B's use of graphic icons to represent the Open and Lock positions for the key, as well as the power, hard disk, and turbo lights. Different AT systems may use different icons, though the lock, light bulb, cylinder, and arrow are quite popular. (Some systems mix text and icons.)

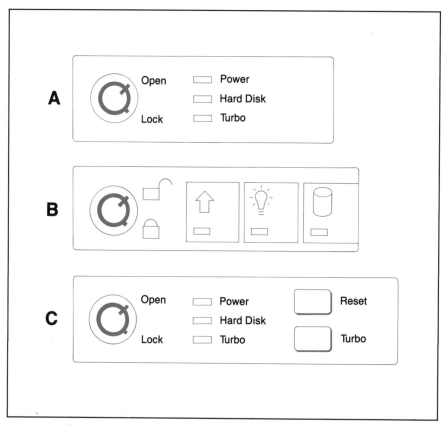

Figure 4.4: Front panel configurations

Panel C shows a variation of panel A, with the reset and turbo buttons on the front panel. These buttons may appear anywhere, with the reset button often recessed so that you don't accidentally press it. The buttons may also have icons or lights by them.

The System Unit

The *system unit* is the main box of your PC. Go ahead and locate the following items on your PC's system unit. If you're working on a number of systems, you should be able to know and recognize these items and where to find them.

You can use the drawings to help you look, but remember that they represent only generic examples. Also, not every PC is going to have all these items. So the emphasis here is on finding and recognizing those components your own PC has.

Figure 4.5 shows a front view of a standard AT system unit, and Figure 4.6 shows a rear view.

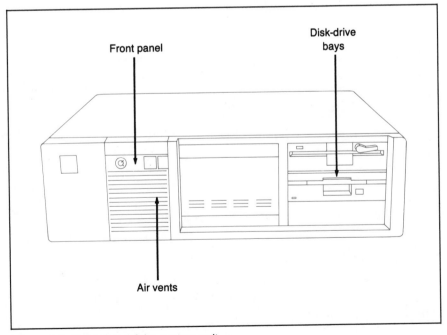

Figure 4.5: *Front view of the system unit*

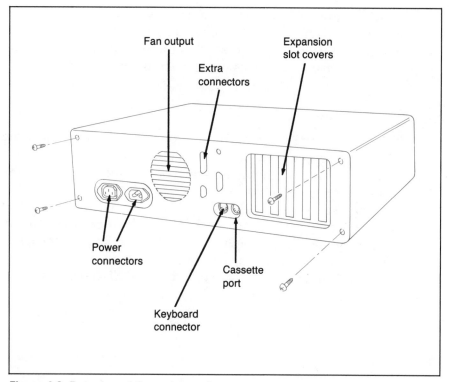

Figure 4.6: Rear view of the system unit

The Front Panel

Try to locate any lights (LEDs) and what they represent, the key switch, turbo buttons, and the reset button.

The Disk-Drive Bays

The disk-drive bays are on the right side of the case.

Air Vents

The air vents are a pattern of slits on the front of the case. The power supply's fan draws in air through these vents to cool the computer's components.

The Power Switch

You use the power switch to turn your PC on and off. It's generally located in the right rear of the PC. Some variations have the power switch on the front of the machine.

Note that 1 is used to represent *On* and 0 is used to represent *Off.* These numbers may be used alone or in addition to the words "On" and "Off."

Power Connectors

The typical power supply on a PC has two connectors, one for the main cable to the wall (from which the PC draws its juice) and a secondary one into which you can plug the monitor. The power connector has three prongs, and the monitor connector has three holes.

To use the monitor's power connector, your monitor must be equipped with a compatible cable. Since most monitors have this cable, it saves an extra connector on your wall socket or power strip. If your monitor lacks the special cable, then it can be plugged into any standard socket.

The Fan Output

The power supply contains a fan (sometimes two) that draws air in through the vents in front of the PC and forces it out through the fan output in the back of the PC. (This is why you may see a black mark on the wall behind your computer.)

Make sure the fan output vent isn't obstructed. If it's caked with dust (which happens after a time), then use a can of compressed air to blow off the dust—be careful not to blow the dust back into the PC.

Extra Connectors

Some systems may have extra connectors or holes for connectors between the power supply's fan and the expansion slot covers. For example, if your system has a built-in parallel or serial port, these connectors will be located on the back of your PC.

Some systems also have connector-size plate covers in the same position. These plate covers can be removed with a screwdriver. You can thread cables through them from your expansion cards if necessary.

The Keyboard Connector

The keyboard connector is a round connector into which you plug your keyboard cable. The holes in the connector are spread out so there's only one way to connect the cable. The connector is notched at the top to make it easier to connect the cable.

A few systems have the keyboard connector in front of the system unit, but most PCs have the connector in back, a good three feet from where the keyboard sits.

Cassette Port

Next to the keyboard connector is the cassette port, found only on IBM's original PC. If you have an original PC, you may be confused because the port is in the same position and has the same number of holes as the keyboard connector.

The cassette port is on the right as you're facing the back of your PC. If you accidentally plug the keyboard into the cassette port, you'll get a **301** POST error message when you start the PC.

Expansion Slot Covers

The right side of the back of your PC is an open area composed of expansion slot covers. On the other side of this area are the motherboard's expansion slots, into which you can plug various expansion cards and options. From the back, you see either the back mounting plate of those cards or the metal slot covers that fill in the holes when a slot is unoccupied. Many expansion cards have connectors on the back of them.

Case Screws

There can be anywhere from two to five screws closing up your computer's case. Four of the screws are located in the corners on the back and one is located in the top center.

The original IBM PC had only two flathead screws on the lower-left and lower-right sides of the back case. Most of today's PCs have five screws (usually Phillips), one in each of the four corners and one in the top center.

Power-Supply Screws

The power supply is anchored to the back plate of your PC by four screws. These screws are usually smaller than the main case screws, but it's easy to be confused.

The power-supply screws are evenly spaced in a rectangle around the fan output and power plugs. Even if you have a good view of your PC's back, it's not hard to miss them—even a seasoned professional sometimes mistakenly unscrews a power-supply screw when she means to take off the case.

Keyboards

There are many different types of PC keyboards. This has been one of the more humorous aspects of PC computing for the past decade or so: IBM, the company that patented the touch typist's dream keyboard, the IBM Selectric, just can't make up its mind on a keyboard for the PC computer line.

Today there are lots of keyboard types, with different key patterns; lights to denote Caps Lock, Num Lock, and Scroll Lock; different positions for the Ctrl and Alt keys; keyboards with touch pads; rows of extra keys; and so on.

The two main parts of the keyboard are the keyboard itself and the cable. Inside the keyboard are a microprocessor chip and some support chips, which generate special codes each time you press a key. The codes are then sent down the cable to the system unit, where they're transferred to the BIOS for use by your software.

You can use your air can or a special vacuum cleaner with a tiny nozzle to clean your keyboard. Otherwise, replacement is your best bet to fix a malfunctioning keyboard. The three major PC keyboard variations are the original model, the PC/AT keyboard, and the enhanced keyboard.

The Original Keyboard

The original IBM PC keyboard has a lot of faults. The Tab, Shift, and Backspace keys aren't marked; they have arrows on them instead. The Enter key is too small and too far to the right, so many people press the accent grave key by mistake. And the backslash key is where the left Shift key should be.

Variations of this keyboard proliferated. Placement of the back-slash key varies a lot, which wouldn't be bad if DOS didn't rely upon this key so much.

The PC/AT Keyboard

The PC/AT keyboard's biggest improvement on the original keyboard was moving the numeric keypad away from the standard typewriter keypad. It improved the Enter key by making it Selectric-size, and it labeled all keys with words in addition to cryptic symbols. The AT keyboard also has indicator lights for Caps Lock, Num Lock, and Scroll Lock.

But problems remain. The Esc key is too close to Backspace. Because pressing Esc usually erases a whole line, if you accidentally press it instead of Backspace, you may have a lot of retyping to do.

The Enhanced PC Keyboard

The enhanced PC keyboard has a smaller Enter key than the AT keyboard. It names the Tab key and puts Esc back where it belongs. It has a separate cursor keypad as well as a numeric pad, which makes working with spreadsheets easier. But the function keys are at the top of the keyboard, and the Ctrl and Caps Lock keys are backward.

There are other kinds of keyboards as well. Laptop computers have the worst keyboards. Other companies make custom variations. But the enhanced PC keyboard seems to be becoming the standard in the industry—even Apple has borrowed from its design.

Monitors

The monitor is the final component in your basic PC setup. Since you should never take apart your monitor, there are only a few things you need to know about it.

There are two major types of monitors: color and monochrome. Color monitors give you color and more exciting graphics, and monochrome monitors give you outstandingly crisp text. You must have a corresponding adapter card inside the PC to drive the monitor—something to plug it into.

There are a lot of variations between different types of monitors; color monitors are generally larger.

Like TVs, monitors have brightness and contrast knobs, as well as vertical and horizontal control. Additionally, there may be picture-size, left-right, and up-down positioning controls. Color monitors sometimes have saturation and hue controls.

You can usually fix trouble with a monitor by adjusting its knobs. For example, a classic mistake is thinking your monitor is broken, when in fact the brightness is turned down all the way. But you don't want to turn up the brightness too much. To find a happy medium, follow these steps:

1 Find the brightness and contrast knobs on your monitor.

2 Turn up the brightness so that you can see the entire scan area of your picture tube. (A bright rectangle will appear on the monitor, surrounding any displayed text.)

3 Adjust the contrast. Make sure that the characters stand out, that any bright characters appear bright, and that any dim characters are still visible and well defined.

4 Turn down the brightness so that the rectangle disappears from the screen.

If you're forced to run your monitor with the brightness turned all the way up, there may be a power-supply problem inside the monitor. If this is the case, you should have a professional look at it, as you should do with any monitor problems.

◤ *The Inside of the PC*

The internals of your PC are in the system unit. There are four main items you should look for and be able to recognize:

- Disk drives
- Power supply

- Motherboard

- Expansion cards

The information covered in this section is general in nature. You don't need to pry open your PC to find these things. Just follow along with the examples and illustrations. Toward the end of this chapter, you will open your PC and locate some important items on the motherboard.

Figure 4.7 shows the inside of a generic AT-style PC—you can refer to it throughout the sections that follow to help orient yourself. Your own PC will probably look more complex than the one shown in the figure.

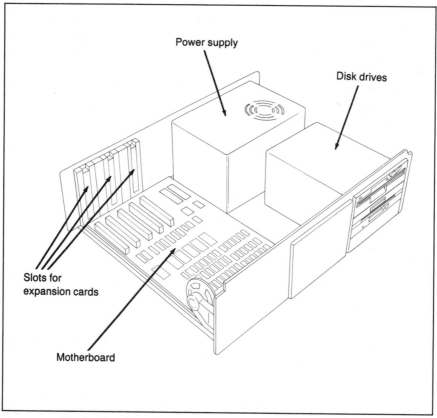

Figure 4.7: The inside of the generic PC

*T*he Disk Drives

Disk drives are located in the front right of the system unit. They're either stacked top to bottom, as shown in Figure 4.7, or left to right, as shown in Figure 4.8 (PC/XT-style).

Note that the PC/XT-style case doesn't leave much extra room inside the computer for expansion cards. The hard drive, usually on the left side, sits over part of the motherboard and partly blocks room for some expansion slots. (This prohibits the use of full-length expansion cards, but half-length cards are available.) This problem occurs in some AT-style cases as well, where the hard drive sits internally, with no access through the front of the system unit. A hard drive in the middle of a PC isn't a problem as long as you have a hard-drive light on your front panel.

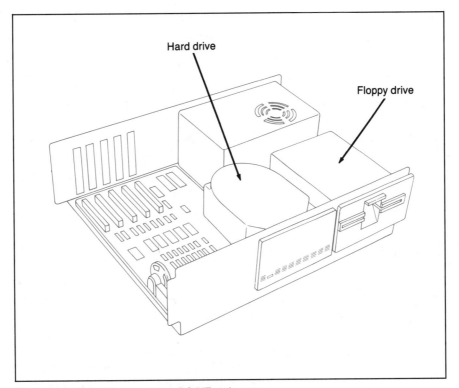

Figure 4.8: Disk drives inside a PC/XT-style case

Every drive has at least two cables. One is a *power-supply cable*. It is a multicolored grouping of four wires that originates in the left side of the power supply and plugs into the back of the drive. Both hard and floppy drives use the same type of connector; it doesn't matter which cable you plug into, as long as the drive is plugged into the power supply.

In addition to the power-supply cables, every drive has a *controller/data cable*. For floppy drives, this is a 34-wire ribbon cable that connects to the back of the drive. The other end of the cable connects to either a floppy-disk controller or a hard/floppy (combination) disk controller expansion card, or plugs directly into the motherboard. If you have two floppy drives, they're both on the same cable.

For hard drives, there are two cables in addition to the power-supply cable. The first is a 34-wire ribbon cable, similar to the floppy's cable (so don't confuse them!). This cable is used to send control information to the drive. A second, narrow 20-wire ribbon cable is the data line. It transfers the data to and from the drive. Both of these cables connect to the hard-disk controller.

The hard and floppy controllers may be the same thing. Also, you should note that two floppy drives and two hard drives can generally be handled from one controller. Both floppy drives use the same cable. Both hard drives use the same control cable, but the second hard drive requires its own data cable.

Disk drives also may have jumpers on them, as well as *terminating resistors*. The jumpers and resistors are used by the hardware to determine the last drive in your system and the order of the drives. (Jumpers and resistors are covered later in this book.)

The Power Supply

The power supply is located in the right rear corner of the system unit, directly behind the disk drives. In fact, there's usually less than a finger's worth of space between the drives—just enough room to bend a few cables. If you need to check your power supply, you will probably have to unscrew and slide out your disk drives.

The power supply is anchored by four screws on the back of the case, and it slides under a clip on the bottom of your PC. The main power, or On/Off, switch sticks through the side of the case on the right side of the PC. The fan and two power outlets stick out the back.

On the left side of the power supply is a whole bunch of cables. The disk-drive power cables are groupings of four wires: two black, one red, and one yellow. The group ends with a white, boxlike connector that's plugged into the end of the drive. Older power supplies only have two of these types of cables; modern power supplies have four drive cables or more.

The second type of cable is the motherboard's power-supply cable. There are two of them, each having five or six wires of various colors. These wires attach to the motherboard, plugging into two adjacent sockets.

All power-supply cables are notched, so you can't plug them in backward. It is possible, however, to plug the motherboard's power cables in bottom to top instead of top to bottom.

On top of each power supply is a rating, listing both voltage and watts. The watts value is important because it tells you the actual power output of your power supply. Nearly every PC/XT should have a minimum 150-watt power supply. That's also OK for most AT systems and 386s, but you should preferably have 200 watts or more.

The Motherboard

The motherboard is located on the left side of your PC's case, on the bottom. It's usually a green sheet of fiberglass, populated with silicon chips, resistors, and electronic circuits. (The motherboard may be hard to see, especially if you have lots of expansion cards—it may be hidden beneath all the electronic chop suey.) Figure 4.9 offers a close-up view of its basic components.

Again, this is a generic and exaggerated figure. But it should help you locate the parts your motherboard does have and help you recognize parts you may not have seen before on other motherboards.

The Microprocessor

The microprocessor is a long wide chip, or a large square chip, usually located on the right side of the motherboard, near the middle.

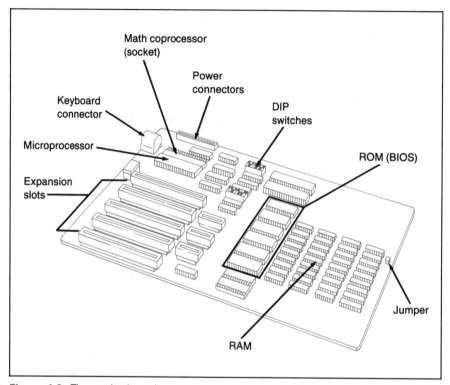

Figure 4.9: The motherboard

The chip can be identified by an inscription on its top. The inscription lists the chip's number, which could be any one of the following:

8088

8086

80C86

V20

V30

V40

80286

80386

Some of these numbers will be followed by other numbers, which typically indicate the chip's speed in megahertz. In 8088s these numbers indicate dual-speed chips.

The microprocessor may be hidden under the hard drive or the power supply. If you can't find it, but see that the motherboard extends under the hard drive, then that's probably where the microprocessor is located.

The Math Coprocessor

The math coprocessor is adjacent to the microprocessor. It's usually the same size as the microprocessor, though sometimes smaller. The chip's number is nearly the same, but ends with a 7 instead of a 6.

Since a math coprocessor is often an option, it's usually just an empty socket, sometimes with a stenciled label on the motherboard that says ''math'' or ''coprocessor'' or has just a number.

The Expansion Slots

The expansion slots are located to the rear of the motherboard on the left, along the back. There can be any number of them, but five and eight are typical. You plug your expansion cards into these slots.

In some PCs there may be only two cards, for example, a video controller and a hard-disk controller. In other PCs, every slot may be full. (It can get crowded inside the case.)

The expansion slots are also referred to as the *system bus* or just the *bus*. The slots themselves aren't the bus, but if you look carefully, you'll see tiny rows of wire traces running left to right, perpendicular to the expansion slots. These wires, plus some support chips located nearby, constitute your system's bus. The bus is a direct line of communication between your microprocessor and the expansion cards.

Some slots have a small extension on them. These are the 16-bit slots. The slots without the extension are 8-bit slots; these are the only types of slots found in PC/XT-compatibles.

All the slots are numbered, usually by a small stenciled number on the motherboard. Though the number does not indicate which card gets plugged into which slot, one special slot is No. 8, found on the XT System board. If you have a ''slot 8,'' then you should only plug special slot-8 adapter cards into it.

ROM

The ROM contains your computer's BIOS. There can be anywhere from one to several chips for your system's BIOS.

It's hard to pinpoint the location of the ROM chips, though they are commonly found in the left center of the motherboard. If you know who makes your PC's BIOS, then their name on the chips will be a big hint that you've found it. Look for names like IBM, COMPAQ, Phoenix, AMI, DTK, and Award.

RAM

One of the motherboard's main residents is RAM, usually found in the bottom center. It's easy to spot because it typically is made up of several rows of chips that all look alike.

There are variations to memory, however. The traditional type of memory consists of four banks of nine RAM chips each. Since more memory can now be put on a single chip, some computers may have only one bank of nine chips. Other computers may have tiny slots for SIMM memory, which is made up of nine chips on a tiny expansion card-like holder. SIMM memory plugs into a socket on the motherboard (but it's not an expansion card).

The Proprietary RAM Connector

The proprietary RAM connector is found only in 386 systems; a special 32-bit memory slot is often included. This allows you to add full 32-bit memory. Otherwise, if memory were added in an expansion slot, the 32-bit microprocessor could only access it 16 bits at a time, slowing the computer down.

The 32-bit memory connector varies with each 386 model. (Since IBM never produced a standard, there are dozens of variations.) Some connectors are extensions of the expansion slot on the far left. Others are long slots or multiholed connectors on the lower-left side of the motherboard.

You can get the card that plugs into this special RAM connector from your dealer only. Once you have it, you can continue to add RAM to your 386 system.

Support Chips

Not marked in Figure 4.9 are several smaller chips that serve support functions for the motherboard. They control the keyboard, the computer's timing, interfaces, and other miscellaneous jobs, most of which are beyond the scope of this book.

DIP Switches

PC/XT and some AT systems have DIP switches on the motherboard. They are used to set your system's configuration, number of disk drives, and memory. The original IBM PC and most PC clones have two sets of DIP switches. Some AT clones have a smaller DIP switch that is used to set the video display. (Most AT and 386 systems use the CMOS RAM and the setup program.)

Note that the two sets of DIP switches are labeled differently. One is SW-1, the other is SW-2. Your PC's manual should give you the approximate locations of each. The SW-1 or SW-2 is stenciled on the motherboard next to the appropriate switch.

Jumpers

Jumpers are found on nearly every PC, from the first IBM to the latest 386. They specify the type of video adapter you have, the configuration of your hard drive, memory on the motherboard, and the speed (turbo or slow) the computer starts in.

Jumpers are located all over the place. You'll need your PC's manual to find out where they are and what they do.

The Power Connectors

The two cables that run from the power supply to the motherboard plug in near the right rear of the motherboard, just below where the cables come out of the power supply.

The Keyboard Connector

The keyboard connector is in the right rear of the motherboard, just above the power connectors. It sits up, off the motherboard a bit, and juts out through a hole in the back of the case. (Your computer may have the keyboard connector on the front.)

Other Connectors

The motherboard has a row of tiny prongs onto which you plug cables for the speaker, the reset and turbo switches, and LEDs on the front panel. How many of these connectors you have and what kind they are depend on what you have on your front panel.

Some motherboards are obscured by the hard drive and power supply (not to mention any expansion cards you may have). If you need to access the motherboard, you may have to yank out a few components. But don't worry, it's not that tough and it does make working on the system easier.

Also, some computers don't have the traditional type of motherboard. In some systems the motherboard is in an expansion slot, leaving the real estate on the bottom of the PC empty! This allows you to upgrade your PC to a new platform by simply swapping motherboard cards.

If your system's motherboard is on a card, then you will still be able to locate the items mentioned in this section. They'll just be harder to see because you'll be looking at them from an angle.

Expansion Cards

Expansion cards are located on the left side of the system unit. They plug into the slots on the rear of the motherboard. They can occupy any amount of space, from the back of the system unit to four inches into the case, or all the way to the front of the case. Figure 4.10 shows the location of an expansion card relative to other items in the PC. A card is held in place by up to three elements. The first, and most important, is the slot in the motherboard into which it plugs. This slot also serves as the card's power source and its line of communication with the PC.

A card is also held in place by its mounting bracket, which attaches to the back of the PC. The bracket replaces the expansion slot cover on the system unit. It also helps to slide the card into its slot. Additionally, there may be connectors on the mounting bracket for cables through which the card communicates with the outside world.

If a card is long enough to stretch to the front side of the PC, certain guides may be available for keeping the card in position.

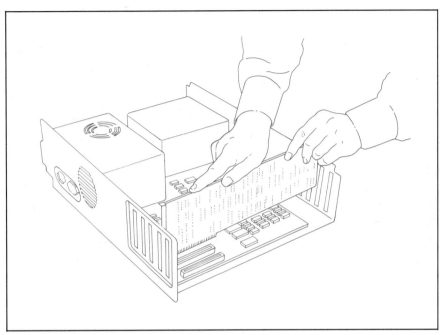

Figure 4.10: An expansion card

Nearly every PC has at least two expansion cards. The first is for the video adapter, the second is a combination hard-disk/floppy-disk controller. Older PCs routinely have more cards, because they offer fewer features on the motherboard.

The location of the cards is not crucial, though if you have a "slot 8" in your system, you should only put special slot-8 cards into it. And it's a good idea to put 8-bit-only cards into 8-bit slots, rather than waste a 16-bit slot on an 8-bit card. Other than that, there are no real rules, but I do offer the following suggestions.

Video cards are traditionally put toward the left side of the motherboard. Eight-bit video cards can go in the far-left 8-bit slot, and 16-bit video cards can go in the far-left 16-bit slot.

The hard-disk and floppy-disk controllers are usually put in the slot farthest to the right, which will accommodate the card but not interfere with the space taken up by the hard drive. (If it's a short card, it can go in the far-right slot.) Again, there's no real reason for this, though it prevents a long stretch of the cables over to the disk drives.

*M*iscellaneous Parts

The miscellaneous parts of the PC that you should locate are all attached to the motherboard, generally toward the front left of the computer case. Several of them are illustrated in Figure 4.11.

The LED connectors on your front panel originate in the motherboard; they indicate power and turbo speed, plus whatever else the manufacturer deems important. Note that the LED connector for your hard-drive light comes from the hard-disk controller, not the motherboard.

The AT's internal clock and all the setup information saved in the CMOS memory are kept alive by the battery when the computer is

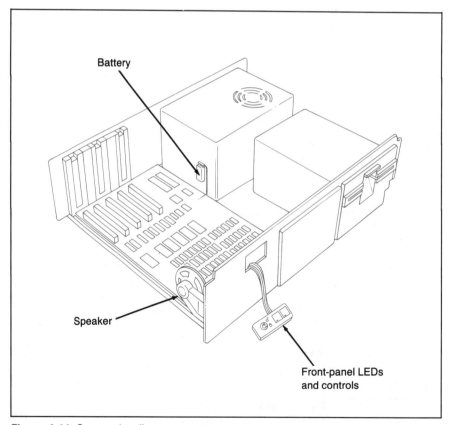

Figure 4.11: Some miscellaneous parts

turned off. The location of the battery varies with the manufacturer, but it's often located just inside the front of the case. It may also be clipped onto the motherboard. In a few rare instances, the battery is soldered to the motherboard.

The last several sections have covered all the major parts inside your PC. Anything aside from the items I've already mentioned is probably something particular to your brand of PC.

If you find something in your computer and don't know what it is or why it's there, then you should refer to your PC's manual for information. The odds are pretty good it will not be something you want to mess with and nothing you can upgrade yourself anyway. But it is good to know what an unknown part is and what it does.

Tower Configurations

My discussion of parts has been limited to the desktop configurations of most PCs. But there are a few floor-standing tower models out there. Although the parts are the same, the internal arrangements of these tower models are a little different from what you'd normally expect. It is possible to upgrade a tower model, but, as with the desktop model, you should know what it is you're looking for and where to find it. The locations of individual items, especially those on the motherboard, are similar to those in desktop PCs.

Note that the power supply in a tower model PC is always at the top. This ensures the best possible airflow. Heat rises, so the air vents in a tower model PC are on the bottom. The heat from the components and air from the vents rise through the case, drawn up and out by the fan in the power supply.

You can put your desktop model on its side, if you want it to be like a tower model. There are floor mounting brackets to let you stabilize a desktop model in a tower position. Make sure the power supply is at the top of the case, allowing for proper airflow through the computer. Also some experts say you won't have any disk-drive problems with a PC mounted vertically. Others recommend that you format your hard disk when the drive is in the vertical position. Still others say you should have the hard drive mounted horizontally (as most tower cases do). My own advice is that if you want a floor-standing PC, buy one in the first place.

Taking a Look Inside

This section tells you how to remove your PC's cover. You will not be taking your entire computer apart. This is all basic training for the upgrades you'll be doing, so read carefully.

You're going to be doing some work in this section, so set out your tools and get ready for some hands-on adventure. You will be making no permanent changes to your system, so nothing you change is going to affect the way your computer works. As long as you follow the instructions, you'll be OK.

You will be in no danger—just make sure you unplug your PC from the wall before you even lift a screwdriver. If there's no possibility of power coming into your PC, then you can't hurt yourself.

You may be tempted to only *read* this material. But that's not how you learn to upgrade your own PC. While reading *before* doing is always highly recommended, you should eventually follow the steps outlined here to remove your PC's case.

One more important thing to remember: Don't forget technical support! There's nothing wimpy about calling your dealer, developer, or hardware OEM if you get stuck—the pros do it all the time. Most hardware manufacturers have support lines for people just like you.

A General Strategy

Here are ten basic steps to follow when working on your PC:

1 Read before doing.

2 Power down.

3 Unplug the computer.

4 Create a work space.

5 Get your tools.

6 Take apart the PC.

7 Install/upgrade/remove the item.

8 Test the PC's configuration.

9 Put the PC back together.

10 Plug in the PC.

Read Before Doing

Before even thinking about lifting a screwdriver, read what it is you're about to do. This chapter has described what you'll find inside your computer; from the diagrams, you should get a rough idea of where everything is. Familiarity with the instructions is very important.

Power Down

Powering down your system involves a little more than just flipping the power switch. Before you shut off your computer to perform a hardware upgrade, you should do each of the following:

- Save the data in any programs you're working on.
- Back up important data or the entire hard drive.
- Park the heads on your hard drive.
- Turn off any peripherals, printers, monitors, modems, etc.
- Turn off the PC's power.
- Unplug the box from the wall.

Make sure you've done each step, especially the second one. Should anything happen to the hard drive, you will want to have duplicate data on another disk. Even if the upgrade involves memory or something seemingly unrelated to the hard drive, back it up. (You don't need to back up the entire hard disk, just important data files.)

Head-parking programs, such as PARK, SIT, and SHIP, will position the hard drive's delicate read/write head over an unused portion of disk, eliminating any data loss resulting from head crashes. Some versions of these programs may even lock the read/write arm in place.

Unplug the PC

Unplug the computer from the wall, then unplug the cord from the power supply. (This will save you if some bozo sees the cord unplugged and decides to "do you a favor" by plugging it in. I know, it's happened to me more than once.)

Create a Work Space

You're going to need some elbowroom to work on your PC. Clear your desk. You might have to move the monitor and keyboard off to one side or move some peripherals.

Get Your Tools

Each upgrade in this book requires little more than a screwdriver. But in some cases, specific tools are required. You should set out all your tools.

Take Apart the PC

After unplugging the system and giving yourself some elbowroom, you can remove the PC's lid. Once that's off, you're ready to work on your computer's innards.

Install/Upgrade/Remove the Item

Even though everything inside the PC screws, snaps, or slides in place, you may still have some work to do. Some PCs are jammed full of stuff, so getting to where you want to go takes time.

You'll be working a lot with cables and connectors inside the PC. While this book is quite clear on identifying cables, their source and destination, and their proper orientation and connection, you may want to give yourself a little extra help. This is where you can use sticky labels to label the ends of your cables. You can make two labels with "A" on them and then put one on the cable and the other on the connector. This helps you to remember where to reconnect a dangling cable.

Test the PC's Configuration

After you do an upgrade, you should always plug in the PC and test it with the lid off. Power up and make sure the new hardware device is working properly *before* putting the lid back on. This is completely safe (as long as you're careful). And it saves the hassle of repeating steps if you notice something isn't working right.

If everything checks out, turn off the power, unplug the system, and replace the lid. If everything does not check out, the computer is open and ready for you to troubleshoot.

Here is a good trick to use when doing more than one upgrade at a time: Do the first upgrade, turn on the system to make sure it checks out, do the second upgrade, and check it out as well. That way you don't have to bolt the lid back on just to check something out.

Put the PC Back Together

You should reassemble any internal items you've removed and put the lid back on the PC, screwing it on snugly. You should also reconnect any cables you disconnected when you first took off the lid.

Plug in the PC

Plug the computer back into the wall. Turn on the power and watch your computer boot.

Removing the Lid

Follow these steps to remove the lid of your PC:

1. Power down your PC.

2. Turn off all peripherals.

3. Unplug your computer from both the power supply on the back and the wall socket.

4 Remove the screws on the back of the PC's case. There will be anywhere from two to five screws (more on some models). As you remove each screw, set it aside in a convenient, safe location. Use a small dish if you have one.

5 Grab the rear of the lid on the sides of the system unit and slide it forward slowly (see Figure 4.12). Be careful that the top of the lid doesn't snag anything inside the PC. (Don't press on the disk drives to push the lid forward.)

Once the lid is far enough forward, lift it up the front and off. The sides of the lid hook under a metal lip, so you may have to jiggle the lid's sides to bring it free of the PC. Once it's off, set it aside.

If the lid won't come off, then maybe your key is locked. Be sure the key is in the open position before you slide off the PC's top.

Locating Components

Now that you have the lid off your PC, it's time to scope out the interior and get to know where things are.

First, you should locate the four major parts of your system unit: the power supply, the disk drives, the motherboard, and the expansion cards.

Right away you'll notice that your PC is a little more crowded and complex than the illustrations in this chapter. But the basic parts are in the same locations.

Next, after hunting down the four biggies, you should take the time to locate the following items on your motherboard:

- Microprocessor
- Math coprocessor or a socket for one
- ROM, particularly the BIOS
- Expansion slots
- RAM
- Proprietary RAM connectors
- Various support chips and electrical doodads

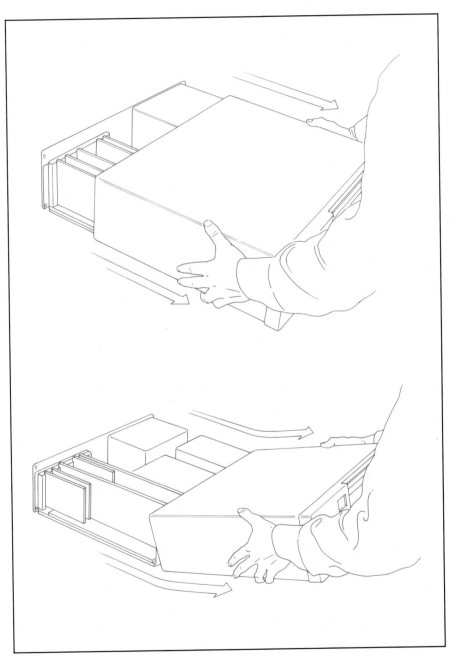

Figure 4.12: *Removing the lid*

- DIP switches (if any)
- Jumpers (if any)
- Power connectors
- Keyboard connector
- LED connectors to the front panel (if any)
- Speaker
- Battery (if you have an AT or 386 system)

You may also want to trace a few cables to see where they come from and where they go. The cables from your hard drive go to the hard-drive controller card. The cables from your floppy drive may go to the same place or to a separate floppy controller card.

Look at how the cards are arranged in the back of your PC and find the video adapter.

After you're done looking around, it's time to put the lid back on your PC. At this point you can fire up the PC and use it (though it's not FCC-approved without the case on because it can interfere with radio and TV transmissions). You can do this as an interim step to make sure everything is working properly. There's nothing in the case that will leap out and shock you; all the dangerous stuff is contained inside the power supply's case. You can even touch the chips while the computer is running. Just don't do any of the following:

- Spill anything inside the PC.
- Touch an expansion slot or use a tool on anything metal.
- Install something with the power on.

*P*utting the Lid Back On

Putting the lid back on your PC is the tricky part. That's usually when you encounter a snag—the case can grab and pull a cable from its socket if you're not careful. (There is a metal lip in the center of the top edge of the case where one of the screws fastens.)

1 Position the lid over the case, lining everything up.

2 Gently push the case back. The sides of the case will usually fit under a lip on the bottom of the system unit. Make sure the sides of the case are positioned properly before you push back. If you notice the sides are bowing a bit, then you probably don't have it on correctly. As you push, keep an eye on the cables and expansion cards. You don't want to snag one and tear it out.

3 The case will go back nearly all the way. For some reason, no computer case lid has ever slid back all the way. You always have to push it a bit to get it back that final one-eighth of an inch to the screw holes. Also keep an eye on the right side where the power supply's On/Off switch is. If the lid doesn't go back all the way and is about a half-inch to an inch short, then the key has probably flipped into the locked position. Make sure it's open and try again.

4 Line up the screws with the holes and tighten them into position. You might want to start with the top-center screw, though it's best to start with whichever screw hole is lined up properly.

5 Once all the screws are back in position, reassemble the PC. Put the monitor back on top, rearrange your desk, and get ready to flip the power switch. Your work is finished!

6 Put away your tools. My dad always told me to do this. After I lost five hammers, I finally learned.

Summary

This chapter gave you a complete overview of your PC's hardware. You learned about the external components of your PC, including the system unit, the keyboard, and the monitor. You also learned about the inside of your PC, including the disk drives, power supply, motherboard, and expansion cards.

At the end of the chapter, you learned the general strategy for taking apart your PC. Then, you actually removed the lid from the case and located all the components that you read about. Now you have all the background information that you need to begin doing upgrades to your PC.

5

Upgrading
Memory:
The Software
Side

MEMORY HAS ALWAYS BEEN AN IMPORTANT ELEMENT OF the PC. The first PC had the ability to access up to 640K of RAM (memory). That was a high value back in the days when 64K was standard. What could you do with all that memory? But soon prices on RAM chips dropped, and eventually software developers found out how to use all that memory. Now 640K just isn't enough. And the future trend shows that as PCs hold more and more memory, software will find new ways to use it all. So more memory is on the top of just about everyone's upgrade wish-list.

This chapter is the first of two about upgrading memory. Why two chapters? Because plugging in chips isn't everything a RAM upgrade is about. What's more important than that is knowing what to do with the memory and how to use it. What's the point of having a potential 16Mb of RAM in your PC if you have nothing to do with it? There are ways to put all that memory to work in your computer—right now. Even if no program you own requires more than 256K, there are benefits to having a PC with lots of memory installed, which is why it's one of the most important upgrades you can make.

The subject of what to do with your computer's memory—the software side—is covered in this chapter. The actual installation of chips—the hardware side—is covered in the next chapter.

The first part of this chapter deals with general memory concepts, bytes and K's, how DOS uses memory, and the different types of memory in a PC. The second part tells you how to use software to get the most from the RAM in your computer. The last part of this chapter covers what can be done with memory, with specific concentration on expanded memory and how it can be useful.

 ## How Memory Is Used

Computer memory is commonly referred to as RAM, which stands for random access memory. It is temporary storage, controlled by the PC's microprocessor and used by software to let you create and manipulate information. It's really quite versatile and the more you have, the more your PC can do.

The microprocessor is your PC's brain. You can think of it as a high-speed calculator. But the calculator is absentminded; it has nowhere to put the results it calculates, so extra storage is needed. Storage can be either temporary or permanent.

RAM is temporary storage, because when you turn off the power, RAM's contents are lost. To complement RAM, the computer has disk drives to store data permanently. Information saved to disk memory isn't erased when you turn off the computer's power.

But the microprocessor cannot directly manipulate information stored on disk. It only works directly with RAM. In fact, in addition to the microprocessor's mathematical duties, one of the things it does best is to manipulate memory. That's where it stores values and compares, copies, and moves around information. All this happens automatically, so don't lose any sleep over it. The more memory you have, the more information you can store and the more information the microprocessor (as directed by your software) can manipulate.

◣ *B*ytes, *K's, and Megs*

When computer storage is measured, the *byte* is used as the basic unit. To understand memory, you'll need to know this term, as well as two others: kilobyte and megabyte.

What is a byte? You can consider a byte as equivalent to a single character: a letter of the alphabet, symbol, or punctuation mark. The word byte is four bytes long—it contains four characters and would be stored in four bytes of computer memory.

Bytes are composed of *bits*. A bit is a binary digit, a one or zero. Computers count using bits. These bits are grouped into sets of eight to make one byte.

At the next level, bytes are grouped into kilobytes and megabytes. They're terms used to describe memory storage. The *kilobyte,* usually abbreviated as *K,* is 1024 bytes. Since computers deal with binary digits—base 2—1024 is the power of two closest to 1000 (2^{10} = 1024), and K is the common abbreviation for 1000. So when you refer to 1K, you're referring to 1024 bytes, or about half a page of written text.

The *megabyte,* abbreviated as *M,* or *Mb* (the convention used in this book), represents about one million bytes, or exactly 1024K. In bytes that's 1024 times 1024, or 1,048,576 bytes of information.

Memory Basics

The amount of memory a computer can use is related to the design of its microprocessor. The amount of memory a microprocessor can use directly is referred to as its *address space*. For example, the 8080 microprocessor, common in many older CP/M computers, can address 64K.

The first IBM PC used an 8088 microprocessor. It can directly address up to 1024K, or 1Mb, of memory. The 1024K is divided into sixteen 64K chunks. Each 64K chunk is called a *segment* of memory, and they are numbered segments 0–9 and then A–F. Figure 5.1 shows a PC's *memory map* and illustrates the locations of RAM and ROM in a typical IBM-compatible computer.

Segments 0–9 are designated for RAM. This is the standard 640K that holds programs when you are using them. It's often called *conventional* memory or *low* memory. Segments A–F, called *high* memory, are reserved for special RAM locations, such as video display memory and ROM (such as your PC's BIOS and the hard-drive controller). Other locations, not currently used, are marked "reserved" by IBM. For example, segment E is used for ROM in the PS/2 system. But most PCs don't use these areas.

ROM

ROM is read-only memory. It is accessed like RAM, but it cannot be written to. It stores information permanently, so the information can only be read (hence *read-only*). The contents of ROM are not lost when the power is turned off.

Computers use ROM for a variety of purposes. The PC's BIOS is stored on a ROM chip. ROM chips are used for EGA and VGA video controllers and your hard-disk controller.

You should know about ROM because, like RAM, it supplies memory locations in your PC. The locations supplied by ROM subtract from the amount of memory that can be provided by RAM and therefore further limit the total amount of RAM available to your programs.

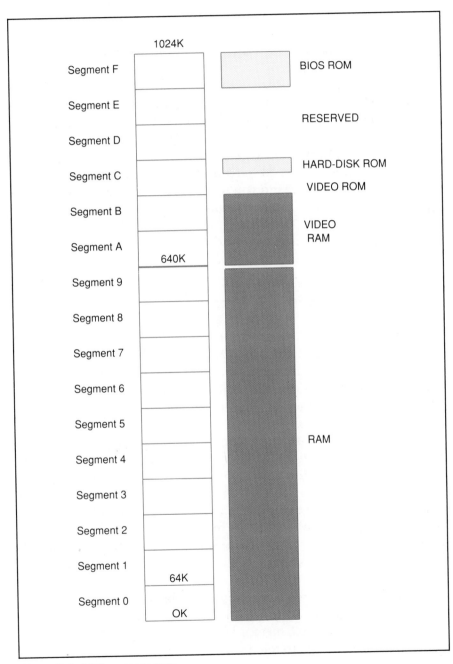

Figure 5.1: A PC memory map

Contiguous Memory

Other than the 1Mb limit on a PC's usable RAM under DOS, you should also know that memory in a PC is *contiguous*. You can't have logical "holes" in a PC's RAM. RAM must start at memory location 0 and increase from there without skipping any memory locations. It helps to think of your PC's memory as if it were composed of bricks stacked on top of one other. Each brick is a segment of memory.

Why is this important to know? Because when you upgrade your PC's RAM, you must do so from low to high memory locations. If your PC only has 256K and you want 512K, you must add the extra 256K on top of the first. Memory must be placed into the machine in a contiguous manner. There can't be any holes. You can't overlap memory either—this results in conflicts and POST errors.

Upgrading Memory—A History

When the first PC came out, it was equipped with only 64K of RAM. A 16K version was also available, but without disk drives. The memory potential for the machine at that time was only 512K. Later, it was boosted to 640K. But the basic PC had room for only 64K on its motherboard. Extra memory had to be added by means of expansion cards.

Later PCs came with more memory on the motherboard. During the reign of the PC/XT, 256K was standard. The introduction of the 384K memory expansion board made it possible to add 384K to give you 640K. You bought an expansion card, packed it full of RAM chips, and installed it in your PC. You told the card that it had the full 384K, and then you told it that its memory started at location 256K (the memory already in the computer). Finally, you set the DIP switches on the motherboard, telling the computer how much RAM it now had installed.

The DIP switches were very important, but confusing for many PC owners. DIP switches were used in two instances: first, to tell the expansion card how much memory it had installed and where the memory started, and second, to tell the PC how much total memory it had.

It was more confusing if you had one of the earlier 64K or 128K motherboards. Adding a 384K expansion board to a 64K system meant you had a total of 448K of RAM in your PC. You told the computer this by setting the motherboard's DIP switches. You also had to tell the expansion card it had 384K of RAM and that the RAM started at address 64K. If you added another 192K of RAM (to give you the full 640K), you had to fill a second expansion card with 192K, tell that expansion card it had 192K of RAM installed, and also tell it that the RAM started at address 448K.

Currently, most PCs come with at least 640K of RAM already on the motherboard. If not, you can upgrade by adding chips directly to the motherboard. And if that's not possible, you can buy expansion cards to zoom you up to 640K. Many AT and 386 computers come with 1Mb of RAM installed, and there are ways that you can take advantage of the extra memory. I'll explain these ways later in this chapter.

How to Find Out How Much Memory You Have

There are two DOS commands you can use to check the amount of memory in your system.

The first command is CHKDSK. It looks for lost files and attempts to fix them if any are found. When CHKDSK is done, it also displays the amount of memory in your system. For example, you may see a message like the following:

```
C:\> CHKDSK
Volume TOO LOUD   created Sep 24, 1988 5:03p

33409024 bytes total disk space
358400 bytes in 6 hidden files
133120 bytes in 61 directories
27451392 bytes in 1150 user files
5466112 bytes available on disk

655360 bytes total memory
567808 bytes free
```

CHKDSK displays information about the disk, its volume label, the date the label was attached, the disk space and number of files, and the total amount of memory. According to the output, this PC has 655,360 bytes of total memory, of which 567,808 bytes are free. The rest is used by DOS (or any memory-resident programs).

The second command you can use to check on memory is *MEM* (available only in DOS 4.0). Unlike CHKDSK, MEM displays all sorts of information about memory, such as the following:

655360 bytes total memory
655360 bytes available
566000 largest executable program size

3145728 bytes total extended memory
3145728 bytes available extended memory

This display shows you the maximum memory in your system, the amount available, and the largest program size you can load (which is *really* the total amount available). Below this are values showing the amount of extended or expanded memory available (if any).

MEM also has two optional switches: /PROGRAM and /DEBUG. The /PROGRAM switch lists the addresses, names, and sizes of all programs loaded into memory. The /DEBUG switch lists the same information, but includes additional details describing how memory is used. The details of the MEM command are only of real use to programmers.

Getting the Most Out of 640K or Less

Not every program you run on your PC will take up lots of memory. Some programs run just fine in only 40K of RAM. And for a long time, it seemed as if any program on the PC was swimming in 640K of RAM. So a lot of people thought of interesting uses for that extra memory.

Memory-Resident Programs

The most popular way to take advantage of unused memory is to use *memory-resident programs*. These are programs that don't release the RAM they use when they quit. Instead, they stay in memory. (The term *TSR,* often used to describe memory-resident software, comes from the DOS function called *Terminate and Stay Resident.*)

Memory-resident software usually monitors some state in your PC. For example, it may monitor the clock and display the current time on the screen 24 hours a day. Or it may monitor the keyboard, waiting for a special key combination to be pressed. When you hit those keys, the program comes alive and "pops up" on top of whatever you're doing. Other types of memory-resident software modify the way your PC works, emulate a certain printer or graphics adapter, or give DOS more features.

RAM Disks

Another popular use for extra memory is to use it in a *RAM disk.* A RAM disk, also called an electronic disk or VDISK (virtual disk), is a disk drive that uses RAM for storage instead of a physical disk. A device driver is loaded by CONFIG.SYS to set aside an area of memory. Then DOS is fooled into thinking that the RAM is actually a disk drive. It proceeds to format it and assign it a drive letter. From that point on, you can treat the area of RAM just like a disk drive.

The RAM disk has the advantage of being much faster than a physical disk, but otherwise it's treated the same as any other drive in your system. The only drawback is that, like all RAM, when you turn off the power, the contents of the RAM disk are lost.

Disk Caches

A *disk cache* is a storage area in memory. It monitors all disk activity and, over the long run, makes all disk access much quicker.

Any time DOS reads information from disk, a copy of it is kept in the cache memory. If the same data needs to be read again, the cache program picks it up from cache memory, instead of reading it from disk. Since most disk access is repetitive, this greatly speeds all disk operations. And unlike a RAM disk, the cache only keeps a copy of information already on disk. Information is still written directly to disk, so nothing is lost if the power goes out.

Print Spoolers

A *print spooler* is an area of memory that stores characters waiting for the printer to print them. The printer is the slowest device in your computer system.

Most of the time, the computer waits for the printer to begin printing. A print spooler sets aside a small area in memory, so all characters sent to the printer go to memory first. They wait there while the spooler program dishes them out to the printer a handful at a time. During this time you can continue using the computer. The spooler will only steal computer time when the printer is ready to print. This allows you to get your printing done while you're using the computer for something else.

 # Smashing the 640K Barrier

You probably know the saying by heart: DOS is limited to running programs in 640K of RAM, the first ten 64K segments of memory in your PC. Memory above that is used as High DOS memory, for your video RAM, hard-disk-controller ROM, and the BIOS. And DOS can't access memory beyond 1Mb. So that leaves you with 640K of RAM. Or does it?

Internally, DOS only loads programs in Conventional DOS memory, your basic 640K of RAM. But the programs themselves could really sit anywhere in that 1Mb of DOS memory. After all, there is no brick wall at 640K. So to take advantage of more memory, you can resort to several interesting tricks:

- Stealing video memory
- Using High DOS memory other than video memory

These are both legitimate ways to sneak in more memory under DOS. The first simply expands DOS's usable memory space. The second allows you to move memory-resident software and certain device-drivers out of Conventional and into High DOS memory, making your basic RAM space larger. Both of these tricks are possible through the hardware and software of LIM 4.0 EMS.

Stealing Video Memory

Refer back to the PC memory map (Figure 5.1). You see that video memory starts right after the 640K DOS barrier. Actually, video memory doesn't fully occupy that amount of space. Instead, the memory used depends on which display adapter you have. Figure 5.2 shows how each display adapter uses video memory.

The Monochrome Display Adapter (MDA) and Color Graphics Adapter (CGA) graphics adapters use only a part of segment B for their RAM. But the Enhanced Graphics Adapter (EGA) and Video Graphics Array (VGA) use two full segments of memory, 128K, providing they're both fully equipped.

Since EGA and VGA are both compatible with CGA, it's possible to run them both in the CGA mode. In that mode, the video display only uses RAM in the upper half of segment B. That's only 32K from the 128K supplied with the card and leaves 96K of video RAM left over. Using the right software, that 96K can be added right to the basic 640K of RAM in a PC, giving you 736K of usable memory under DOS.

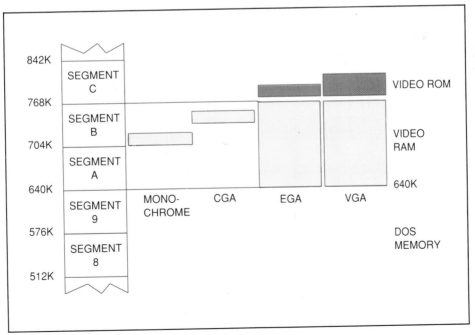

Figure 5.2: How the various PC video displays use memory

There are quite a few software packages that do this, including some in the public domain. All the software packages listed later in this chapter can do the job for you. But note that you must have fully equipped EGA or VGA graphics in your system to do this. Also, you forgo the advanced graphics capabilities of these adapters when you run them in the CGA-only mode (which means you can't take advantage of fancy graphics packages when you have 736K of DOS memory). Finally, not every program will recognize or use the extra RAM. Some will, especially if you're using one of the memory management packages covered later in this chapter.

*U*sing High DOS Memory Other Than Video Memory

One of the main benefits of LIM 4.0 (discussed in the section "Expanded Memory") is its memory mapping abilities. If you use an LIM 4.0 memory expansion board that has hardware registers in combination with a good EMS device driver, you can do fancy things with memory. (On a 386, you only need a capable memory device-driver.) These memory mapping abilities allow you to squeeze EMS RAM into any part of your PC's basic 1Mb of memory. This includes High DOS memory and the holes left there—space unused by ROM or video RAM.

For example, on most PCs, segments D and E are left empty. Using LIM 4.0 and a device driver (such as Quarterdeck's QRAM or Qualitas's MOVE'EM), you can fill in the holes in High DOS memory with usable RAM. Programs can't run "up there," but it is possible to load device drivers, such as the mouse driver, network drivers, ANSI-.SYS, and so on. When you put these memory-resident programs and device drivers into High DOS memory, it frees up your basic 640K of RAM, giving your programs more breathing room.

Also, by using LIM 4.0 and special software drivers, you can "fake" extra video memory—even in systems that don't have EGA or VGA. QRAM or MOVE'EM will fill in unused memory in segment A and allow you to have up to 736K of RAM.

Remember, a 386 PC is also capable of these memory manipulations. You don't need LIM 4.0 EMS hardware on a 386, however, because the 386 microprocessor has more powerful memory-management abilities built in. But you do need a capable device-driver. Two of the best are Quarterdeck's QEMM and Qualitas's 386MAX. Both offer features similar or identical to QRAM and MOVE'EM, but they are customized for the 386 environment.

Adding Memory Beyond 640K

You can add memory so that you have access to more than 640K. This memory comes in two forms:

- expanded memory
- extended memory

Of the two, expanded memory is more useful under DOS.

Expanded Memory

Lack of memory was first noticed by spreadsheet users. Spreadsheets require a lot of RAM, and Conventional DOS memory (the basic 640K) just doesn't cut it. So Lotus, Intel, and Microsoft got together and developed the *Expanded Memory Specification,* or *EMS.*

EMS defines expanded memory. This memory isn't really part of the DOS memory, and it doesn't start at address 1024K on the memory map. Instead, it's a pool of RAM—a storage area that can be up to 8Mb in size. (The current version of EMS, LIM 4.0, allows for up to 32Mb of expanded memory.)

Expanded memory is accessed via one of the reserved segments in High DOS memory, for example, segment D or E. (High DOS memory consists of all memory locations from 640K to 1024K.) That segment provides a 64K window into the larger pool of EMS memory. Through that window you can access any part of EMS memory. And then your software can access that memory, which has since been copied into segment D or E.

The reserved segment is called the *page frame.* It contains four 16K windows, each of which contains a copy of a chunk of EMS memory found somewhere in the memory pool. To access that memory, a program uses the EMS device driver. (The device driver controls EMS memory and how it's accessed.)

Accessing up to 8Mb of RAM, using only four tiny 16K windows, may sound kind of awkward. But when you consider that your hard drive is accessed only 512 bytes at a time, and that memory is faster than disk, then you can see the speed involved. And EMS solved the basic problem: It gave spreadsheet users access to larger amounts of memory.

Eventually, quite a few software packages took advantage of EMS memory. They only used it for storage, because you cannot run programs in EMS memory—only in the basic 640K. And if there is any extra EMS memory left over, you can use it to create RAM disks, disk caches, or print spoolers.

After a time, a second expanded memory scheme was developed. Called EEMS, it offered many advantages over the first LIM EMS. Developed by Ashton-Tate, AST Technology, and Quadram, EEMS didn't limit expanded memory access to four 16K pages in a single 64K page frame in High DOS memory. Instead, using EEMS, you could swap out a major chunk of memory just about anywhere in the PC. This had tremendous advantages in speed, storage, and flexibility.

Eventually, the two standards were merged under LIM 4.0 EMS. Under this expanded memory specification, any amount of memory at almost any location in the PC's RAM can quickly be swapped to expanded memory. This has two advantages. The first advantage is that more data can be moved quickly using LIM 4.0 EMS. Instead of swapping a spreadsheet into memory 16K at a time, you can swap in, say, 348K at a time. The second advantage is that programs can also be swapped in and out of memory. Under the guidance of the proper software, several applications can be swapped in and out of memory at a time, allowing you to easily switch between them. Of course, the programs can't run once they've been swapped to expanded memory. That memory is used only for storage; no software can run from there. But it does add an extra level of convenience to using a PC, and it helped to legitimize the DOS program switcher as usable software.

Extended Memory

Expanded memory was developed for the PC/XT. It works under DOS, which can directly address only 1Mb. But the newer 286 and 386 microprocessors are capable of directly accessing much more memory, so-called *extended memory*.

Extended memory is memory beyond 1Mb in a PC/AT, 286, or 386 system and cannot be used by DOS. It can only be accessed when the 286 or 386 is operating in its *protected mode.* This is an advanced mode of the microprocessor, whereby memory is protected and allocated to each program. DOS was developed for *real mode,* which is the 8088-compatible operating mode of both the 286 and 386. When these microprocessors run DOS, they're in real mode and cannot access or use extended memory.

Extended memory is, in effect, shut off from use by DOS. However, extended memory can be converted into the more useful expanded memory under DOS. This is done by means of a software driver that converts the extended memory into LIM 4.0-compatible expanded memory.

If you have an AT- or 286-compatible system, you can choose from among several programs to "change" extended into expanded memory. (Strictly speaking, these programs allow for emulation of expanded memory.) Four of the best are Above DISC from Above Software, MOVE'EM from Qualitas, Turbo EMS from Merrill-Bryan Enterprises, Inc., and QRAM (pronounced "cram") from Quarterdeck Office Systems.

The 386 systems deal with memory differently from 286 systems. If you have a 386 PC and would like to convert your extended memory into expanded memory, I recommend two programs: 386MAX from Qualitas or QEMM from Quarterdeck.

Additional information on using these packages to enhance memory in your PC is covered later in this chapter. But talking about all these conversion programs brings up an interesting question: What good is extended memory?

Extended memory is used primarily for protected-mode operating systems, such as Xenix, UNIX, and OS/2. In those environments, the 286 and 386 microprocessors operate in their native, protected mode and can access their megabytes of RAM directly.

Under DOS, the 286 and 386 operate in real mode, where DOS lives. There, extended memory is either ignored, or converted to expanded memory by means of a device driver.

There are several applications that run under DOS *and* use the 286 and 386's protected mode. These programs use software programs known as *DOS extenders* to switch between protected and real modes. That way, the software can take advantage of extended memory, the microprocessor's power, and the protected mode and still be compatible with DOS. Examples of such applications include Lotus 1-2-3 Release 3 (and later versions) and AutoCAD 386.

Using software enhanced with a DOS extender, you can take full advantage of your 286 or 386 computer's power and still keep your other DOS software. But keep in mind that a DOS extender is part of a program. You don't buy it separately; it's used by the program developer to create DOS-extended software.

If you're going to be packing your PC full of RAM, you might as well put it all to use.

 ## *U*sing Expanded Memory

Expanded memory was developed to give DOS users more memory storage. Remember that expanded memory is actually a memory storage device, a pool of memory in which data can be stored. You cannot run software in expanded memory.

The computer industry, long a lover of standards but always short on following them, has settled on the Lotus-Intel-Microsoft Expanded Memory System, version 4.0, abbreviated LIM 4.0 EMS. It's a set of rules governing hardware and software that control expanded memory.

*E*MS Hardware

On the hardware side, LIM 4.0 is available on LIM 4.0-compatible expansion cards. If you buy one of these cards, make sure it's hardware-compatible at the register level. The box must specify "register level," because it can be LIM 4.0-compatible without hardware registers (in which case you lack the full benefits of the LIM 4.0 system).

Also, on the hardware side, to get the most from LIM 4.0, you should disable as much of your motherboard memory as possible. Usually this is done in your 286's setup program or by means of the DIP switches on a PC/XT. Simply tell the motherboard that it has only 256K (or less, if possible) of RAM. The rest of your Conventional DOS memory will be supplied by means of the LIM 4.0 expansion card, through a technique known as *backfilling.*

Backfilling memory is the best way to get the most from LIM 4.0 on a PC or AT (286) computer. If you have a 386 system, you already have built-in memory management equal to LIM 4.0 in your micro-processor. (You only need the software to take advantage of it.) But for other systems, replacing motherboard memory with LIM 4.0 memory means that memory can quickly be swapped out to the EMS pool of RAM. The LIM 4.0 software driver can deal with RAM more efficiently if all of it is on the EMS memory board, as opposed to your system's motherboard.

EMS Software

On the software side, your LIM 4.0-compatible memory card needs an LIM 4.0 driver. The driver comes with the card and is called something like *EMS.SYS.* You install the driver in your CONFIG.SYS file by using the format

DEVICE = EMS.SYS

From there, any software you use on your PC that takes advantage of EMS memory can access it. Under LIM 4.0, you can have up to 32Mb of EMS RAM in your PC. Though you may not use all that, any amount you have can greatly improve the performance of some software.

But to get the most from all that EMS memory, you really need a superior memory-management application. The four best for PC- and AT-level systems are Above DISC, MOVE'EM, Turbo EMS, and QRAM. MOVE'EM and QRAM will even remap EMS memory into High DOS memory, as well as load device drivers and memory-resident soft-ware there. If you have EGA or VGA graphics, video memory can be used to boost DOS to 736K.

PCs with 386 microprocessors already have advanced memory-management capabilities built into their systems. However, a mem-ory driver is necessary to emulate LIM 4.0, as well as to convert extended memory into expanded memory. The two best packages for that purpose are 386MAX and QEMM. Additionally, these pack-ages control the 386's virtual mode, allowing you to run multiple DOS applications on a 386 system.

So the memory situation under DOS isn't that bleak. Lots of software supports LIM 4.0, as well as the basic Expanded Memory Specification. The key advantage of LIM 4.0 is its ability to quickly swap out major portions of DOS memory to EMS memory (and it does it more quickly when you have backfill). This comes into play with certain applications known as *program switchers*. They allow you to quickly switch between several programs, swapping unused ones out to EMS memory. And on the basic level, EMS memory will always be there for programs that need a lot of memory to store their data.

Using Extended Memory

Extended memory is a white elephant under DOS. Any time you add memory beyond 1Mb to an AT, 286, or 386 system, you're adding extended memory. DOS is a real-mode operating system. Extended memory can only be used in the 80286 and 80386's protected mode. Therefore, the memory just sits around wasted under DOS.

A few DOS applications can use extended memory directly. VDISK and other DOS utilities can be loaded into extended memory. Outside of DOS, other operating systems like OS/2 and UNIX use (and need) extended memory directly. But under DOS, extended memory is only useful when you convert it to expanded memory.

However, a recent development has been the so-called DOS extender. A DOS extender isn't a program you can buy off the shelf. Rather, it's a subprogram that software developers can include in the applications they create. It lets DOS, a real-mode-only operating system, run protected-mode programs. These protected-mode programs can then take advantage of extended memory.

DOS extenders give you the best of both worlds. On one side, you have an application that takes full advantage of your 286 or 386's powerful protected mode and extended memory. And on the other side, you're still running familiar old DOS. You don't have to move up to a more powerful operating system to get the most from what you already have.

Several DOS-extended applications are currently available. The most popular is Lotus 1-2-3 (the 286/386 version). More packages will appear as time goes by, eventually peeling the white elephant label from extended memory. But until that happens, just remember that it's possible to convert extended memory into expanded memory for use under DOS.

◣ Summary

You can't be too rich, too thin, or have too much RAM in your PC. But having all that RAM isn't enough. Your PC can be filled with RAM chips, giving you many megabytes of storage, but the key is putting all that RAM to use.

Under DOS, memory is put into three categories. The basic category is DOS memory. It has two parts: Conventional DOS memory (RAM up to 640K), where your programs run and where you get your work done, and High DOS memory, where the BIOS, video RAM, and other ROM chips are. Programs don't run in High DOS memory.

Given the limitations of DOS memory, expanded memory was developed. It's basically memory storage outside of DOS memory. Currently, expanded memory is governed by the LIM 4.0 EMS standard. That standard allows for up to 32Mb of expanded memory to be used for a variety of purposes.

EMS memory is still used only for memory storage. However, there are ways to get more out of it. Using backfill, you can take advantage of LIM 4.0's advanced memory-mapping and swapping power. And using the right device-driver, you can relocate memory-resident software and other device drivers in High DOS memory, freeing up your basic RAM space.

Extended memory is memory beyond the 1Mb level in a 286 or 386 system. It's only used by those microprocessors in their protected mode. Since DOS runs in real mode, it can't access extended memory. Therefore, to use that memory under DOS, you need to convert it into the more flexible expanded memory. Device drivers are available for both the 286 and 386 to make this possible and to allow you to reap the benefits of LIM 4.0 EMS memory in your PC.

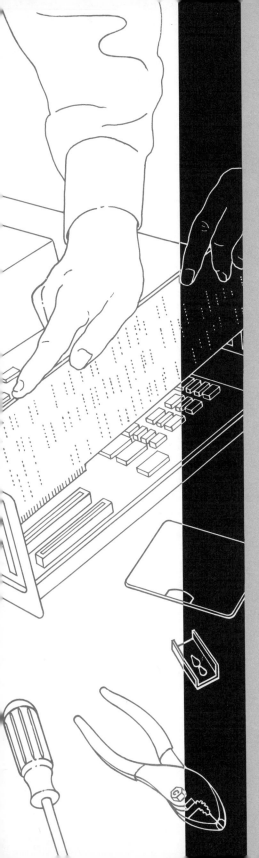

6

Upgrading
Memory:
The Hardware
Side

IT ISN'T THAT TOUGH TO ADD RAM TO YOUR PC. IT'S ONE of the basic upgrades, requiring only a bit more skill than plugging in Lego blocks, but a lot more patience. There are no secrets, no tricks, nor is there anything hidden from you. You can buy chips just about anywhere and plug them in yourself.

This chapter covers the physical aspects of upgrading memory—plugging chips into sockets.

 ## All About Chips

In the early days of computer memory, RAM was stored on a grid of wires. A magnetic "doughnut" was looped through an intersection of two wires, and it held a positive or negative charge, representing a bit somewhere in memory.

Today RAM comes on chips. These chips come in a variety of sizes, hold different amounts of memory, run at different speeds, and can be installed in the PC in a number of ways.

There are two types of RAM chips: *static* and *dynamic*. Static RAM (SRAM) chips are high-speed, and they don't require constant *refreshing* to retain their contents. (Refreshing is the process of writing information to a chip after it has been read from.) But they're expensive. If you have them in your PC, they're probably soldered into the motherboard and used for RAM caches to speed up the microprocessor. Static RAM is rarely used as part of your DOS memory.

Dynamic RAM (DRAM, pronounced "Dee-RAM") chips are more common than SRAM chips, and they're usually what we refer to when speaking about a PC's RAM. They're slower than SRAM chips. DRAMs are inexpensive and widely available. They also constitute the majority of the chips you'll be installing in your PC.

DIPs, SIMMs, and SIPs

There are three basic types of DRAM chips you'll find in a PC:

- DIPs
- SIMMs
- SIPs

The most common type of RAM chip is the DIP, or *dual in-line package,* chip. (This is different from a DIP switch.) It's a flat, black rectangle with several metal legs on either side.

Figure 6.1 shows a rendition of the typical DIP-style RAM chip. It's a thin black rectangle, a little under an inch long and about ⅖ of an inch wide. On the long sides of the chip are rows of eight metal legs. The legs plug the chip into a similar-size socket—just like Lego blocks. This is the basic type of RAM chip.

SIMM is an abbreviation for *single in-line memory module*. It's actually like a mini-memory expansion card. About half the size of a playing card, a SIMM is fitted with nine DIP chips. One of the long ends of the SIMM usually has a row of tiny metal connectors. That edge plugs into a slot. (Figure 6.2 shows a typical SIMM.)

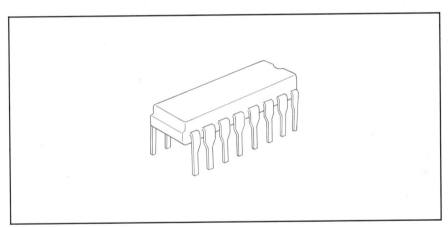

Figure 6.1: A typical DIP-style RAM chip

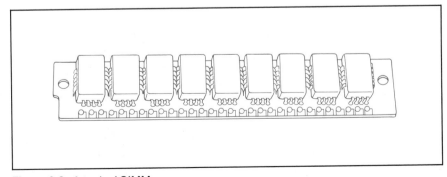

Figure 6.2: A typical SIMM

SIMMs were developed to help prevent chip damage. It's much easier to plug in a sturdy card with DIP chips already on it than to plug the chips in one by one and risk damaging them. Unlike the DIP-style RAM chip's legs, SIMM connectors don't bend or break easily. And one side is notched so you can't plug them in backward.

There are two kinds of DIP chips you will find on a SIMM. Some SIMMs use standard DIP chips, which are plugged or soldered directly into the SIMM card. Other SIMMS use *surface mount* chips. The surface mount chips are smaller, making the SIMM thinner and more suitable in cramped situations. You can tell a surface mount chip primarily because its legs are thinner and are soldered onto the surface, as opposed to through, the card.

Finally there are SIPs—SIP stands for *single in-line package*. SIPs are like SIMMs in every way, except for how they're installed. Unlike a SIMM, which uses an edge connector to plug into a slot, a SIP has a row of pins that plug into holes (it looks like a mustache comb). SIPs are not as common as SIMMs, and they are more fragile. Normally, they're installed at the factory and are not intended to be user-upgradeable items. But if you have to plug one in, be very careful.

Chip Capacities

Chips are rated in terms of their capacity and speed. Capacity is the amount of K the chip stores. RAM chips are grouped into *banks*. Only a number of chips grouped into a bank are capable of storing information.

The capacity of a chip is measured in bits. For example, the common sizes of RAM chips are 16K, 64K, 256K, and 1024K. So if you buy a 256K chip, you're really buying a 256-kilobit chip. A 1024K chip is a 1-megabit chip.

A bank of RAM in a system with 8-bit architecture has nine chips. Because there are 8 bits in a byte, it would seem that there is an extra chip—the ninth chip is the parity chip. It's used to verify and check the contents of the other eight chips. This is one way the PC ensures against RAM errors.

In the 286- and 386-based systems, a bank of chips may have 18 chips, double that of the PC/XT's 9 chips (it includes two chips for parity checking).

At present, the two most popular sizes of chips are the 256-kilobit and 1-megabit chips. The 16-kilobit and 64-kilobit chips still exist, and you can upgrade older PCs with them. An oddball 128-kilobit chip was used in the original PC/AT, but it is no longer used.

Chip Speeds

The second way a chip is rated is in terms of its speed, the maximum rate at which it will function—which determines the rate at which the microprocessor can write to the chip. The speed of a chip is measured in *nanoseconds,* abbreviated as *ns.* (A nanosecond is one-billionth of a second, or the time it takes a beam of light to travel just under 12 inches.) An 80-ns chip, for example, can be written to by the microprocessor at intervals of 80 ns; a 120-ns chip is slower because the intervals are 40 ns longer.

In the early days, 200- and 250-ns chips were needed for most microcomputers. But at present, speeds of 150, 120, 100, and 80 ns (from slowest to fastest) are popular. PC/XTs and ATs can use the 150- and 120-ns chips. But fast 386s and very fast 286s require 100- or 80-ns chips to keep up with the speed of the microprocessor. And the chips get more expensive as the speed increases.

When you buy a lot of chips, you'll want to make sure you get the right speed for your system. Chips rated at 150 ns or 120 ns are fine for most PCs. But if you have a 386, you will need the faster chips.

You can mix chip speeds in a bank, though its best to mix in only faster chips. Putting a 120-ns chip in a bank of 80-ns chips slows down your computer, and the chip may overheat, fail, or cause parity errors. But there's nothing wrong with sticking a 120-ns chip in a bank of 150-ns chips, though it's a waste of money.

Chip Quantities

With few exceptions, most chips are packaged in groups of nine. So if you want to add 256K to your system, you need to buy nine 256-kilobit chips.

If you're upgrading memory by using SIMMs (which is dependent upon having SIMM sockets on your motherboard or memory expansion card), they come with all nine chips installed. To add 256K to your system, you buy a 256K SIMM; to add 1Mb, you buy a 1Mb SIMM. Some expansion schemes require upgrading in given increments, such as 512K.

Some motherboards may have an odd memory scheme to fill out the final 128K of Conventional DOS memory. In these cases, the memory chips used won't be of the typical 256K × 1-bit variety. For example, to fill in that last 128K of RAM you may use four 64K × 4-bit chips plus two 64K × 1-bit chips. That's only 6 chips, but it still comes out to 128K.

In some 286 and 386 systems, memory must be upgraded by given increments. For example, there's no such thing as a 386 with 1.5Mb of RAM. All memory in a 386 must be installed within the 1Mb limit. Even then, the number of megabytes in some systems must be a specific number: 1, 2, 4, 8, 10, or 16. This is all based on the design of the system and how it uses memory (the number of SIMMs that can be installed).

Chip Numbers

Finally, you should be familiar with the code that's printed on the top of every RAM chip. This code tells you what kind of chip you're looking at, its capacity, and its speed. Knowing how to read these values comes in handy when you find a loose chip or when you're shopping so that you know you're getting what you paid for.

On top of a chip, there's usually a design logo, the name of the country where the chip was made, and a lot of numbers. A seasoned RAM chip guru, for example, could tell you that a chip with KM41256AP-12 on it is a 256-kilobit one running at 120 ns.

The chip's capacity is always listed first. It's usually the last part of the first group of numbers on the top row of numbers. Common values are listed below:

Number	Meaning
164	64K × 1 bit
264	64K × 2 bits
1128	128K × 1 bit
2128	128K × 2 bits

Number	Meaning
1256	256K × 1 bit
2256	256K × 2 bits
4256	256K × 4 bits
11000	1024K × 1 bit
21000	1024K × 2 bits
41000	1024K × 4 bits

There may be additional numbers before the numbers listed here. (Usually the first number is a *4*.) And there may be letters before or after the number. But typically, the numbers will be followed by a hyphen and two other numbers. It's these numbers after the hyphen, which make up the *suffix,* that tell you the chip's speed. In the example KM41256AP-12, the numbers are 1 and 2, which indicates a speed of 120 ns. Here are some other chip numbers and their meanings:

Number	Meaning
– 15	150 ns
– 12	120 ns
– 10	100 ns
– 80	80 ns

Not every chip (or manufacturer) adheres to these rules. And there will be other speed values as well: – 85 for 85 ns, – 20 for 200 ns, and so on. Some chips may even use one number, such as 8 for 80 ns.

An experienced eye can read a chip's code in no time to decipher what kind of chip it is and how fast it runs. Here are the numbers from the tops of several different chips and what they mean:

Chip Numbers	Meaning
8810 8 USA MT 1259-12	256-kilobit chip, 120 ns
KM41C1000AJ-8	1-megabit chip, 80 ns
53C464S-10	64K × 4-bit chip, 100 ns
4164C-15	64-kilobit chip, 150 ns

In the first example, 1259 refers to a 256K × 1-bit chip. The 9 probably indicates that it's one chip in a bank of nine. But since the numbering scheme comes close to no other value, you can assume it's a 256-kilobit chip.

Some values are likely to throw you. For example, the early 16-kilobit chips on the first IBM computers had the following numbers on them:

AM9016DPC
8132WMP

These chips don't follow today's conventions, but you can still make out the 16 in the first number, which is the tip-off that it's a 16-kilobit chip. You may occasionally come across other chips that don't appear to follow any conventions, but it's not hard to take a guess at their speed and their capacity. If you are at all unsure, consult your documentation or your vendor.

Where Chips Go

There are three places inside your PC where you'll be installing RAM:

- The motherboard
- An expansion slot
- A proprietary slot

The motherboard is probably where most (or all) of your basic memory is stored. Why? Because that's the best arrangement. A lot of RAM directly on the motherboard is usually a sign of a well-designed PC.

Some systems may have room for megabytes of RAM to be installed on the motherboard. Others may have room for only 640K or less. Whatever the case, it's best to first pack your motherboard full of RAM. In fact, the only time that will work against you is if you have a PC or AT system (not a 386) and are using an LIM 4.0-compatible EMS card. (Refer to Chapter 5.)

After your motherboard is loaded full of RAM, you can add extra memory by means of an expansion slot and a memory card. The memory card can do two things for you: It can bring your basic memory up to 640K (if there isn't room for it on the motherboard), and it can give you expanded memory.

Finally, the last place you can add memory to your system is in a proprietary, or dedicated, memory slot. This slot is actually an extension of motherboard memory, not memory that comes on an expansion slot. A special memory-expansion board is plugged into the proprietary slot. It's called *proprietary* because there are no standards for this type of memory card. Each manufacturer devises its own scheme for the card.

The proprietary slots appear mostly on 386 systems. The 386's microprocessor works best if the memory it accesses is in full 32-bit mode. Memory on an expansion card can only be accessed in 16-bit mode via the PC's bus. Therefore, to get the most from the 386, the special memory slot is used.

In all three locations, you'll be installing RAM chips in banks of nine, or all nine at once if you have a SIP or a SIMM. Some motherboards may have memory installed in banks of six chips, but most PCs have banks of nine.

Also, 386 computers have specific memory-upgrade requirements. You must add memory in given increments. The design of the 386 requires that memory be added in specific amounts so that you get the most from the system. It can get expensive, but what you get in performance is worth the cost.

Buying Chips

When you buy RAM chips, there are several things you need to know in advance:

- The amount of RAM you're going to install
- How many chips you need
- The capacity of the chips
- The speed of the chips

Normally, if you want to add 1Mb of RAM to your PC, you'll be buying a set of nine 1-megabit chips, or four sets of nine 256-kilobit chips. (Four times 256K is 1Mb, and you need 9 times 4, or 36, chips to equal 1Mb.)

The amount and capacity of chips you buy is determined by where you're putting the memory and what type of memory is required. For example, if you have an upgrade card that requires four banks of 256-kilobit chips to make 1Mb of RAM, then those are the chips you buy. If you're putting 1Mb on the motherboard and it requires a 1Mb SIMM, then that's what you buy.

After you know the amount (total RAM) and quantity (number of chips), you need to know the capacity and speed of the chips. Capacity is related to the total amount of RAM you're installing and the number of chips. Again, you could have nine 1-megabit chips or four banks of nine 256-kilobit chips. It all depends on where you're installing the memory and what types of chips are required. I recommend that you go with the highest capacity wherever possible. In the long run, buying 1-megabit chips will save you money, even though individually they are more expensive.

You also need to keep in mind the speed of the chips when you shop for them. Your PC's manufacturer will probably have set certain guidelines for RAM speed. But generally speaking, 150 or 120 ns is fast enough for a PC/XT system, 120 ns or 100 ns is fast enough for most ATs and 286s, and anything from 120 ns to 80 ns is fast enough for 386 systems. And if you're really uncertain, sometimes the people you buy the chips from will have suggestions, based on your PC's clock speed (in megahertz).

You can buy the chips from just about any source, including a local dealer, mail-order house, or even at a swap meet (you should avoid ''pulled chips,'' which are used chips pulled from older computers).

Chips come in static-free tubes. You should keep them in the tubes until you're ready to upgrade. The tubes are transparent, so you can look through one to see if it has chips of the proper size and speed. You may notice that not all the chips are made by the same manufacturer. Some people insist on using all Toshiba or Micron chips. But that's not crucial to the operation of your PC (it only makes each bank of RAM look identical).

Remember to count the chips in the tube to make sure you have enough. Nothing is more disappointing than coming home with 16 chips when you need 18. And keep the tube after you've finished your upgrade, as it's the best thing to use to store chips you may have lying around.

A *General Strategy for Upgrading RAM*

Unlike adding an expansion card, hard drive, or power supply, which are fairly standard installations on all PCs, adding memory is different with each system. The basics are the same; you're still plugging chips or SIMMs into sockets. But where you plug in the chips (into an expansion card or your motherboard or some proprietary memory card) is different for each system. The instructions here are generic.

Remember to be very careful about grounding yourself while working with chips. Sit still! And before touching a chip, touch your PC's case or the power supply. This will drain off any static you have built up, static which could damage the chip if you touch it.

Know Where You're Installing the Chips

If you're installing the chips on an expansion card or a proprietary memory board, you should install them *before* you put the card in the PC. Create a work space and set the card down flat in front of you. If the card came in a static-free envelope, set the card on top of that or on a piece of cardboard. Don't put it on a carpet.

If you're installing the chips on your motherboard, you may need to remove some expansion cards. Putting memory on the motherboard is more difficult than sticking it on an expansion card. Your work space is hindered by the PC's case, and it's hard to inspect your job afterward to make sure all the chips are seated properly.

Work on One Bank at a Time

When upgrading RAM, you should work on one bank of chips at a time. First, locate the bank of RAM you're upgrading. It really doesn't matter which order you plug chips in, top to bottom or left to right. For example, if you're installing four banks of 256-kilobit chips, install each bank individually as opposed to plugging in chips at random. This also helps you to prevent plugging in chips of different capacities into the same bank. Try to keep as many chips in the tube as possible. This keeps them safe and in one place.

Orient the Chip Correctly

Unlike some other items in your PC, RAM chips can be plugged in wrong. To make it easier, each chip has a notch or dot on top. To properly orient the chip, position the dot or notch against the corresponding notch on the socket or the stencil underneath the socket. Figure 6.3 shows how to orient a chip.

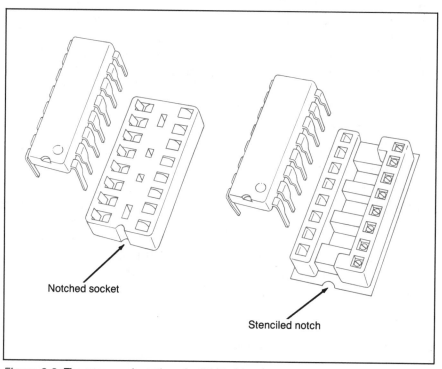

Notched socket

Stenciled notch

Figure 6.3: The proper orientation of a RAM chip

Insert the Chip

Once the chip is properly oriented, insert it. Line up its legs with the holes in the socket. Then press down firmly. (See the end of the chapter for specific, step-by-step instructions.)

Inspect Your Work

After installing a bank of chips, look over all the chips. You may notice that the bank is uneven, with some chips to the left and others to the right. This is fine. But you should keep an eye out for chips with their legs out of the sockets.

Occasionally, one of a chip's legs won't make it into the socket. It's usually one of the legs on the end of the chip, and it will be twisted and bent up in the air. Don't panic. It's possible to correct this and still use the chip. Finally, make sure all the dots on the chips are all lined up. For chips from the same manufacturer, the numbers on top should read the same way.

Tell the PC About Its New RAM

The final step in the upgrade process is to tell the PC the location and amount of RAM you installed. If you have a PC/XT machine, you set DIP switches on the motherboard. If you have an AT machine, you run the setup program.

Remember, there may be DIP switches or jumpers on an expansion card you may have to set as well. Since these cards operate differently, refer to the card's manual to see what must be set.

◤ Removing Chips

Occasionally you may need to remove some RAM chips. This is usually to change from a bank of 256-kilobit chips to 1-megabit chips. After you make the switch, remember to tell the expansion card that it now has 1-megabit chips. Some systems require no other changes and will recognize the newer chips, but check to make sure.

Procedure: Removing chips

Tools: Chip puller or tiny flathead screwdriver

1 Park your hard disk if it does not automatically park itself when the power is off.

2 Power down your PC.

3 Unplug everything.

4 Remove the lid.

5 Locate the chips you want to remove.

If the chips are on an expansion card, remove the card and lay it flat in its own work area. If the chips are on the motherboard, you may need to remove some expansion cards to get at them.

6 Remove the chips one at a time.

Never remove only part of a bank of chips or leave a bank incomplete. To remove a chip, position the chip puller on either of the short sides of the chip. Gently rock it back and forth to loosen it from the socket. Then pull it straight out. If you are using a flathead screwdriver, wedge the screwdriver under alternating sides of the chip. Twist the blade slightly to raise the chip a fraction of an inch at a time. Eventually the chip will lift out of the socket.

7 Put the chips in a static-free tube for storage.

As you remove the chips, place them in a static-free tube. Alternatively, you can plug them into static-free foam. If any chips have bent legs, you may want to straighten them before storing them.

8 After removing the chips, reset any DIP switches or jumpers.

You have to tell the PC or expansion card that it now lacks memory it once had. Check and set any necessary DIP switches or jumpers. If you're installing new chips in place of the ones you just removed, then you can skip this step and all remaining steps in this section.

9 Reinstall any expansion cards.

10 Test the PC, and if everything checks out, close it and fire it up. (If you have to make a change, make sure you unplug everything first.)

An AT system may give you a POST error and require you to run the setup program to tell the PC how much RAM it has. Your system now has less RAM, which may be what you want. But removing chips is usually done so that larger-capacity chips can be installed in their place. This task is covered in the section ''Installing Chips.''

Removing SIMMs

Using SIMMs is a much better way of dealing with memory than fumbling with chips. You'll make fewer mistakes, and SIMMs are easier to deal with in the long run. But as with DIP-style RAM chips, you may occasionally need to pull a few 256K SIMMs to replace them with 1Mb SIMMs to give your system more memory.

Procedure: Removing SIMMs

Tools: Tiny flathead screwdriver (optional)

1 Park the hard disk (if necessary).

2 Power down your PC.

3 Unplug everything.

4 Remove the lid.

5 Locate the SIMMs you want to remove.
   If the SIMMs are on an expansion card, remove the card from the PC and put it in its own work area. If the SIMMs are on the motherboard, you may need to remove some expansion cards to get at them.

6 Remove the SIMMs.

SIMMs are anchored on either side by a hook-and-hole mechanism. Hooks on the SIMM mount go through two tiny holes on either side of the SIMM. You may need a screwdriver to assist you in bending the hooks out of the holes. Sometimes you can do it with your fingers. Once the hooks are free from the holes, tilt the SIMM forward and then pull it up and out. Handle the SIMM by its edges.

7 Put the SIMM in a static-free tube for storage.

8 Reset any DIP switches or jumpers.

Be sure to tell the PC or expansion card about the memory you just yanked. If you're replacing the SIMM with one of a higher capacity, you can skip this step and the remaining steps in this section.

9 Reinstall any expansion cards.

10 Test your PC, and if everything checks out, close it up. (If you have to make a change, make sure everything is unplugged first.)

If you have an AT system, you'll probably get a POST error. Run the setup program to tell the computer how much memory is now installed.

Installing Chips

Upgrading RAM means plugging in chips. Whether you're filling an empty bank or swapping for higher-capacity RAM, plugging in chips is a major part of the upgrade. During the entire procedure that follows, make sure you're grounded; touch the PC's power supply before handling each chip. Sit still.

Procedure: Installing chips

Tools: Chip inserter tool (optional)

1 Park the hard disk (if necessary).

2 Power down your PC.

3 Unplug everything.

4 Remove the lid.

5 Locate where you want to install the chips.

    If the chip sockets are on an expansion card, remove the card and lay it flat so you can work on it. If you're inserting chips on the motherboard, you may need to remove some expansion cards to give yourself some working room.

6 Slide out a bank of chips from the static-free tube.

    You'll need nine chips. If you're upgrading two banks with different-capacity chips, make sure all the chips you're installing in one bank are the same size.

7 Put the chip into the chip inserter tool. (If you don't have a chip inserter tool, then go to the next step.)

8 Position the chip over its socket.

    Make sure the dot or notch in the top of the chip lines up with the notch in the socket or a stenciled notch on the motherboard or expansion card. If you've already stuck the chip into the inserter, you may need to remove it to double-check its orientation.

9 Line up the pins with the holes in the socket.

    Position the chip so that each of its legs fits over a hole in the chip socket. If you're not using a chip inserter, you may have to bend the legs a bit so that they'll fit. To do this, rest the chip on its side on a hard, flat surface. With the legs pointing toward you, carefully bend the chip toward you. Repeat this procedure for the other side of the chip.

10 Press down firmly but carefully.

11 Repeat steps 7–10 for each chip in the bank.

12 Inspect your work.

Always look over each bank after you've installed it. Check to see that each chip is properly oriented and that all pins are in their sockets.

13 Install any additional banks of memory.

You may be upgrading several banks of memory. The number depends on what you're upgrading and in what size increments you're upgrading. For example, many expansion cards allow upgrades in 512K or 1Mb increments.

14 Set any DIP switches or jumpers.

If you're upgrading memory on an expansion card, check it for DIP switches or jumpers. Set them according to the card's manual and the amount of memory you've installed. If you're upgrading memory on the motherboard of a PC/XT-type system, you also have to set DIP switches. However, if you're upgrading memory on a 386's motherboard or proprietary expansion board, you only have to modify your setup program.

15 Reinstall any expansion cards.

16 Test the PC and, if everything checks out, close it up. (If you have to make a change, make sure you unplug everything first.)

Installing SIMMs

Because all PCs require nine chips in a bank, some genius developed the SIMM. Not only is it sturdier than single RAM chips, it's easier to install. Most of today's high-end PCs and memory expansion cards are equipped with SIMM sockets.

Procedure: Installing SIMMs

Tools: None

1 Park the hard disk (if necessary).

2 Power down your PC.

3 Unplug everything.

4 Remove the lid.

5 Locate where you want to install the SIMM.

   If you're installing the SIMM on an expansion card, remove the card and lay it flat, giving yourself ample work space. If you're installing it on the motherboard, you might have to remove some expansion cards.

6 Slide the SIMM out of the static-free tube.

7 Position the SIMM over the socket.

   Make sure you have the SIMM positioned over the proper slot. Quite a few upgrade schemes require you to insert SIMMs in every other slot; others have you fill the slots in a certain order.

8 Insert the SIMM at an angle, guiding it into the slot.

   The long edge of the SIMM with the metal connectors goes into the slot. One side of the SIMM is notched, so you can't put it in backward. You should back the SIMM in, with its chips facing downward. Once the SIMM is in the slot, straighten it up so it is perpendicular. Guide the two hooks in the SIMM mount into the holes on either side of the SIMM. You may have some trouble doing this, so you can bend the hooks slightly by using a pair of pliers.

9 Make sure the SIMM is properly seated.

   SIMMs really do snap into place. They'll sit either perpendicular or at an angle. Make sure the SIMM is in all the way and that the edge is fully in the slot.

10 Repeat steps 7–9 for each SIMM you're installing.

11 Inspect your work.

Unlike when you install individual RAM chips, you don't need to check for SIMMs with bent legs or SIMMs put in backward (because you can't put them in backward). You might want to gently hold the top of the SIMM and wiggle it to make sure it's sturdy and properly seated.

12 Set any DIP switches or jumpers.

Some memory expansion cards may require you to set DIP switches or jumpers to tell the card how much RAM has been installed and where the RAM starts in memory. Since SIMMs are rarely used in PC/XTs, you probably won't have to set any DIP switches on the motherboard—but check to be sure.

13 Reinstall any expansion cards.

14 Test the PC, and if everything checks out, close it up. (If you have to make a change, make sure you unplug everything first.)

Start-up Advice

If any chips or SIMMs aren't working, you may get a POST error when you start the computer. On AT-level systems you always get a POST error after adding memory. The error indicates that memory sizes don't match. To fix things, you have to run your setup program and tell the computer how much RAM you've installed. (You get an error message because on AT, 286, and 386 systems extended memory is tested by the POST.)

Expanded memory boards in a PC/XT don't usually report any errors when you power up (the first time). You must install the expanded memory manager in your CONFIG.SYS file, then reboot the computer if any auto-testing is to take place. And some boards come with diagnostic software that you can use to test your RAM. The software may even give you the exact location of a malfunctioning chip on the card.

◢ **P**otential Problems

Upgrading memory has the potential for quite a few problems. These are rare, but when they occur it helps to know what to do and how to deal with them.

Parity errors are the bane of most RAM upgrades. They're an indication of either an improperly installed chip or a dead chip somewhere in RAM.

The PC lets you know about a parity error, usually by means of a POST error message. After that, the machine freezes and displays a message for you like "Parity error" and a cryptic number. If you're lucky, the number can be deciphered and the malfunctioning chip located.

The format of the typical parity error message is

PARITY CHECK x

xxxxx

The x on the first line is either a 1 or 2. If it's a 1, the bad RAM is on the motherboard. If it's a 2, the bad RAM is on an expansion card.

The second row of x's tells you the location of the malfunctioning chip. The first two numbers indicate the bank the chip is in, the other numbers reveal the position of the individual chip itself.

Individual manufacturers use different schemes for parity-check numbers, so there's no point in listing them all here. If your memory expansion card or PC has a diagnostic disk, you can use it to track down the location of the bad chip. But chances are that the chip is misinstalled.

Bending one leg of a chip up, as shown in Figure 6.4, is a common installation error. It's occasionally hard to spot, especially if you're installing several banks of DIP chips. (This error won't happen on a SIMM because the chips are soldered into position.)

To correct the problem, carefully pull out the chip. Then lay it flat and bend the leg back into position using either needle-nose pliers or a flathead screwdriver. The legs are metal and will break off if you bend them back and forth too much, so be careful. Straighten it as best you can and reinstall it. If you break off the leg, the chip is useless.

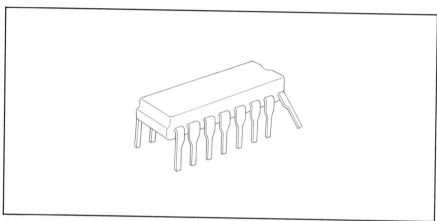

Figure 6.4: A chip with a bent leg

Summary

Upgrading RAM is simple: You plug RAM chips or a SIMM into a socket, tell the PC about the new memory either by setting DIP switches or by using the setup program, and you're ready to roll.

Chips are rated in terms of their capacity and speed. The capacity of the chip tells you how much information it will store. Chips are grouped into banks of nine, the ninth chip checking parity. So 256-kilobit chips are used in a bank of nine to make 256K, and 1-megabit chips are used in a bank of nine to make 1Mb.

Chip speed is measured in nanoseconds (ns), or billionths of a second. Slow RAM chips, suitable for PC/XTs and some AT systems, are rated at 150 to 120 nanoseconds. Faster chips, suitable for fast 286 and 386 systems, are rated at 100 to 80 ns.

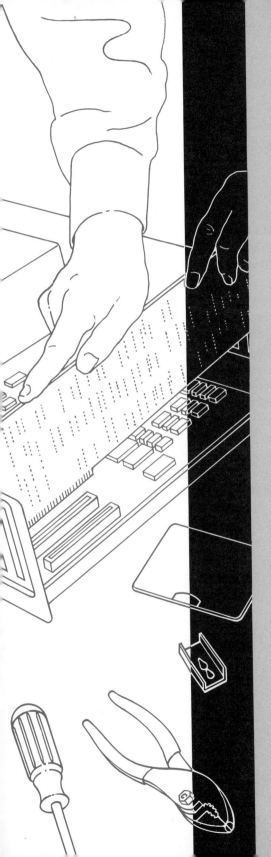

7

Floppy-Disk Drives

THE FLOPPY DRIVE IS THE MOST MECHANICAL THING IN your computer. Everything else (except for the power supply) is a mixture of electronic circuitry, chips, and cables. Because floppy drives have moving parts, they are usually the component most likely to break after you've had your PC awhile. There also may be a time when you want to upgrade or replace a floppy drive. For example, you may want to exchange a 5 1/4-inch unit for a 3 1/2-inch unit that is compatible with your laptop; you may want to add a B drive to a single-drive system; or you may want to replace your old 360K full-height drive with two 1.2Mb half-height drives.

Upgrading or installing a floppy drive isn't really a hard thing to do, but there are a few different items to keep track of. You'll need to know some background information before you pull out your old floppy drive and replace it with the latest model.

Upgrading floppy drives isn't as common a procedure as upgrading memory. But it's something quite a few users with older systems should consider doing. Currently the PC industry has settled on the 1.2Mb format for 5 1/4-inch disks and the 1.4Mb format for 3 1/2-inch disks (although 360K 5 1/4-inch and 720K 3 1/2-inch disks are still common). Software is still distributed on the lower-capacity 360K 5 1/4-inch disks and 720K 3 1/2-inch disks. But having a large-capacity floppy drive makes transporting data and backing up the hard drive a lot easier.

 ## How Floppy Drives Work

There's a lot more to your floppy-disk drives than the slot into which you slide your disks. It's important to be able to identify the parts of a disk drive before you go about upgrading one.

There are two main parts of a floppy drive: the drive unit itself, though there can be more than one, and the controller card. A cable connects the two. Also, there is a power-supply cable attached to the back of the drive unit.

The Drive Unit

The disk drive itself is a light, compact unit. It's about 6 inches wide, 1 1/2 inches tall, and 8 inches deep. The front of the drive consists of the following parts:

- The slot where the disk slides into the drive
- The disk activity lamp (LED)
- The door latch or eject button

Figure 7.1 shows these components on two generic floppy-drive faceplates.

The locations of the activity lamp and door latch or eject button vary. Different drive manufacturers put them in different locations, but they do the same things on each drive: The activity lamp lights up when the computer is accessing the drive, and the latch closes the slot, clamps the floppy disk in place, and touches the read/write

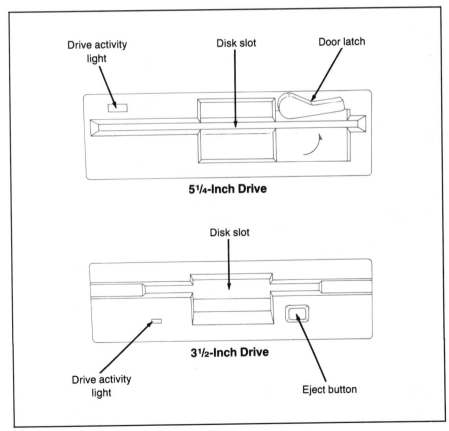

Figure 7.1: *Floppy-drive faceplates*

heads to the disk. (Older drives actually have a hinged, doorlike device.)

The eject button on a 3½-inch drive is only used to push the disk from the drive unit. Inserting a 3½-inch disk into the drive is all that needs to be done to clamp it in place; there's no latch to close.

The important thing about examining a drive's faceplate is knowing which side is up; it's often hard to tell. Older drives have doors on them that always shut downward. For the most part, today's 5¼-inch drives have latches that shut with a quarter-turn down; whether the latch turns clockwise or counterclockwise depends on who made the drive.

The orientation of the drive is important because you're always supposed to insert your disks label-side up. If you find your newly installed drive doesn't read any of your old disks, then stick a disk in upside down. If it works that way, then you've installed the drive upside down.

On both sides of the drive unit you'll find mounting holes. There are two sets of two holes each, for a total of four on each side.

The bottom or top of the drive (depending on who made it) contains the drive's logic board. This is usually a green fiberglass sheet full of chips and other electronic doodads.

Your drive's logic board may have jumpers. Some installations may require you to set these jumpers. This subject is covered later in this chapter.

The back of the drive contains your two vital connectors: the power-supply connector and the control/data-cable connector (which is the drive's umbilical cord).

The power-supply connector is an open white plastic rectangle containing four metal pins and is attached to the power supply by four colored wires. The corners on one side of the open end are beveled, which prevents you from plugging in the power connector upside down.

The control/data cable attaches to the drive by means of a 34-pin *edge connector.* You'll notice that there is a notch at one end of the edge connector. This corresponds to a stopper in the connector on the drive's cable. As with the power connector, you can't plug the drive's umbilical cord in upside down. If the cable does not have a notch, align the colored stripe on the side of the ribbon with pin 1 on the edge connector.

Inside the drive unit are the guts that make your floppy drive work. At the beginning level of upgrading, it isn't wise to mess with any of the following internal items. But you should know what they are, where they are, and what they do.

The Drive Spindle and Spindle Motor   The drive spindle clamps the center of the disk, and the motor spins the disk.

The Head Assembly   Most drives contain two heads for reading both sides of the disk at the same time. The head assembly contains the read/write heads, which are responsible for reading from and writing to your disks.

The Stepper Motor   The stepper motor moves the head assembly (mounted on rails) in and out, over the surface of the disk. The stepper motor positions the read/write heads over an area of the disk. (All this is controlled by DOS, which issues commands to your floppy-disk controller.)

Other parts inside the drive are designed to glide the disk into the drive and to clamp the disk into position when you close the latch. There is also circuitry for the drive's activity lamp, plus a second LED by the spindle that senses the disk's index hole. Finally, there's a small switch on one side of the drive that detects whether or not a disk is write-protected.

The floppy-drive unit is one compact package. Drives for 3 1/2-inch disks are especially confusing because they're usually mounted in a 5 1/4-inch drive bracket and then completely sealed inside a metal case. But as far as you're concerned, you only need to know the basics:

- Which way is up
- Where the mounting screw holes are
- Where the power-supply connector is
- Where the control/data edge-connector is

The Controller Card

To interface the floppy drive with your PC you need a controller card, which is an expansion card that plugs into one of the slots on your PC's bus. Some newer PCs have the floppy controller (the circuitry) built into the motherboard—the floppy cable plugs into the motherboard directly. The floppy controller may be combined with a hard-disk controller on one card, or it may be part of a multifunction card containing a printer port, clock, memory, and so on. The best way to find it is to trace the cable from your floppy drive to the controller. A floppy-disk controller is illustrated in Figure 7.2.

You should be able to identify the following parts:

- Drive-cable edge-connector
- Bus edge connector
- External connector
- Circuitry

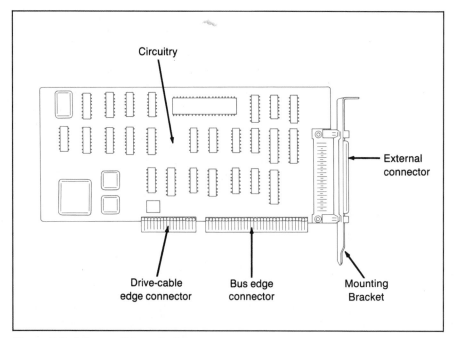

Figure 7.2: A floppy-disk controller

The drive-cable edge-connector is found on the end of the card (which is an unusual location because it sticks out). It's notched, just like the edge connector on the floppy-drive unit. There's no way you can plug in the cable wrong.

The 62-pin edge-connector is for the PC's system bus and plugs into an expansion slot on the motherboard. It's how the drive controller interfaces directly with your PC's microprocessor.

The floppy-disk controller may also have an optional connector on the rear mounting bracket for external drives. This connector will probably not appear on hard/floppy-controller combinations, nor on drive controllers that also serve other functions. Any connectors on the controller may be for the card's other functions.

Circuitry is made up of chips, resistors, and timers on the board itself. As far as internal positioning goes, there is no designated slot for your floppy-disk controller. It is helpful, however, to place the controller close to the floppy-drive unit(s) so that you don't have to stretch the cable too far.

*T*he Cable

One of the few tangles you may encounter when installing a floppy drive is with the cable. The cable connects your drives to the drive controller. The way you hook up the cable, plus a few other items, is what determines which of your drives is A and which is B.

The controller cable itself is a 34-line ribbon cable. A ribbon cable is flexible, so you can bend it. It was made this way, so don't be shy about tweaking it at 90-degree angles to weave the cable through your system unit's internal jungle. There are three connectors on the cable. Two of them go to drives A and B, the third hooks into your floppy-disk controller.

There are many ways to figure out how the cable connects to the drives and the controller card. Basically you have two concerns when installing the cable. First, since the edge connectors on the drive and controller card are the same, you have to know which end of the cable connects to which part. Second, you have to know which connector hooks to drive B and which hooks to drive A.

Here are some easy mnemonics for figuring out the floppy-drive controller cable:

- The connectors go *A-B-C,* for drive *A,* drive *B,* and the controller.

- The drive *B* connector is *b*ackward.

Most cables have the drive A and B connectors quite close to one end. Also, you should notice that the cable is switched, twisted in the middle, right before the drive A connector. So you always plug that end into your first (or only) floppy drive. The other end, the one far away from the other two, goes to the controller card.

I always remember that the middle connector is for drive B because it's backward. If you lay the cable flat, you'll notice that the two end connectors face one way, but the middle connector faces the other way.

Other than remembering which connector on the cable goes where, it's really no sweat to hook things up. Remember, everything is usually notched. If you have drive A, you plug the A connector on the cable into it, then the power supply, and you're set. You do the same thing with drive B.

If the edge connector isn't notched, then you have to use another method to find out which way to connect it: Look for pin 1. Pin 1 is identified by a stenciled *1* on the edge connector or somewhere nearby. The gold strips on the edge connector are numbered. For the drive cable, it's numbered 1–33 on the odd side and 2–34 on the even side.

The cable also has numbers, but they're wire numbers. (Some connectors have wire numbers on them as well.) Wire 1, which corresponds to pin 1, is marked on most cables with a red line. To connect an unnotched cable properly, put wire 1 on the cable on the same side as pin 1 (or pin 2) on the edge connector.

If you plug it in wrong, usually nothing bad happens—your drive just won't work. No power comes through the cable (that comes through the power-supply connector), so you can't "fry" anything. But matching up wire 1 on the cable with pin 1 on the edge connector is guaranteed to work.

How can you tell which one of your drives is drive A and which is drive B? There are other differences between drive A and drive B, besides their position on the umbilical cable. There are two things you need to look out for:

- The Drive Select, or DSx, jumper
- The terminating resistor

When you buy a new drive, you should specify whether you want a drive A or drive B so that your vendor can configure the drives properly. Even given their position on the cable, each drive has a jumper that can be set to make the drive A or B. The jumper has a stenciled label by it, DS0 for drive A or DS1 for drive B. (Some drives may specify DS1 for drive A and DS2 for drive B.)

Normally in PC drives, the jumper is set to DS1 for drive B. This is because there is a twist in the drive's control cable. If the cable doesn't have a twist, then you must set the jumper to DS0 for drive A, and DS1 for drive B.

The terminating resistor is a device, sometimes a jumper, attached to the last drive in your system, drive A. (Remember, drive A is on the end of the cable.) The resistor saps the excess signal sent down the cable from the controller. It should only be on drive A.

The best way to be sure of all this is to specify a drive A or B when you buy it. If the dealer says it doesn't matter, then he's probably right. But check the drive's manual to see if you have a DSx jumper or the terminating resistor. Other jumpers on the drive may need to be set depending on your installation options. These options are covered later in this chapter, as well as in the drive's manual.

Types of Drives

The components covered in the previous section are common to all types of drives. But there are differences, including the following:

- The drive's formatted capacity
- The drive height

- The number of sides and heads
- The disk size

The drive's formatted capacity is usually all you need to know to determine which floppy drive you need. Currently, there are four standards in PC computing:

- 1.4Mb, 3½-inch
- 1.2Mb, 5¼-inch
- 720K, 3½-inch
- 360K, 5¼-inch

The formatted capacity is an indication of the drive's physical size. Disks that are 720K and 1.4Mb are 3½ inches wide, and disks that are 360K and 1.2Mb are 5¼ inches wide. So when you buy a drive, you can pretty much get by with just saying which formatted capacity you want. But there are other considerations as well.

The drive height used to be a consideration when two sizes were common: full-height and half-height. Today, nearly all floppy drives are half-height so that more can be fit into the system. You only need to specify the height when you're dealing with hard-disk drives.

The number of sides and heads on a drive is really a moot point today. Originally, disk drives had only one read/write head (on the top). The bottom side of the disk was unused. Because of this, the drive was said to be single-sided. Today, all drives have two read/write heads, one on the top and one on the bottom. These drives are all said to be double-sided.

The final difference is the physical size of the disk that goes into the drive. The 5¼-inch square disk has been around since 1978. At that time, you could only put some 140K on the disk—but that was a lot in those days. Today, a 5¼-inch disk can be formatted to 1.2Mb, depending on the drive and media used.

The introduction of the Macintosh computer brought about wide use of the 3½-inch disk format. Especially popular on laptops, these disks are more compact, can store more information, and are more durable than 5¼-inch disks.

◣ **W**here Floppy Drives Go

Disk drives are mounted internally, in your PC's system unit. Most of the drive sits inside the case. The faceplate is outside the case and is usually designed to match the color and style of your PC's case.

Floppy drives—and hard drives as well—are mounted in drive bays. The number and the size of the bays vary from model to model.

The typical floppy-drive bay is full-height. This is the way it is on the original PC, which has two full-height floppy drives. Most PCs that imitate the original PC's case style have this arrangement. However, AT and tower cases may have lots of drives, usually up to five half-heights (or two full-heights and one half-height).

If you end up with some odd combination that leaves a hole in a drive bay, you can purchase a blank faceplate to put over the empty spot. (Dealers should give them to you for free.) My IBM PC has two half-height floppies and one half-height hard drive. A half-height faceplate fills in the missing hole.

There are no hard-and-fast rules to follow in deciding where to position the drives you install or upgrade. Drive A is traditionally on top of, or to the right of, drive B. But since you can do anything you want (as long as you get the cables right), you can switch the drives. For example, my PC system has drive A on the bottom, and my AT system has drive A on the top.

The hard drive is usually positioned on the left, which is best because that bay is usually hidden inside the PC. However, there's nothing wrong with a single hard-and-floppy-drive system where both drives are in the visible bay.

External drives are mounted outside the PC in their own case and often with their own power supply. A cable connects them to your floppy-disk controller or to a proprietary controller of their own. A second cable may plug them into a wall socket, or they may draw juice directly from the computer.

The positioning of your drives isn't that big a deal—unless you're in an office where you want to maintain consistency with other PCs.

Buying a Floppy Drive

Buying a drive is probably the hardest part of the upgrading process. So you should consider the following things when you go drive hunting.

Know What You Want   You could add a drive B to your system, you could change drive A to a 1.4Mb 3½-inch drive to be compatible with your laptop or PS/2 system, or you could replace a dead drive. New drives off the shelf cost under $100. Compared to downtime and labor costs to fix a drive, that's nothing.

Know the Size   Remember the four basic formats for a drive. Most 3½-inch drives come with 5¼-inch mounting gear that lets you plug them into standard 5¼-inch drive bays. (The exceptions are tower units that have 3½-inch-specific mounting.)

Tell the Dealer Which Computer You Have   You should also tell the salesperson which type of PC you're installing the drive in: a PC/XT or an AT or a 386 system. This may not make any difference, but some older PC/XTs have special jumpers set on the cards. The older BIOS and the floppy-disk controller couldn't recognize and format the drive to its full capacity. Normally, a drive installed in such situations will work, but no matter what its full formatted capacity, it will only be formatted to 360K under DOS. This can be adjusted by setting the proper jumper on the drive or by using DRIVER.SYS in your CONFIG.SYS file or by doing both.

Buy Brand-Name Equipment   As far as brand names go, take your pick. But steer clear of unknown names, no-name clones, and swap-meet drives or anything without a warranty. Documentation is nice—if it's provided. But don't expect it, and if you get it, don't expect it to read like English.

Look at Prices   Cost is a factor, but the differences in prices between drives are minimal. Some people swear by Sony drives; others insist upon Teac. Most of the time a reputable dealer will stock only what gives him the least amount of hassle.

Look at Color   The choices are usually beige and black to match your PC's case.

Request Drive A or Drive B   If possible, try to request a drive preconfigured for positioning as drive A or drive B. If the dealer scratches his head or mumbles that "all drives are alike," then he's probably right: All PC drives are configured as drive B, with DS1 set. However, if your controller/umbilical cable doesn't have a twist in it (between the A and B connectors), then the DSx jumpers must be set. Drive A (not B) must have a terminating resistor.

Buy a Faceplate   If you're replacing a full-height drive with a half-height, you're going to need a half-height faceplate to install in the hole.

Note the Case Style   PC/XT-style cases may need a mounting bracket to handle a half-height drive. Since these cases were designed around full-height drives, there are no screw holes for any drives on top. If you have an AT-style case, you're going to need plastic mounting rails to install the drive (see the section "About Mounting Rails").

Shop at the Right Place   Forget about buying a drive in a national-chain computer store. Even if they have what you want, it will be overpriced. Go to a local dealer or order through the mail. Since drives only differ slightly between manufacturers, you only need to specify the necessary items mentioned in this section and you'll be fine. Personally, I've ordered all my drives, both hard and floppy, by mail order. Everything has always arrived on time and in excellent condition.

About Mounting Rails

On a PC/XT-style case, the screw holes on the side of the disk-drive unit are used to anchor the side of the drive to the drive bay. The drive is anchored on one side only—the left side for the left bay and the right side for the right bay. (This will make sense when you install the drive.)

AT-style cases use a more secure method of anchoring the drives: mounting rails. Mounting rails are the plastic, pontoon-shaped things that screw into the side of your drive. You must screw a mounting rail into both sides of your drive. The drive bay in an AT-style case doesn't have screw holes. But it does have grooves into which you slide the drive. The mounting rails actually slide into these grooves. You position your drive in front of the bay, line up the grooves with the rails, and slide the drive back.

Once the drive is in position (and after you've attached the cables), you screw two angle brackets into the front of the case. These brackets keep the drive in position, anchoring it to the case. This is a more secure way of anchoring a drive, a lot more sturdy than the way half-height drives are attached to a PC/XT-style case.

Removing a Floppy Drive

You may have to remove a floppy drive to install a new one or to replace it with a hard drive or tape backup unit. If so, remember to remove your B drive, not your A drive.

Procedure: Removing a floppy drive

Tools: Medium Phillips screwdriver

1 Park your hard disk, if necessary.

2 Power down your PC.

3 Unplug everything.

4 Remove the lid.

5 Locate the drive you want to remove.

Find the floppy drive you want to remove, located in one of the bays. Note which cables connect to it and where the screws are.

6 Unscrew the mounting screws.

The screws are on the side on an XT-style case and in front when there are mounting rails. If the screws are on the side, and your drive is in the left bay, you may need to remove some expansion cards to get at them. Otherwise, the screws will be on the right side of the case and easily accessible. If you have an AT-style case, the screws are in front, on either side of the drive's faceplate. After you've removed the screws, set them aside for installing the new drive. Don't lose the angle brackets if you have mounting rails.

7 Slide the drive forward a bit. This will give you finger room to remove the cables behind the drive.

8 Unplug the power-supply cable.

The power-supply cable has four wires, with a white plastic box on the end. Grab the box and pull it firmly to unplug the cable. All power-supply connectors are the same, for both floppy and hard drives. So it doesn't matter which one you plug into your drive. Simply bend the connector out of the way.

9 Unplug the umbilical cord.

The umbilical cord slides off the edge connector when you pull it. Sometimes sliding the drive forward causes the connector to slip off. You may want to label the connector A or B. Note that you're not removing the cable from the controller card. Keep all other ends of the floppy cable attached. If you have only one floppy, there will be two free connectors when you unplug the cable from the drive.

10 Slide the drive all the way forward and free. All drives, floppy and hard, pull out through the front of the drive bay.

11 Set the drive aside.

After you remove the drive, you can put it anywhere, but the best place is in the box it came in. If it's a dead drive, remember to label it *DEAD* on the box. Otherwise, label the box with the drive type and put it in storage. If the drive has mounting rails and you plan to install a new drive, you may want to unscrew them at this time.

If you aren't replacing the drive, you should install a blank faceplate over the drive-bay hole.

Installing a Floppy Drive

If you're putting in a new drive that requires a new controller card, you should also upgrade the controller card at this point. Remember that you can use the same cable that's already in your PC (unless, of course, the cable is damaged).

Procedure: Installing a floppy drive

Tools: Medium Phillips screwdriver

1 Park your hard disk, if necessary.

2 Power down your PC.

3 Unplug everything.

4 Remove the lid.

5 Remove the old drive (see "Removing a Floppy Drive" or "Removing a Hard Drive," Chapter 8), or remove the faceplate covering the drive bay.

6 Set any jumpers or switches on the new drive.

If it's drive A, make sure that the terminating resistor is installed, if necessary. If you bought the drive off the shelf as an A or a B, then just double-check everything. If your floppy controller cable doesn't have a twist, set DS0 for drive A and DS1 for drive B.

7 Attach mounting rails to the drive.

The pointy end goes toward the rear of the drive. If there is no pointy end, the brackets will be clearly marked so that you don't screw them onto the drive upside down. If you're putting a half-height drive in a PC-style case, you may need to add a mounting bracket to support the half-height drive in the top position: Remove the screws from the lower drive's position, install the bracket, and put the screws back on the lower drive.

8 Slide the drive in from the front.

Position the drive in front of the drive bay and push it back. If it has rails, then it will naturally slide into place. Otherwise, you may have to rest the drive on the one below it or on the bottom of the drive bay until it's properly anchored into position. You shouldn't slide the drive back all the way at this point. Be careful that you're not installing the drive upside down.

9 Attach the power-supply cable.

Plug the white power-supply connector into the white receptacle on the drive's logic board. The connector only fits one way, so don't force it. It does require a bit of pressing, however, to push the connector in all the way.

10 Attach the umbilical cord.

The umbilical cord is notched, so don't force it. If you can't get it on, or it only attaches at an angle, then flip it over and try again. If the connector switch is not notched, make sure wire 1 (red or blue) is attached to pin 1. If you're also adding a new controller at this stage, attach the cable to the controller as well.

11 Slide the drive in all the way.

Once the cables are attached, slide the drive into the bay as far as it will go.

12 Tighten the screws.

If you have a PC-style case, match the screw holes on the side of the drive with the holes in the drive bay or mounting bracket. Only two screws are required to anchor the drive— use whichever holes line up best and position the drive properly. If there are mounting rails, put the angle brackets into the drive so that they hold the drive in the bay and wrap around to the front of the case over the screw holes.

13 Make sure all connections are sound.

Make sure the umbilical cord and power-supply cable haven't come off. Just reach back with your fingers (or simply look) to make sure everything is still attached.

14   Test the PC and put the lid back on.

Before putting the lid back on, fire up the PC to make sure the drive works. (Just keep your hands out of it.) Put the lid back on, and you're ready to use your new drive.

If you ever install a second 5 1/4- or 3 1/2-inch drive that's of a different capacity than your first drive (for example, a 720K drive A and a 1.4Mb drive B), you might want to label the drives on the faceplates using one of those raised-letter marking-tape machines. This helps prevent any future confusion, especially when someone else uses the computer.

Once you're done, turn on your PC and access your new drive. If you get a POST error, you may have forgotten to set DIP switches or to run your AT's setup program. Run SETUP or turn off the system, open the case, and set the DIP switches. If you have a PC/XT-style system, you may even want to power up with the case still open. That way, if you need to set a DIP switch, the case is already open for it. (But power down before putting your hands inside the open unit!)

If the computer starts up fine, then the best way to make sure you did everything properly is to use the FORMAT command on a disk in the drive. If the drive formats the disk to its given capacity, everything's OK. If not, you'll either have to try using DRIVER.SYS in your CONFIG.SYS file or recheck your jumper settings.

DRIVER.SYS only needs to be used if the drive you installed can't be properly configured as an integral drive, either because the DIP switch settings or the setup program can't recognize it. In such a case, DRIVER.SYS allows you to configure the drive as an external drive.

Replacing a Full-Height Drive

Quite a few disk upgrades involve replacing a full-height drive with two half-heights. If you're going to do this type of upgrade, keep the following points in mind:

If you're replacing an old full-height drive A with an A and a B, remember which drive is which. Unless you buy them off the shelf as A and B, you may have to set jumpers and put a terminating resistor on drive A. Note the cable position between the drives.

If you do have full-height disk drives, the odds are pretty good that you have an older controller card. Consider getting a new controller card or a hard/floppy-disk controller combo.

Full-height drive bays may only have screw holes on the bottom. If so, you'll need a half-height-drive mounting bracket to give you that extra set of screw holes necessary to anchor a half-height drive in the top position.

Older PCs with full-height drives only have two drive connectors on the power supply. If you have such a PC, you'll need a power cable splitter, also called a Y cable. But before installing it, you may want to consider upgrading your power supply. Older power supplies that have only two drive connectors are rated at only 65 watts. Today's PC systems need at least 135 watts, preferably 150 watts; AT systems need 200 watts or more. If your power supply is rated at 65 watts, replace it.

If you're replacing a full-height drive with a single half-height, you'll need a half-height faceplate to cover the hole.

Software Considerations

Upgrading a floppy drive involves more than just hardware. On the software side, there are three main issues:

- Formatting your disks
- Using DRIVER.SYS
- Exchanging disks

Formatting is necessary because you can't use the drive without having formatted disks to put into it. DRIVER.SYS is required for some PCs with external floppies, or computers with older BIOSs that don't recognize the high-capacity formats. And, thanks to the variety of PC disk formats, exchanging disks has become a real part of life for anyone who uses more than one computer.

Using DRIVER.SYS

If you're installing a 720K 3½-inch disk drive in an older PC (with an old BIOS), or you're adding an external drive to your system, or you're using a version of DOS earlier than 3.3, then you have to specify the DRIVER.SYS command in your CONFIG.SYS file to have DOS properly recognize the drive.

Problems occur most often when you add a 720K drive to an older PC system. Unless you use DRIVER.SYS, DOS will only format the drive to 360K. Why? Because it still assumes you have a 360K drive. (The BIOS doesn't know about a 720K drive.) The drive may not function at all.

To make the drive act like a 720K drive, you should add the following line to your CONFIG.SYS file (assuming it is in the C:\DOS subdirectory):

DEVICE = C:\DOS\DRIVER.SYS /D:1 /T:80 /S:9 /H:2 /F:2

Remember to specify the full pathname for DRIVER.SYS in your CONFIG.SYS file.

The only problem with this solution is that DRIVER.SYS fools DOS into thinking you have an *external* drive D, because that's the drive that supports the 720K format. If you refer to drive B as B:, then it's only 360K. But if you access the *logical* drive D (which is the same as the *physical* drive B), you get your full 720K. This really isn't as confusing as it sounds. Just don't be fooled into thinking that DRIVER.SYS didn't work.

The format for DRIVER.SYS is as follows:

DEVICE = *pathname*\DRIVER.SYS /D:ddd [/T:ttt][/S:ss][/H:hh][/C][/N][/F:f]

The *pathname* is the location of the DRIVER.SYS file on your hard drive.

/D:ddd is the only required switch. It indicates the physical number of the drive you're modifying, starting with 0 for drive A. Drive B is /D:1, as seen in the previous example. If you have two internal hard drives, then /D:4 is your fifth drive—an external drive if you install one.

The /T and /S switches specify the number of tracks and sectors that the drive has. The default value for /T is 80, for 80 tracks. The default for /S is 9, for 9 sectors.

The /H switch is used to specify the number of heads that the drive has. The default is 2, which all types of floppy drives commonly have.

The /C switch, available with DOS 3.3, is used for some AT drives and all PS/2 drives that have change-line support.

The /F switch specifies the drive's form factor. For all low-density 5¼-inch disks up to 360K in size, the form-factor value is 0; for 1.2Mb disks it's 1; for 720K disks it's 2; and for 1.4Mb disks it's 7.

Exchanging Disks

There are four popular disk formats, so exchanging data between different PCs can be a real hassle. Here are a few tips to help make it easier.

Format a Disk at Its Rated Capacity

Format 360K disks to 360K, format 1.2Mb disks to 1.2Mb, format 1.4Mb disks to 1.4Mb, and format 720K disks to 720K.

Problems arise when you format a disk for a size other than what it's intended to be. You can format a 1.2Mb disk for 360K, but it's a waste of media. Few 360K disks will be able to read the drive because of the high-capacity media's tighter storage of information. Also, you won't be able to reformat the disk back to 1.2Mb, unless you completely erase the disk using a bulk eraser.

It's OK to Format 360K Disks in a 1.2Mb Drive

Formatting a 360K disk to 360K in a 1.2Mb drive sometimes formats it better than formatting it in a 360K-only drive. It used to be said that formatting a 360K disk in a 1.2Mb drive rendered the disk unreadable by other 360K drives. This isn't true.

There's also no problem in formatting a 720K disk in a 1.4Mb drive. Moving 3½-inch disks between different-capacity drives isn't a problem either.

Don't Format a 360K Disk for 1.2Mb

You can't format a 360K disk for 1.2Mb. The magnetic density of the 1.2Mb disk is much greater than that of the 360K disk. Although DOS will proceed as you direct it, the 360K disk will usually come up with more than 50 percent bad sectors.

Also, the close proximity of the tracks to each other on such a low-density magnetic surface will lead to dreaded *magnetic migration*. After a time, the magnetic particles will slowly be corrupted, rendering your data useless.

Don't Format a 720K Disk for 1.4Mb

Some people figure that since both 3½-inch disk formats have 135 tracks per inch (TPI), all they need to do is to punch a hole in a 720K disk to make it into a 1.4Mb disk. (And there are even companies that sell tools to punch the hole.)

But punching a hole in a 720K disk to make it 1.4Mb is stupid— 1.4Mb disks have a higher magnetic density than their 720K brothers. That's why they cost more. While punching a hole will fool the drive and DOS into formatting the 720K disk to 1.4Mb (the disk may actually work for a while), eventually magnetic migration will begin, especially if you write to the drive again.

Also, if you've been using a disk for a long time and it suddenly becomes unreadable, the problem isn't in your drive. It's age—disks don't last forever. You should make backup copies of your disks every once in a while, especially those you use often. Otherwise you may suddenly find that the disk you've used every day for three years just doesn't work anymore.

 ## Summary

The primary reasons for upgrading your floppy drives are to give yourself a higher-capacity disk format and to maintain compatibility with other computers, primarily laptops and desktop PCs that use the 3½-inch disk standard.

The upgrade process itself is rather simple. The most difficult part is determining which drive is A and which is B. Other than their positions relative to the cables (where drive B is in the middle), both drives have jumpers to set their position. Drive A should also have a terminating resistor.

On the software side, many people have problems with exchanging disks between different drive formats. The rule of thumb is to format all disks to their maximum capacity, either based on the size of the drive or the full capacity of the disk. You only run into problems when you force a drive to format a disk to a higher capacity than its rating.

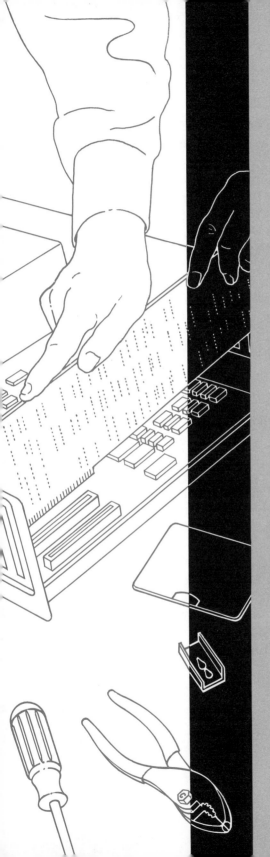

8

Hard-Disk Drives

BACK IN 1983, WHEN IBM TOSSED IN A BULKY OLD XEBEC 10Mb hard drive with their PC/XT, a hard disk in a PC was an oddity. But businesses, individuals, and eventually the hardware and software branches of the PC industry came to see they had a hot item. Today, you just can't live without a hard disk (or two) in your computer.

Upgrading the hard drives is very similar to upgrading floppy drives—the only difference is an extra cable on the hard drive you have to deal with. But there is some information specific to hard drives that you should know.

Nearly every PC sold today comes with a hard disk installed. If your PC does not have one, this chapter will tell you how to install one. Even if you have a hard drive already, there is probably room for another one inside your PC. And because software applications are getting larger and larger, having more hard-disk storage is tops on just about everyone's hardware wish-list.

Differences Between Hard and Floppy Drives

Physically, hard and floppy drives are about the same size and are removed and installed in the same manner. Internally, they have similarities as well. But that's where the direct comparison ends. Hard drives are faster, store more information, and store it more reliably than floppy drives. Floppy disks are more likely to be defective right out of the box. In constant use, hard disks outlast floppies.

Hard drives use a lot of the same techniques for storing information as floppy drives. They have a spinning disk, magnetic media, and read/write heads. The difference lies in the hard drive's controlled environment. The hard drive is sealed, and the mechanical tolerances of the drive are much higher than for floppies, allowing for more information to be stored and retrieved quickly.

The trade-off is that hard disks are fixed; you cannot remove or store them as easily as floppy disks. Over the years, removable hard disks have surfaced. But usually the disk remains fixed inside the computer (which is why it is sometimes referred to as a fixed disk).

◣ *H*ow Hard Drives Work

A hard drive contains a disk like a floppy drive, though often it holds more than one disk, which are stacked on top of one another like pancakes. Also, unlike a floppy disk, a hard disk is rigid, usually made of aluminum and coated with a thin film of magnetic oxide.

The reason a hard disk is "hard" is because it spins at a very high speed—usually at 3600 revolutions per minute, or ten times faster than a floppy disk spins. It's that rapidly spinning disk that makes retrieving data from a hard drive so fast.

Also, the hard drive is encased in an almost airtight environment. Unlike a floppy drive, which you can see inside of, a hard drive is sealed to keep out dust and other particles that could damage the media or the delicate read/write heads. This is important because the read/write heads float some ten-millionths of an inch above the surface of the rapidly spinning disk. It's the smallness of that distance and the density of the magnetic media that allow tracks on a hard disk to be written so close together; consequently, a hard drive holds much more information than a floppy drive.

Because the hard drive is in an almost airtight environment, you should *never* attempt to open its protective shell. At a beginning level of upgrading and maintenance, if there's a problem with the hard drive, it's better to replace the entire drive. More important, it's best to keep a software backup of your hard drive's information as extra insurance. You can do serious damage to a disk if you attempt to break into its sealed case to fix something only experts know anything about.

In your upgrading adventures, you'll never be tearing into a hard drive's sealed case. (You can try opening up one on a dead drive, but you need a special type of screwdriver.) Figure 8.1 should give you an idea of what's going on inside the drive.

As in a floppy drive, the disks spin around a spindle that's powered by a motor on the drive unit itself. Each disk is called a *platter*. And like most floppy disks, both sides are used. Yet, because there are so many platters (up to six in some drives), the sides are numbered from top to bottom. The typical hard drive, with three platters, has sides 0–5, with the even-numbered sides on top of the platters and the odd-numbered sides on the bottom.

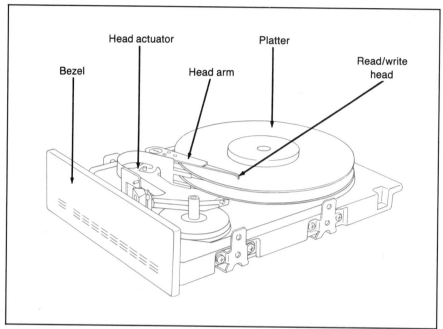

Figure 8.1: The inside of a hard drive

There is a read/write head on each side of the platter. All the read/write heads are mounted on a single unit, the head assembly. They all move together, each accessing a different track on all sides of the disk at once. It's the physical locations of all those tracks in space that really gives meaning to the formatting term *cylinder*. Three platters with six sides makes for six circular tracks in space—a cylinder.

The read/write heads are moved in and out as a unit by the *head actuator mechanism*, similar to the device that moves the read/write heads in and out over a floppy disk. But that's where the similarities end.

The tolerances of the head actuator mechanism are very precise. There are usually two types: stepper motors and voice-coil actuators. Stepper motors cost less but are slower than voice-coil actuators. Unlike the stepper motor, which moves the head assembly in given increments, the voice coil uses a magnet to position the head assembly. The magnet works like the magnet in a stereo speaker that moves the speaker cone in and out.

Other than the special environment and high tolerances inside the hard disk, it's basically just one big floppy drive. Don't let the multiple platters, tracks, and read/write heads throw you. The physical aspects of installing each kind of drive are very similar.

The Drive Unit

Since hard drives occupy the same drive bays as floppies do, they're very similar in size, though the hard drive is heavier. If you want to examine a hard drive as you're reading this, be careful with it! Always keep it level, don't jerk it around quickly, and don't drop it. It's robust but not designed to take punishment.

Hard drives come in two sizes: full-height and half-height. The full-height drive still exists, especially for very large capacity hard drives. But for most of the average-size drives, even up to 100Mb or more of storage, half-height is the standard size.

On the front of the drive is the faceplate, which really isn't part of the drive at all. It's a plastic bezel, colored to match the color of your other drives, and has a red or green drive-activity light. Most drives have a series of air holes on the front. Though the drive itself often lacks a fan, the air holes draw in air for the computer's power supply.

The bottom of the drive holds the logic board, which is usually facing up into the drive so that all you see is a green Plexiglas pincushion. The top of the drive has the metal bubble that contains the sealed disk, read/write heads, and mechanisms.

On each side of the drive there are up to four screw holes by which to mount the drive. On older cases you have to screw the drive directly into the drive bay; on newer cases you have to attach mounting rails to the drive and then slide the drive into the bay.

As on a floppy drive, there is a white box for the power-supply connector and a 34-pin edge connector. But in addition, there is a second 20-pin edge connector. You might also see some jumpers and terminating resistors. These determine the position of the drive (as on a floppy drive), either as your first hard drive, C, or the second one, D.

Your first hard drive, usually drive C, must have a terminating resistor and have its DS0 jumper set. If you upgrade and buy a drive D, you will need to remove its terminating resistor. Unlike floppy drives, all hard drives are sold as *C*, so you must remove the resistor on your D drive. But resetting the jumper to DS1 isn't always necessary. (This subject is covered in the upcoming section on cables.)

Every connector on the back of a hard drive is notched. There's no way to plug anything in backward. (And if a connector isn't notched, you simply match line 1 of the cable to pin 1 of the connector and you're in business.) But there are two edge connectors instead of one. The 34-pin edge connector is for the drive's control cable. The 20-pin connector is only for data.

The Controller Card

The hard-disk controller interfaces the hard disks to the PC itself via the bus. In some cases, the hard-disk controller may be on the motherboard, as is the case with IBM's PS/2 line of computers. Other cases may have a dual floppy/hard-disk controller.

Your hard-disk controllers should be able to handle up to two hard drives. Most PCs only have one, though adding a second one isn't that hard. But having more than two can lead to problems. If you're considering a move to three or more hard drives, think about replacing your existing drives with ones of a larger capacity. More drives can only be added by using compatible controller cards.

Generally speaking, your drive type and controller card should match. Since drives and controllers are often sold together, the salesperson can help you match them up. But be aware that there are differences. The biggest mistake you can make is buying what's known as an RLL-type drive and using it on a non-RLL-type controller. Other than that, drives and controllers should match up without any problems; your choice depends only on the type of drive and the system you're installing it into.

In some cases, if you're changing controllers, you may need to reformat the hard drive. On some hard drives, especially the low-end models, it's the controller card that determines the drive's format. When you change the card, it may not be able to read the format created by the previous controller. In that case, you'll need to reformat the drive using the new controller. But don't panic. Remember to back up your entire hard disk before swapping controllers (if possible).

The generic example in Figure 8.2 shows you all the highlights of a hard-disk controller.

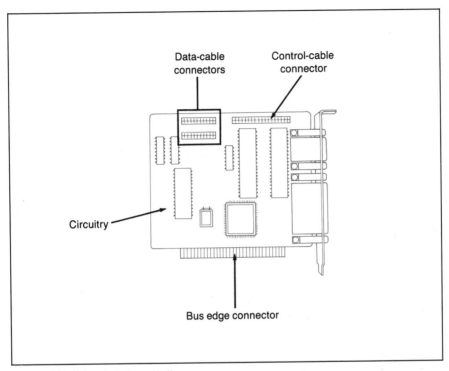

Figure 8.2: A hard-disk controller

These are the key things you need to look for:

- Any jumpers or switches
- The two 20-pin data-cable connectors
- The single 34-pin control-cable connector

It may be necessary to set jumpers on some computers (the settings depend on the capacity of the drive—see your documentation). Certain controller cards may conflict with other cards in your system, such as mouse cards. (In that particular instance, you change the mouse card, *not* the hard-disk controller.) For example, some SCSI interface cards may have trouble with some internal modem or serial port cards. These problems are resolved by setting the right jumpers. But for the majority of cards, the factory settings are adequate.

A special jumper or connector you may want to look for is one that controls the hard-drive activity light on your front panel.

The cable connectors on the hard drive controller are different from those found on most floppy controllers. Instead of edge connectors, they're pin connectors. So be careful with them: The pins are easy to bend. If you do accidentally bend a pin, gently straighten it out again using needle-nose pliers. Don't twist it.

There are two sets of 20-pin data-cable connectors. One is for drive C, the other is for drive D. Each will be marked with a number, stenciled somewhere nearby. The one for drive C will have the lower of the two numbers, for example, J2 instead of J3 (which would be for drive D). The single 34-pin connector hooks into a single cable that services both hard drives.

Note that the connectors may not have any indication on them as to how to hook in the cable. Some may have missing pins, which correspond to a blocked hole in the cable's connectors. Others will just be "straight through." The only way to determine that the cable is on correctly in those instances is by matching up pin 1 on the connector with line 1 in the cable. Pin 1 will have a stenciled 1 (or 0) by it on the card, and line 1 will be colored on the cable.

In addition to those two connectors, a combination hard/floppy-disk controller may have an edge connector for the floppy drive. There may be other connectors on the controller as well, depending on what type of controller it is and how many other options the manufacturer has put on the board.

Unlike the standard floppy-drive controller, there are several types of hard-disk controllers. The controller type depends on the drive, and it also describes the method by which information is recorded on the drive.

Data Encoding

MFM stands for *Modified Frequency Modulation,* and it refers to the magnetic encoding scheme by which bits are put onto the magnetic media. Of all the controller types, this one is the least expensive and also the least efficient at storing information.

RLL stands for *Run Length Limited.* It stores information in a much tighter format than MFM, so RLL drives have nearly twice the formatted capacity of similar MFM drives. But be warned: These benefits are only accrued when both the drive and controller support the RLL format.

Device Interfaces

ESDI stands for *Enhanced Small Device Interface*. These types of drives and controllers are very fast and hold a lot of data. They're typically found on high-end PCs. Also, because ESDI drives have minds of their own (so to speak), you can run any ESDI drive with any ESDI controller. There's no need to reformat when switching controllers.

SCSI, pronounced "scuzzy," stands for *Small Computer System Interface*. SCSI is actually more than a disk-drive interface. Up to seven devices can be chained to one SCSI card. So you can have seven hard drives, or one hard drive and a printer, scanner, digitizer, or any number of SCSI-compatible devices running off one controller card. Also, like ESDI drives, SCSI drives are smart, fast, and come in a variety of sizes.

Interleave

The *interleave* factor determines how the information is organized on each track of the hard disk. Some PCs are just too slow to read the information from a spinning drive as it rotates under the read/write head. They need time to digest the information, so the sectors in each track are laid out in an interleaved pattern.

A 3:1 interleave means that three sectors of information pass under the read/write head for every one sector that the drive, controller, and computer are capable of reading. To make the most efficient use of the drive, the sectors are scattered about each track so that the next sector in sequence on disk is ready to be read from once the previous sector has been digested. This interleave means no time is wasted waiting for the next sector to rotate under the read/write head. Figure 8.3 shows three different interleave ratios.

The interleave factor is important because a bad interleave can really slow down a disk. It's one thing to use an interleave in favor of a slow PC. But too great an interleave means the computer waits too long for the proper sector to come under the read/write head. All that waiting takes time and slows down the drive.

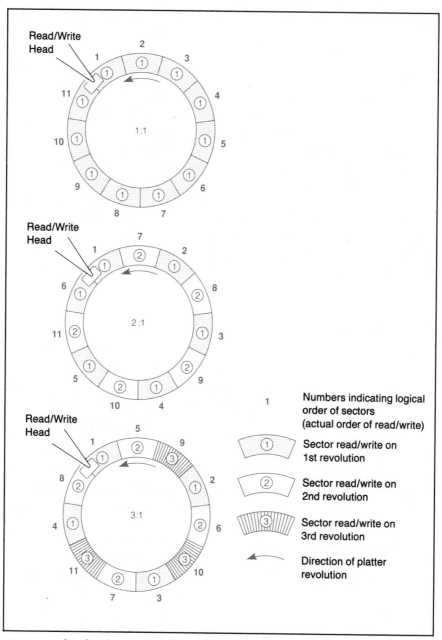

Figure 8.3: Interleaving

Cables

There are two sets of cables that hook your hard drive to the controller card:

- The 20-line data cable
- The 34-line controller cable

Each hard drive has its own 20-line data cable. It goes from the 20-pin edge connector on the back of the hard-drive unit directly to a row of pins (the connector) on the hard-disk controller card.

The edge connector on the drive is usually notched, so installing it isn't difficult. But the pins on the controller card may not have a key or an obvious orientation. For that end of the cable, remember to line up pin 1 on the connector with line 1 on the cable. Also, since each controller card can support two hard drives, make sure you plug the data cable into the proper connector (refer to the previous section for instructions).

The 34-line controller cable is remarkably similar to the cable used to connect your floppy drives. But it's not the same cable!

Like the floppy cable, the typical hard-disk controller cable supports two disks. One end of the cable plugs into the hard-disk controller, the middle connector goes to drive D (if available), and the end connector goes to drive C. But the twist between drive D's and drive C's connector is different from that of a floppy cable's. Don't confuse the two. (Actually, since most hard-disk controller cables connect to the controller card via a pin connector and not an edge connector, you're not likely to make this mistake.) Just remember that the twist in the cable is before the C drive.

Before moving on, note that some PCs may have a special straight-through cable, without a drive D connector in the middle. When this is the case and you need to add a drive D, you'll need to buy the dual-drive cable. If the dual-drive cable *lacks* the twist between the D and C connectors, remember to set the Drive Select jumper on drive D. Once you've done that (and have removed drive D's terminating resistor), you can proceed with installation.

Buying a Hard Drive

The following four items are the most important when choosing a new hard drive:

- The type of PC you have
- The size of the hard drive
- The drive's speed
- The controller card interface

Make sure you get the proper drive for your system. You'll need to know the size of the hard drive in megabytes. How much is enough? You need at least 3Mb per application, 4Mb or more if the application involves graphics. Total up your estimates and then double or triple that value. If you're using your PC at work, a minimum size to consider is 40Mb—which even then may not be enough.

You also need to think about how fast a hard drive you want. Hard-drive speeds are measured in milliseconds, abbreviated *ms*. This value is known as the *average access time*. A fast hard drive has a speed of 12 to 30 ms. The lower the number, the faster the drive. Average hard drives have speeds from 30 to 60 ms. Anything over 60 ms is considered a slow hard drive.

Finally, you need to consider the *controller card interface*. In some instances, it may be determined by the drive. If you select an ESDI drive for your 386, you need an ESDI controller. Normally, dealers recommend controllers for the hard drives they sell. But if some controllers offer features and performance that you need, find out if they will match your selected hard drive.

Other items that play an important role in hard-drive selection include the following:

- Whether the drive uses a stepper motor or voice-coil mechanism
- The drive's MTBF rating
- The drive's bezel color

If possible, you should select a hard drive that uses a voice-coil mechanism to position the read/write heads. The drives that have a voice coil are more expensive, but they are better systems. The key advantage is that a voice-coil drive automatically *parks* the read/write heads when they're inactive. This prevents the chance of a head crash should the power suddenly go out.

MTBF stands for *Mean Time Between Failure*. It's a rating, usually given in hours, that indicates how long a life your hard drive should have. For example, an MTBF rating of 10,000 hours means the drive should work for ten thousand hours (that's a little over a year) without any problem. You should get a drive with an MTBF rating of 20,000–30,000. But as with most ratings, it should only be used for comparison. You'll probably get a lot more time out of your drive than the MTBF value indicates.

Finally, there's the aesthetic issue of your hard drive's faceplate—the bezel—and whether or not its color clashes with that of your PC. Since the bezel is a separate part of the hard drive, you can usually choose between a light- or dark-colored one to match your system. Also, if you're putting a half-height drive in a full-height drive bay, you can get a full-height-drive bezel to fill in the hole.

After you buy the drive, you should know the following items about it:

- The total number of cylinders
- The number of heads (or platters)
- The drive type or form factor

Most of this information is required by the AT system's setup program. Most manufacturers spare you from having to know these details, but they are good things to know.

Because nearly every drive has bad sectors on it, the hard drive itself comes with an error map, either in the box or attached in a pouch on top. Normally, when the drive is formatted, the bad sectors are plotted and avoided. Or the drive may be preformatted and already know about the bad sectors. Some software installation programs may require you to enter the bad sector numbers, though this is rare. If you have to do this, remember to photocopy the error map, or keep it on your computer hardware documentation shelf.

A General Strategy for Upgrading

The basic steps for upgrading a hard drive are identical to those for upgrading a floppy drive (see Chapter 7). The drives go in the same location, with hard drives usually placed in the left drive bays. And they're mounted the same, either directly on the side or by means of mounting rails.

Since the drives are the same physical size, you only need to concern yourself with the cable connections. Two of the hard drive's three cables work just like those on a floppy drive, and the third cable, the data cable, isn't any big deal either.

The only additional concern you should have is the extra 20-pin edge connector on the hard drive. Floppy drives don't have this connector; you must connect it to the hard drive for the drive to work properly.

Like the 34-pin edge connector, the 20-pin connector is notched, both on the card and cable. (If not, match up pin 1 with line 1 and everything will work fine.) There is one cable for the 20-pin edge connector, and it goes directly to the hard-drive controller. If you have two drives, they'll both have their own 20-line cable.

Removing a Hard Drive

When you upgrade a hard drive, you may first need to remove an older hard drive or remove a floppy drive that you're replacing with the hard drive. If you are removing a floppy drive, make sure it's your *B* drive, not A. Also, you should install the hard drive in the left drive bay.

Procedure: Installing a second hard drive

Tools: Medium Phillips screwdriver

<u>1</u> Power down your PC.

<u>2</u> Unplug the CPU.

<u>3</u> Remove the lid.

<u>4</u> Locate the drive and remove its screws.

For a PC-style case, the two mounting screws are on the side of the drive. AT-style cases have mounting rails on the drive, which have screws on either side of the drive's front. Remember to remove the mounting rails and set them, and all other screws and brackets, aside for installation of the new drive.

<u>5</u> Slide the drive forward a bit and detach the power-supply cable, the 34-line control cable, and the 20-line data cable. Move them out of the way.

If you've removed drive D but still have drive C, you can also remove drive D's 20-line control cable. Detach it from the hard-drive controller and keep it with the drive, or store it if you're throwing the drive out.

<u>6</u> Slide the drive forward and free.

You can now set the drive aside, put it into a box, or throw it away. Remember to keep the mounting rails for any new drives you may install.

<u>7</u> Replace the drive, or cover the empty drive-bay hole with a blank faceplate and restart your system. (If you're replacing the drive, keep the PC open.)

If you're removing a drive D or drive B, then there is nothing else that needs to be done.

If you're removing all hard drives from your system, you should also remove the hard-disk controller card. Removing expansion cards is covered in the next chapter. Otherwise, close up the case and you can continue working.

If you have an AT computer, you will need to modify the setup program to instruct the battery-backed-up RAM that a hard drive has been removed.

◢ *Installing a Hard Drive*

This section covers the physical side of installing a hard drive in your PC. This is really only half the job; hard drives also require some software setup, which is covered in the final part of this chapter. If you're installing a second hard drive, please refer to the following section.

This procedure assumes that the hard-disk controller has already been installed in the system and that the cables are already connected to it. Information covering that installation is described in Chapter 9.

Procedure: Installing a hard drive

Tools: Medium Phillips screwdriver

1 Power down your PC.

2 Unplug the CPU.

3 Remove the lid.

4 Remove the old drive or faceplate covering the drive bay.

5 Check any jumpers on the new drive.

Since adding a drive D is covered in the next section, you should look for the following on drive C: a terminating resistor (which comes standard on nearly all hard drives) and a Drive Select (DSx) jumper set to DS0 or DS1, whichever is less. Double-check these two items, though they are likely to be set the right way.

6 Attach the mounting rails to the drive. If necessary, screw a mounting rail on each side of the drive.

7 Slide the drive into position. As with floppy drives, hard drives slide in from the front.

8 Attach the power supply and cables to the drive. The power-supply cable, 20-line data cable, and 34-line control cable can only go on one way.

9 Slide the drive into the bay all the way.

10 Anchor the drive in position by tightening the screws.

PC-style cases have screws on the side. For drives with mounting rails, position the angle brackets and then tighten the screws on both sides of the front of the drive.

11 Recheck your connections.

12 Test the PC and close it up.

Remember not to touch the inside of the system or modify it with the power on. If there are any problems, power down again and recheck your connections. Odds are pretty good that if the hard drive doesn't come on (its light won't blink), a connector came loose.

If everything checks out, then you can close the lid on your PC, tighten everything up, and reattach the power cable. You're now ready to proceed with software installation.

 ## Installing a Second Drive

When buying a second drive, remember to buy one that's compatible with your controller card. If you have an ESDI or SCSI controller, then nearly any matching hard drive will do. But other MFM and RLL controllers may require a specific type of drive. If you're unclear, then simply buy a second hard drive identical to the first.

You will definitely need a second 20-line data cable for the second hard drive. The 34-line controller cable you're using may or may not have a drive D connector and twist in it. To be safe, get a dual-drive controller cable when you buy your second hard drive. Nothing is more disappointing than being halfway through an upgrade and finding that you have to go back to the store to buy a cable. (And remember to buy another pair of mounting rails and screws, if you need them.)

Procedure: Installing a second hard drive

Tools: Medium Phillips screwdriver

1 Power down your PC.

2 Unplug the CPU.

3 Remove the lid.

4 Remove the old drive or faceplate covering the drive bay. If the drive bay is internal, it may be left open.

5 Set any jumpers or remove the terminating resistor on the new drive.

> You only need to set switches if you're installing a drive D and the cable is *not* twisted between drive C and drive D. Set the DS1 jumper to DS2; if it's a DS0 jumper, set it to DS1. If the cable has a twist, both hard disks may be set to the same drive number. Also, you must always remove the terminating resistor on drive D. Most drives you buy come as drive C and have the terminating resistor installed.

6 Attach the mounting rails to the drive, if necessary. (If you're installing a second hard drive in a PC-style case, you may need to purchase a mounting bracket to mount the drive.)

7 Slide the drive into position.

8 Attach the power-supply cable and 34-line controller cable to the drive.

> Most power supplies have four connectors, divided into two for floppy drives and two for hard drives. If you don't have enough connectors, you'll need to buy a Y splitter. (And if so, your power supply may not be up to snuff to run two drives.) The controller cable connector you'll use is the one in the middle. Note that both the power-supply and controller cable can only go on one way.

9 Attach the 20-line data cable to the drive. It's usually notched.

10 Attach the other end of the data cable to the hard-disk controller. There should be a second 20-pin connector for it, either below or to the side of drive C's data connector.

11 Slide the drive all the way into the bay.

12 Anchor the drive in position by tightening the screws.

13 Recheck your connections.

14 Test the PC and close it up.

If you have a PC/XT, the drive should come to life right away, but it may be unformatted, so don't expect it to go online just yet. If you have an AT, you'll need to run the setup program to tell the computer what type of drive you've installed.

The AT Setup Program

If you don't have an AT or 386 system, you can skip this section. ATs generally lack DIP switches and come with special battery-backed-up RAM (or CMOS memory) instead. This RAM contains configuration information about the computer, including the disk drives. Because of this, each time you add or remove a hard drive (or just about anything in your computer), you need to run a setup program to alter your battery-backed-up RAM.

Your computer (as part of the POST) detects the presence of a new hard drive when you boot and displays an error message, such as the following:

Invalid configuration information—please run SETUP program

The message may be different on your own system, but don't worry. Take whatever steps are necessary to run your computer's setup program. Depending on your system, you may have to press a function key after the error message is displayed, press a certain key combination while in DOS, or run some setup application. (Refer to your computer's instruction manual for details.)

Once in the setup program, you need to select the hard drive you've installed. For example, if you've just installed a drive C, you may need to select something called *First Hard Drive* or *Fixed Disk 1*.

After you select the hard drive, tell the setup program what type of drive you have. This is where the *drive type* or *form factor* value comes into play. The terms and statistics for each drive are listed in the drive's manual and can be confusing, but there should be a matching type or form factor somewhere on the list. Once you know it, enter it into the setup program according to the instructions supplied with your computer.

In some rare cases, a drive type may not be known. If you're installing a drive and don't know the type, refer to Appendix B to match up cylinder, head, and track counts, or contact the manufacturer's technical support staff. But try Type 1 first, because for some reason, this seems to work for quite a few AT-type systems and their hard drives.

After assigning the drive and type in the setup program, reboot the system. It should come up as normal (providing installation was OK), and you can then continue with the software installation.

 # Preparing for and Installing DOS

Like a floppy disk, a hard disk needs to be prepared for use with DOS. It's done in three steps:

- Low-level formatting
- FDISKing, or partitioning
- High-level formatting

A final step, installing DOS, is necessary if the new drive is your first, drive C. Otherwise, formatting alone is fine for your second drive.

Low-Level Formatting

There are two levels of formatting for a hard drive: low-level and high-level. This leads to a lot of confusion with first-time hard-drive owners. Low-level formatting defines the tracks and sectors on the drive. High-level formatting is done by DOS, and it simply makes sure that the tracks and sectors are in order, readable, and ready for DOS to use.

Some drives are low-level formatted at the factory. If yours is not, you can

- Use a software program
- Access the hard-disk controller's ROM by using DEBUG

There are a number of ways you can find out if your drive was low-level formatted at the factory. The easiest is to use the FDISK utility on the drive. If FDISK says you don't have a hard drive (or a drive D), then you know it isn't low-level formatted. (Additional information on FDISK is covered in the next section.)

When the drive hasn't been low-level formatted, it's up to you to do it. The better-quality drives and those purchased through national dealers come with a disk containing a low-level formatting program. The program is usually called something like HSECT, FSECT, or HDSETUP.

You have to be careful, because a low-level formatting program erases everything on the drive. Make sure you really want to do it, especially for a drive with data already on it.

Some hard drives leave it totally up to you to do the low-level formatting. If you don't have a program, you need to access the hard-disk controller's ROM by using the DEBUG utility that comes with DOS. The low-level formatting program is encoded in the ROM chip on your controller card.

To invoke DEBUG, type **DEBUG** at the DOS prompt and press Enter. DEBUG's prompt, a single hyphen, then appears:

```
A> DEBUG
-
```

The commands necessary to start the low-level formatting program from DEBUG vary, depending on the type of hard-disk controller you have. The general format is *G* (for *go*), followed by an equal sign, the hexadecimal (base 16) value *C800*, a colon, and a number. The number that follows the colon depends on your hard-disk controller. Call the manufacturer of the drive if you can't find the appropriate number in the documentation.

Type the command corresponding to the controller you have at DEBUG's hyphen prompt. If you're in doubt, try

```
G = C800:5
```

The hard disk may be immediately formatted, or you may see a menu of options. Use the defaults and do whatever is necessary to proceed with the low-level formatting. If you have difficulty, call the controller manufacturer's technical support staff.

*F*DISKing, or Partitioning

FDISK is the name of a DOS utility program that partitions your hard drive. Partitioning is done for a number of reasons:

- To get around DOS's hard-drive size limitation
- To have more than one logical drive
- To have more than one operating system

The first reason for partitioning is that DOS, through version 3.3, is unable to deal with a hard drive larger than 32Mb. DOS 4 can deal with a hard drive up to 512Mb in size (although the first partition must be less than or equal to 32Mb), but even then the hard drive must be initialized by FDISK to prepare it for use with DOS.

If you have a hard drive larger than 32Mb and you're using DOS 3.3 or earlier, then you'll want to divide up the hard drive into one or more *logical* drives. Even if you have DOS 4, you may still want to divide the single hard drive into logical drives C, D, and E, simply to help you keep your files organized.

The final reason for partitioning is to put more than one operating system on the drive—for example, both DOS and Xenix.

Whether or not you need to partition a drive, you still need to run FDISK before DOS can use the drive. To run FDISK, type **FDISK** at the DOS prompt, although you may have run it from a floppy. (You can even run FDISK when a hard drive is already installed, simply to check the partition information.) FDISK is a simple, menu-driven program. Its main screen will look something like the one displayed in Figure 8.4.

Four options are displayed. If you have a second hard drive, a fifth option appears, *Select Next Fixed Disk Drive*. If you're installing a drive D, then that's the option you would select now.

```
IBM Personal Computer
Fixed Disk Setup Program Version 3.30
(C)Copyright IBM Corp. 1983,1987

FDISK Options

Current Fixed Disk Drive: 1

Choose one of the following:

    1. Create DOS partition
    2. Change Active Partition
    3. Delete DOS partition
    4. Display Partition Information



Enter choice: [1]



Press ESC to return to DOS
```

Figure 8.4: FDISK's main menu in PC-DOS 3.3

If you have a single new hard drive, your next step is to select option 1, *Create DOS partition*. After you do so, FDISK displays a second screen with two options:

- Create Primary DOS partition
- Create Extended DOS partition

The Primary DOS partition is the main, bootable part of your hard disk. It only needs to be created once, for drive C. The Extended DOS partitions define any additional, logical drives in your system. (Since they're not bootable drives, they're referred to as *Extended DOS* partitions.)

For a new drive, press 1 to create the Primary DOS partition. Depending on the version of FDISK you're using, a second screen may ask how much of the drive you wish to use for the Primary DOS partition.

After FDISK is done, and you've established the Primary DOS partition and any Extended DOS partitions (for drives D, E, F, etc.),

FDISK reboots your machine. This is necessary so that the new information FDISK writes to your disk's boot sector will be loaded into memory.

But you still don't have DOS on the hard drive. It isn't even high-level formatted. So remember to keep a bootable floppy in drive A for the next, final step: formatting the hard drive under DOS. If you're installing a drive D, you don't need to boot off a floppy in drive A; your drive C will still have DOS installed and intact, and you can set up the second hard drive from there.

*H*igh-Level Formatting

The final software step in installing a hard drive is high-level formatting. This is the traditional formatting you've always done to floppies using the DOS FORMAT command. The difference is that with a hard disk, you're dealing with several tracks per cylinder, as opposed to two. Each track does have a side, or *head number,* associated with it.

The total number of cylinders in a hard drive is greater than in a floppy drive. The typical 20Mb hard drive may have 611–619 cylinders. (A 1.2Mb floppy has only 80.) If the disk has two platters, that makes for four disk sides. So the actual number of tracks is 619×4, or 2476.

There are also more sectors per track on a typical DOS hard drive. Usually, hard drives have a 17-sector track. (ESDI drives use 34 sectors per track.) There are still 512 bytes per sector. So a 619-cylinder hard drive with two platters has 619 (cylinders) $\times$ 4 (sides) = 2476 (tracks). Multiply that by 17 (sectors per track) and 512 (bytes per sector) and you get 21,551,104 bytes. Divide it by 1024 and you get 21,046K; if you divide that by 1024, you get 20.55Mb.

Drives are usually sold with an *unformatted* size value. With larger-capacity drives, that number is always greater than the actual formatted size of the drive. For example, a 90Mb drive may actually only format out to 88Mb. Although that's not a big deal, you should be aware of it when you purchase a drive. The drive will say whether the value listed is the unformatted capacity or not.

The high-level format is basically a type of hard-disk verification. Unlike a low-level format, which really does overwrite all information on the drive, a high-level format on a hard drive rewrites part of the hard disk's boot sector, establishes a root directory and a FAT (file allocation table), and then verifies all the remaining tracks and sectors in that DOS partition. (Remember, there can be more than one DOS partition on a hard drive; each one needs to be formatted.)

You format a hard drive just as you format a floppy. Type the FORMAT command after the command prompt, followed by the drive letter of the hard drive you want to format. For example, to format the C drive, you type

A> FORMAT C:

After pressing Enter, the drive will begin to be formatted. If the hard drive is already formatted, you'll see a warning message as follows:

WARNING, ALL DATA ON NON-REMOVABLE DISK
DRIVE C: WILL BE LOST!
Proceed with Format (Y/N)?

Press Y to begin formatting or N to leave the disk (and its data) as is.

Some versions of DOS may ask you to enter the drive's label name as a secondary form of verification:

Enter current Volume Label for drive C:

Only after entering the proper label will you be allowed to complete the format.

Formatting takes awhile, so get a cup of coffee if you want. Remember to format all your logical drives, if you have them. A hard drive partitioned into drives C, D, and E has to have all its logical drives formatted before data can go on them.

Installing DOS

If you're installing a drive C, put a copy of DOS on the drive and make it a bootable disk. This is done by specifying the /S switch after the format command as follows:

A> FORMAT C: /S

The /S switch transfers the system to the hard drive, primarily the two hidden DOS boot files. You may also need to copy the COMMAND.COM file to your hard drive:

A> COPY COMMAND.COM C:

This finishes the software setup of drive C, which is the only hard drive you'll need to transfer the system to. To test the installation, reboot the computer without a floppy disk in drive A. After a few moments, DOS will be loaded from the hard disk, displaying its name and copyright notice and may ask you to enter the date and time. Your upgrade is complete.

Preventive Maintenance

One of the worst things that can happen to a hard drive is a head crash: The delicate read/write head slams into the surface of the disk, gouging it and damaging the data that sits there.

Head crashes occur for a variety of reasons. A small particle of smoke on the surface of the disk is enough to interfere with the read/write head. Even more common is the damage that takes place if you suddenly jar the drive. Sometimes even if the power goes out, the heads come into contact with the disk media (though that's not really a "crash").

To prevent the read/write heads from damaging the drive media, you can park the heads. This moves the read/write heads over some noncrucial area of the disk and may also even lock them into position there. Once they're safely out of the way, you can turn off the power or move the computer without risking damage to the drive media.

Parking is usually accomplished by using a PARK program or utility. The name is different depending on which type of drive you have, though PARK is the most common (each different drive requires its own PARK program). To park the drive, you simply type PARK at the DOS prompt and the program moves the read/write heads over a safe area of the disk.

Drives with a voice-coil mechanism automatically park the drive heads after any disk is accessed. However, a PARK program may still be required to lock the heads into position—especially before moving the PC.

A lot of people use special utilities that park the drive heads every five minutes or so. This is unnecessary. Only if you're going to shut down for the day, move the PC, or leave it unattended for a long period of time should you park the drives. And if your drive has a voice-coil mechanism, then you only need to park the heads if you're going to be moving the computer or leaving it for any duration.

Summary

Hard drives are valuable; if you don't have one, you should get one. If you already have a hard drive, then you should think about buying a second one, or one that's faster and holds more information. Hard drives hold lots of information and can access it quickly, making them a must-have item for anyone who's serious about using a computer.

The physical upgrade process for installing a hard drive is fairly simple, nearly identical to the upgrade process for a floppy drive. The only difference is the extra 20-line data cable that each hard drive has.

A not as well known part of the hard-drive upgrade is dealing with software. You need to low-level format, FDISK, and high-level format the hard drive.

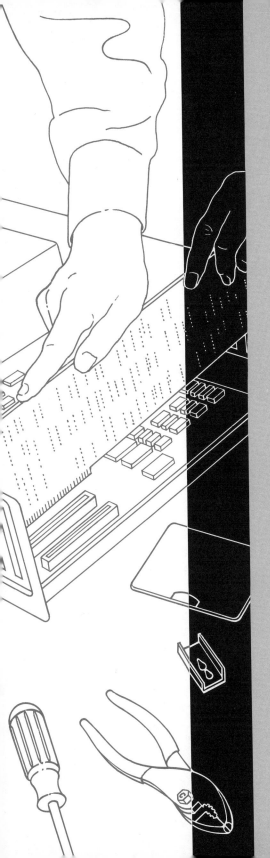

9

Expansion
Cards

THIS CHAPTER IS ABOUT INSTALLING AND UPGRADING expansion cards. The upgrade process itself is rather simple. What makes it complex is the variety of expansion cards that are available. But fortunately, each card is installed the same way.

 ## All About Expansion Cards

Expansion cards are printed circuit boards. They contain chips and other electronics, an edge connector to plug them into the computer, and a mounting bracket by which the card is anchored to the PC's frame.

Parts of an Expansion Card

To illustrate the parts of an expansion card, a generic one is shown in Figure 9.1. This card is a full-height, AT-style card. Other expansion cards may be shorter, narrower, and have only one edge connector on the bottom.

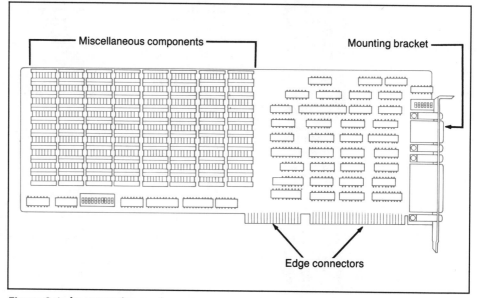

Figure 9.1: *An expansion card*

The Card   The card itself is a (usually green) fiberglass sheet. It's quite stiff, but can be slightly bowed. This is sometimes necessary to fit a card in a poorly designed PC case.

Mounting Bracket   The card is anchored in two, sometimes three, ways. The first is via the edge connector (and the bus). The second is through a metal mounting bracket on the back of the PC. The third, if the card is long enough, is by a slot on the front of the system unit.

Edge Connectors   A standard PC expansion card comes with one or two edge connectors, by which the card plugs into the slot and communicates with the PC via the bus.

Skirt   Some cards have what's called a skirt, which is the lower side of the card that extends below the top of the edge connectors. Note that cards with skirts may not be installed in certain slots. They interfere with chips on the motherboard.

Other Components   All cards have chips, resistors, and other electronic components, almost always on only one side. The other side has rows of tiny pins where the components are soldered on.

Card Sizes

The physical dimensions of cards vary. Before you buy a card, you need to know what will fit in your PC and what won't. For example, cards designed for the AT are often too tall for the PC/XT case. Also, some cards may be too long for some clones. The original Tandy 1000 had too shallow a case for some long PC adapter cards.

Cards are categorized by their height and length and whether they have a 16- or 8-bit bus connector. Figure 9.2 shows a few popular expansion-card configurations.

The two heights available are PC/AT and PC/XT. The AT-style case is taller than the original PC's case, so tall cards, even though they may only be 8-bit, cannot fit in a PC/XT-style case.

The lengths of cards also vary. Full-length cards stretch from the back of the PC's case (where the mounting bracket goes) all the way to the front, a little over 13 inches. There are mid-length cards that are still fairly long. And there are so-called short, or half, cards.

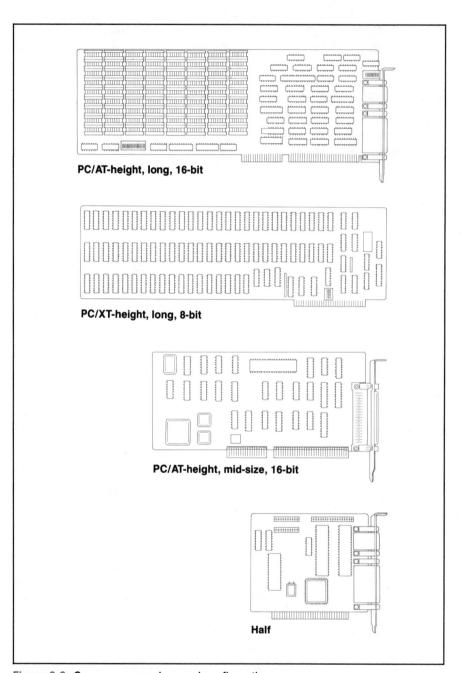

PC/AT-height, long, 16-bit

PC/XT-height, long, 8-bit

PC/AT-height, mid-size, 16-bit

Half

Figure 9.2: Common expansion-card configurations

The card's length really depends on how much circuitry it needs. In the early days, components were numerous compared with today's very large scale integrated (VLSI) circuits. Now cards can get quite small. But certain cards, such as those with megabytes of RAM, are still full-length.

Long cards can only fit in certain slots inside the PC. Short cards were developed primarily to take advantage of those slots on the right side of the bus, behind the disk drives. Since the drives occupy space that would normally be used by a long card, those slots behind the drives are usually referred to as short slots.

Most cards are fairly thin, and you can put them right next to one another without having their components touch. But other cards may have a profusion of cables, or secondary "daughter" boards, that make them fatter than normal. Some hard disks on a card make the card so wide that it really takes up the space of two cards.

Oftentimes, it's possible to put a short card by one of these double-wide cards. That way you don't lose an expansion slot next to a particularly fat card. However, if space inside your PC is at a premium, a fat card may not be what you need.

Card Contents

Most of the electronic doodads on an expansion card will probably be a mystery to you—unless you have some knowledge of electrical engineering. But for upgrading purposes, there are three things you should recognize and know how to deal with on an expansion card:

- Jumpers and DIP switches
- Connectors
- Piggyback and daughter boards

Jumpers and DIP switches set the current configuration of your computer or expansion card. For example, you may have to set DIP switches to tell a memory card how much RAM you've put on it and where that RAM starts in relation to other memory in your system. The instructions for setting the jumpers and DIP switches are in the expansion card's manual.

An expansion card may also have various connectors. Some are on the mounting bracket. For example, a card with a printer port may have the port right on the mounting bracket, making it easily accessible from behind the PC. Other connectors may be on the card itself for internal purposes. For example, a hard-disk controller has two connectors for cables to connect the controller to your hard drive. Other expansion cards may have additional cable connectors, some of which thread to external connectors on the bottom of the PC or elsewhere.

Finally, an expansion card may have special connectors for attaching a piggyback or daughter board, such as an expansion card for an expansion card. Usually, a piggyback card is found on a memory expansion card. It allows you to add even more RAM to the card after all the RAM sockets on the card are full. Keep in mind that piggyback and daughter cards cost more and also make the card wider.

Card Handling

The advice for handling expansion cards is like that for handling RAM chips: Always be careful to prevent static buildup, which can discharge and harm the card. Always ground yourself before picking up an expansion card. If the PC's case is open, touch the power supply before picking up the card.

Handle all expansion cards by their edges, but don't touch the card's edge connector. Occasionally you may need to get a thumb grip on a card, especially when removing it. If so, be very careful and ground yourself before touching the card.

Finally, be aware of the back side of a card. Since expansion cards have their circuitry on only one side, the other side is usually dotted with tiny metal points (where the chips are soldered to the card), which can prick you.

Most cards (the good ones, at least) come in static-free pouches. They're shipped in either foam rubber or some special packing material. Try to keep the card in the pouch and in the packing when it's not in your PC. If you remove a card, put it back in its original box for storage.

Types of Expansion Cards

There are literally hundreds of different types of expansion cards on the market. Not only are there different types of cards, but different manufacturers make variations on each type. When you toss in the so-called multifunction cards, where one card takes on the duties of several cards, the variety is nearly endless.

Standard Cards

There are several types of cards that have become standards in the past ten years of PC computing. Primarily, these are cards that supply such necessary parts of the computer as the serial port, printer port, memory, video display, and floppy controller.

Recently the trend has been to incorporate most of the items on these standard cards in the design of the PC's motherboard. For example, IBM's PS/2 computers have video, memory, hard- and floppy-disk controllers, serial ports, parallel ports, and mouse ports all built into the motherboard. This is a far cry from the first PC, where all these items (except for 16K to 64K of RAM) were on an expansion card.

The five most common types of expansion cards are the floppy-disk controller card, hard-disk controller card, memory card, video adapter card, and serial port card.

Floppy-Disk Controller

The floppy-disk controller was an option on the first PC. Why? Because it had built-in support for cassette-tape storage on the motherboard, as well as BASIC and ROM. Though the Apple II and TRS-80 systems of that time also had cassette-tape storage, it was slow and unreliable, so most people bought the floppy-disk controller and full-height floppy-drive PC configuration.

Hard-Disk Controller

Hard drives are more-or-less standard equipment on the PC/XT and later systems. To interface the hard drive with your PC, you need a hard-disk controller card.

Memory

There are really two types of memory expansions: standard memory and extended/expanded memory. Refer to Chapter 5 for information on each kind.

Video Adapter

The video adapter is the most common card found in a PC, even more so than a memory adapter, because the typical PC has no built-in video-display circuitry. It gives you the advantage of choosing which type of video card, graphics, color, and resolution you want.

The original PC video cards, the Monochrome Display Adapter (MDA) and Color Graphics Adapter (CGA), also came with a parallel port. The parallel port is where you plug in your printer cable (which is why it's also referred to as a printer port).

Serial Port

An extremely popular addition to many PCs is the serial port. It can come on its own card or it can be in combination with other items on a multifunction card.

A serial port provides two-way communications between your computer and some external device. Unlike a parallel port, which is a one-way communications port to the printer, a serial port can both talk and listen to a variety of devices, including modems, printers, plotters, scanners, computer mice, and other devices. (A serial port is also referred to as an RS-232 port.)

Multifunction and Combination Cards

Multifunction cards combine the functions of a lot of single cards, saving slot space. For example, IBM originally had separate adapters available for a serial port, joystick (also called an A/D, or analog/digital, port), real-time clock, and memory. Several third-party developers came up with combination cards that put all these functions on one multifunction card. The most popular was the AST SixPak, which came with memory, a serial port, a parallel port, a joystick port, a real-time clock, and software. Other cards offer other combinations as well.

Today, quite a few of these functions are built into many PCs. Nearly all AT-level machines maintain a real-time clock through their battery-backed-up RAM. Serial and parallel ports are commonly found on the motherboards of the better systems. But there are still multifunction cards available for those PCs that lack these features.

Various cards are also combined today, for example, the hard-disk and floppy-disk controllers. Another combination currently popular is EMS memory with serial and parallel ports. Some video cards have a mouse port as an option.

Mouse Cards

A mouse has been a popular device for the personal computer ever since Apple introduced their Macintosh computer in 1984. The mouse was pioneered on the PC by Microsoft, but today there are dozens of manufacturers making a variety of mice and mouselike pointing devices.

A mouse controls a cursor or pointer on the screen. You move the mouse around on your desk, and the pointer mimics those movements on the screen. Buttons on the mouse are used to select, or click on, items displayed on the screen. The mouse really comes in handy as an editing tool for text, but it's best used with graphics applications and the operating system Microsoft Windows.

More and more PC software is taking advantage of the mouse, so buying one is a good investment. They're not even that expensive, costing from $50 to $150, or less if you can find one discounted.

Mouse Types

The mouse itself is a palm-size device with buttons on top. A cord extends from the front of the mouse and plugs into your PC. How the mouse plugs in determines which type it is: bus or serial.

The *bus mouse* is so-named because it plugs into your PC's expansion bus. The mouse plugs into an expansion card, which plugs into the bus. This expansion card will probably be one of the sparsest, shortest cards in your PC (ideal for a short slot or for the occasional 8-bit slot in an AT-level machine). The ATI VGA Wonder card comes with a bus mouse as an option, and Microsoft's old Mach 20 accelerator had a mouse port as an option.

A *serial mouse* plugs into one of your serial ports. It's basically a computer mouse and cable that hooks up like an external modem.

The bus mouse is better because its dedicated circuitry is more reliable than the serial mouse's. But there are times when you don't have an extra slot into which you can plug a bus mouse card. In those instances, you have to go with a serial mouse. Also, some bus mouse cards will conflict with other cards in your system. To prevent this, they come with a slew of jumpers that must be set depending on what's in your system. Still, I personally recommend a bus mouse over a serial one.

A mouse also has buttons on it. Unlike the Macintosh mouse, which has only one button on it, PC mice usually have two or three buttons. The Microsoft mouse has a left button and a right button. Some mice, such as Logitech's, have three buttons. Most software is built around the Microsoft mouse, so the minimum number of buttons you need is two. A few applications, however, take advantage of a three-button mouse.

Mouse Compatibility

Since there are a lot of companies that make computer mice, and since IBM didn't lead the way with a standard, the most compatible mouse you can get is Microsoft's.

A computer mouse is controlled by a software driver you install in your CONFIG.SYS file. For example, entering a line such as the following will automatically load the mouse driver and activate the mouse each time you start your computer:

```
DEVICE = C:\MOUSE\MOUSE.SYS
```

A second driver, MOUSE.COM, is a memory-resident version of MOUSE.SYS. The original intent of MOUSE.COM, however, was to include it in batch files that run applications requiring a mouse driver. If MOUSE.SYS wasn't in CONFIG.SYS, then the batch file containing MOUSE.COM would load the mouse driver.

There are alternative pointing devices that work like a mouse but offer better features or ease of use, including trackballs and optical mice.

A trackball is basically an upside-down mouse. It has a large billiard-ball-size ball in its center and two buttons on each side. You can move the ball using your fingers and hit the buttons with your thumb. Since it doesn't slide around the desk, many people find a trackball easier to use—especially for large screens—than a traditional mouse.

The standard mouse has a ball bearing in its underside. The optical mouse has two infrared lamps and slides over a special reflective pad. Light sensors inside the mouse detect movement, so there are no moving parts inside an optical mouse. Unlike the traditional mouse, which can roll on any smooth surface, you have to have the reflective pad to use an optical mouse.

Modem Cards

Another popular type of expansion card is the *modem card*. A modem is a communications device that allows your computer to transfer information to another modem-equipped computer by using the phone lines. It takes digital signals from your computer and translates them into sounds. It can also translate the sounds back into digital bytes. This process is called modulation/demodulation, from which the word *modem* comes.

Using a modem, you can dial online networks, remote PCs, or electronic bulletin board systems (BBSs). You can participate in online discussions, digest information, transfer programs, and talk electronically with other modem users. It's a lot of fun. You can also log into the office computer and work if you like.

The two types of modems are the internal modem and the external modem. An external modem is a peripheral you plug into a wall socket, a phone jack, and one of your PC's serial ports. It has the advantage of being visible—you can see its lights flash as it's working (which helps you to diagnose problems). You can turn if off when it's not in use, and you can transfer it to any other computer system that has a serial port, including non-PC systems.

An internal modem comes on an expansion card. They're generally cheaper than external modems, and they don't crowd your desktop or add to the tangle of cables behind your PC as external modems do. If you're short on slot space, then sometimes an internal modem is out of the question.

When you buy a modem, there are two things to look at:

- Speed
- Compatibility

The speed of a modem is gauged in bits per second, or BPS. (The term *baud* or *baud rate* is often incorrectly used.) The higher the BPS, the faster the modem and the greater amount of information you can transmit over a given period of time. Common speeds are 1200, 2400, and 9600 BPS. You pay a lot more for a 9600-BPS modem than you do for a 1200-BPS model.

Compatibility is also an important issue with modems. In the online world, being Hayes-compatible is the big thing. Hayes is the modem manufacturer that developed the original "Smart Modem" in the late '70s. That modem used a series of commands known as AT commands. Since then, PC communications software packages have directly supported the Hayes standard. If your modem is Hayes-compatible, or it supports the Hayes AT command set, then it too will be compatible with a lot of communications software. (Don't buy a modem that is not 100 percent Hayes-compatible.)

An internal modem is basically a combination serial port and modem on a card. Because of this, there may be a conflict between the internal modem and other serial ports in your system. Usually the conflict can be resolved by setting various jumpers, making sure that the modem is assigned to serial port 1 and any additional serial ports are numbered 2 or greater (or by using some other numbering scheme).

Other than that, adding an internal modem to your system is as easy as plugging in the card and hooking a phone cord between your PC (on the back of the modem card) and the wall jack.

Other Types of Cards

The following is a list of 13 additional types of cards. This covers just about every major category of expansion card for the PC, though there are probably dozens more.

Accelerators Accelerators are devices that speed up the operation of your PC. They're like mini-motherboards on a card. You plug them into an expansion slot, then remove your PC's microprocessor and replace it with a cable to the accelerator card. Your system then runs off the faster microprocessor on the accelerator. (Refer to Chapter 13 for more information.)

Bar-Code Readers   Bar-code readers allow you to input bar codes to your PC. This has advantages in reading inventory or can be used for a variety of information input options. The bar-code reader may also interface via a serial port.

Coprocessors   A coprocessor can be a second microprocessor or simply some circuitry designed to assist your microprocessor. One example is the Apple II computer on a card, which gives your PC the ability to run Apple II software. (A Z80-CP/M coprocessor card was on the first third-party expansion cards available for the PC.) Some coprocessor cards also boost the PC's math and graphics performance.

COPY II PC Option Board   Central Point Software makes an expansion card that plugs into your floppy-drive cable. It precisely controls the floppy drive to allow for flawless copies of disks, especially damaged or copy-protected disks.

Debugging Cards   Programmers who work on complex software use debugging cards to snoop around in memory as their software runs. If the software they're testing crashes the system, the debugging card allows them to sift through the wreckage and look for a cause.

Hard-Disk Cards   The hard disk on a card is an excellent option for PCs with no free drive bays or for older PCs that lack proper upgrade options for a hard drive. The hard-disk card is basically a combination hard-disk controller and drive.

Light Pens   A light pen can be used to "draw" on the screen (though a computer mouse is much more popular). There are various ways to hook them up to a PC. The original CGA video adapter had a built-in light pen interface.

Mainframe Communications Cards   Quite a few PCs are shackled to mainframes and used as terminals. Sometimes, to make the proper connections, a dedicated mainframe communications, or terminal emulation, card must be installed.

MIDI   The MIDI, or Musical Instrument Digital Interface, card can be plugged into a PC to record and play back music generated by MIDI-compatible musical instruments, such as synthesizers and samplers.

Network Adapters   To hook up your PC to a network, you need an adapter, which, coupled with networking software, provides the interface between your PC and other computers and peripherals on the network.

Printer Helpers   To speed up the operations of some laser printers, special assistant cards can be plugged into your PC. These cards usually come with megabytes of RAM and support circuitry that make printing go much faster.

Prototype Cards   A prototype card is the size and shape of the typical expansion card but contains no circuitry. (The hacker's term for it is *breadboard*.) It allows you to wire in your own chips or create your own expansion devices.

SCSI   SCSI, pronounced "scuzzy," stands for Small Computer System Interface. It's basically a superfast serial port into which you can plug up to seven different items, from hard drives to printers.

The Bus and Expansion Slots

The bus serves as the direct line of communication between your PC's microprocessor and the devices you plug into the expansion slots. The slots are "on" the bus, so to speak.

The bus is not something you can upgrade; it is part of your motherboard. Only by buying a new computer system or completely swapping out your motherboard (covered in Chapter 13) can you get a new bus.

In order for an expansion card to work with a particular bus, it must meet certain specifications for communications and design. For example, the PC's bus has certain rules on the size of an expansion card. A card must be designed to properly interface with the signals traveling through the expansion slots. A card must operate at a specific speed, as well as be compatible with other cards in the system. The bus also supplies power to all the expansion cards.

The ISA Bus

ISA stands for Industry Standard Architecture and is the bus used in all PCs, ATs, and clones. There are two types of ISA bus connectors, the original PC's 8-bit and the AT's 16-bit.

All PC/XT-level systems have 8-bit slots. AT-level systems have 16-bit slots and 8-bit slots. You can plug an 8-bit card into a 16-bit slot because the two are compatible, but that wastes a 16-bit slot.

The number of slots in a PC varies, though typically there are eight. The original PC has only five, which is too few when you consider that all PCs need a video adapter, hard- and floppy-disk controllers, and a memory card of some sort. (The limited number of slots led to the development of the multifunction card.)

A special slot to look out for in some systems is slot 8 (by the power supply). It's a short slot, designed to send a special signal to one of the PC's chips. (IBM put the slot there to allow the original PC/XT to directly interface with an expansion chassis.) Only cards specifically designed for slot 8 should be placed there. So if you're in doubt, don't stick a card in slot 8.

The ISA bus defined the standards for communications and how to resolve conflicts between the various expansion cards. But it does a really poor job of this. The standard is rather loose, and conflicts between cards happen all the time. (This is why you have to set so many jumpers and DIP switches on each card.) Also, the ISA bus only goes out to 16 bits, half of the width of today's 32-bit 386 and 486 microprocessors.

The MCA Bus

To resolve the problems of the ISA bus, IBM announced a new bus standard, Micro Channel Architecture (MCA), with their PS/2 systems in 1987. (Some of the low-end PS/2s still use the old ISA bus.)

MCA has a much better design than ISA. It offers better communications between cards, resolves conflicts in a more civilized manner, and allows you to configure the cards without ever setting a DIP switch. But it's also incompatible with the older ISA cards. You cannot plug an ISA board into the MCA slot. And the MCA cards are a lot smaller than the older ISA types.

Currently, MCA is at a disadvantage in the industry. Although IBM will license the MCA bus to any clone maker, they require stiff royalties and back payments on all clone-maker sales of MCA bus computers. The cost is just too great for most clone makers, so they've opted to stick with the ISA bus, incorporating proprietary 32-bit memory expansion boards in 386 computers. Consequently, MCA isn't widely available.

The EISA Bus

To combat MCA, several developers of PC compatibles got together and came up with their own advanced bus standard, EISA. EISA stands for Enhanced Industry Standard Architecture. It's a superset of the old ISA bus and adds many of the advanced features of IBM's proprietary MCA bus.

EISA offers the same features as MCA, including the ability to configure cards without having to set DIP switches or jumpers. It also offers faster communications and better resolution of conflicts. EISA is compatible with the older ISA cards, which you can plug into any EISA slot (though there may be problems). For the individual user, EISA offers few advantages over ISA, at least nothing worth paying the high price for.

A General Strategy for Upgrading Cards

Even though there are dozens of different expansion cards, adding any one of them to your system is a basic operation. It's one of the classic plug-in-and-go types of PC upgrades. The only way you can conceivably muck it up is if you plug in a card when the PC's power is turned on.

As with all upgrades you do, upgrading an expansion card requires a little forethought. There are a lot of expansion cards and options to choose from, so you should know in advance what it is you want. If you only need an EMS memory card, then buy just that. If you're getting a second card, for extra hard drives, floppy drives, video adapters, or memory, make sure it's compatible with what's already in your system.

Remember that expansion cards come in different sizes and are of the 8-bit/PC and 16-bit/AT varieties. Make sure you get the right one for your computer.

Do you have room for the card? Nothing is more disconcerting than running out of slots. Aside from that, internal placement of the card is up to you. Traditionally, display adapters go to the left and the hard-disk/floppy-disk controller cards go to the right (conveniently near the drives).

When placing cards inside your PC, consider that a lot of them have cables coming out of them. Most of the external connectors are on the back of the card, on its mounting bracket. But sometimes not all the connectors will fit on that thin bracket. An additional bracket can be installed in an empty slot (by removing its slot cover). Some PCs have blank connectors on the bottom into which you can install the card's connectors. If worse comes to worst, you can always thread the cable over the back of the system unit, just under the PC's lid.

An expansion card slides into place, much as a shelf slides into a cupboard. It's anchored on the bottom by the bus and expansion slot. On the back, it's anchored by the mounting bracket and screw. This keeps the card from wobbling back and forth.

Long cards are also anchored on the front of the PC. Some PCs have a series of grooves on their inside front panel at the same intervals as the expansion slots. If yours does not, most long cards come with a plastic device that can be attached to the front of the case to further secure the card.

◢ *R*emoving an Expansion Card

Removing an expansion card is easy. It can be done for several reasons: The card is incompatible with some new installation, the card no longer works, you have to make room for new cards, you want to replace the card with a newer version of the same card, or you want to make modifications, such as adding memory.

Procedure: Removing an expansion card

Tools: Medium flathead screwdriver; medium Phillips screwdriver (for some expansion slots)

1 Power down the PC.

2 Unplug everything.

3 Remove the lid.

4 Locate the expansion card you want to remove.

If you've installed the card yourself, you probably know where it is. If not, you may have to look around to find it. The biggest clues are the cables connecting the cards. Right away, by tracing cables you can locate the hard- and floppy-drive controllers. Externally, you can find the video controller by tracing its cable to the monitor. Printer cards can be found the same way. RAM cards have lots of chips or blank sockets on them. Some manufacturers stencil the name and type of card on the card itself.

5 Disconnect any external cables from the card, and move any cables obstructing the card out of the way.

Disconnect only those cables on the back of the card, if any. You have to remove any externally connected cables so that you can slide the card up and out. For this, a small flat-head screwdriver may be required, though most cables have convenient thumb twists. Leave internal cables attached for the time being.

6 Unscrew the mounting bracket.

There is a single flathead or Phillips screw on the top of the mounting bracket. On some PCs that have lots of slots, you'll need to be careful to note which screw is holding down the card you want to remove. Sometimes you may even have to remove an adjacent bracket to get at the screw. Set the screw aside. You should always save all the screws from inside your PC.

7 Ground yourself.

Since you might touch electrical circuitry when lifting the card out, ground yourself first. If you're not wearing a grounding wrist-strap, touch the PC's power supply for a moment. Stand still.

8 Lift the card straight up and out.

Grab the card by its edges. The best thing to do is to pinch the top two corners of the card and lift. You may have to rock it longways to release it from the slot. Avoid pinching any chips or electronic parts, though sometimes you may have to.

9 Store the card.

Once the card is up and out, set it aside. If it doesn't have any cables attached, slide it into a static-free bag or preferably its original packing material (which you should always keep). Old cards come in handy when you're trying to diagnose hardware problems.

Before putting the card away, remove any cables or other items you may want to keep. For example, if you want to swap RAM chips from one card to another, now is the time to unplug them (refer to Chapter 6). Also, if removal of the card takes something out of your system, remember to reset any DIP switches on the motherboard. (AT-level systems require the setup program to be run.)

10 Cover the hole.

If you're not planning to install a new card, you can cover the blank hole left by the removal of the old card with a spare slot cover. If you don't have one, put the mounting bracket screw back into its hole so you don't lose it.

11 If you're all done, fire up the PC to test your new configuration. Then put on the lid.

If you have an AT-level system and you've removed some central system component, you may be required to run the setup program to tell the computer about the changes you made. Also remember that there may be some software drivers you have to remove. For example, if you're moving a mouse card to another computer, you'll need to remove the MOUSE.SYS driver from CONFIG.SYS.

Installing an Expansion Card

There are three common expansion cards you have in your PC: the hard-drive controller, the floppy-drive controller, and the video adapter. But you may want to add other cards, add RAM to an existing card, or swap a card.

Procedure: Installing an expansion card

Tools: Medium flathead screwdriver

1 Power down the PC.

2 Unplug everything.

3 Remove the lid.

4 Locate an empty slot.

If you're continuing an upgrade, use the same slot. If not, remember everything in the previous section about card location in a PC. There are 8-bit and 16-bit slots—you'll want to put the appropriate cards in each. Position short cards so that they take advantage of the limited space behind your disk drives, and put long cards where they have room. Put hard-drive and floppy-drive controller cards to the right, where they'll be close to the drives and limit the cable mess.

5 Remove the mounting bracket and slot cover.

Keep the slot-cover screw. You can toss the slot cover out, though it's a good idea to keep two or three of them around as spares. (The new card will have its own slot cover as part of its rear mounting bracket.)

6 Move any cables out of the way.

If you have to move cables, you may have to disconnect them from other expansion cards. To remember where they go, label both ends of the cable and its connector. For example, place a sticker with an "A" on one cable and its connector and move them out of the way. Use "B" on a second cable and its connector.

7 Install the front mount.

If your PC's case does not have front mounts for long cards, check the new expansion card's box for a front mount. Attach it to the inside front of your PC's case.

8 Remove the new card from its package.

The card comes in a static-free bag or other insulated packing material. Be careful when handling the card; ground yourself first and touch the card only on the edges.

9 Make adjustments to the card.

Make sure the card is properly configured for your system. You may have to attach internal cables to the card, set DIP switches and jumpers, or install RAM chips or SIMMs.

10 Line up the card and slide it into the slot.

Position the rear mounting bracket over the slot hole and the edge connector over the slot. If it's a long card, also line up the front mount. Lower the card into position and once the edge connector is over the slot, press down firmly. Make sure the card goes completely into the slot. The rear mounting bracket should be flush with other brackets and slot covers in the system.

11 Replace the screw on the rear mounting bracket and tighten it into position. This helps position the card.

12 Attach any external cables.

Hook up the printer cable, monitor cable, modem cable, or any external connectors. Most cables attach by means of thumb twists, which are easy to work with when you don't want to pull the PC all the way from the wall. Some older cables have tiny flathead screws.

13 Install any additional external connectors on the card.

If the card has a second slot cover with connectors on it, install it in an empty slot. If your PC has blank holes for you to install connectors, take advantage of them. Otherwise, just lay the ribbon cable on the top of the system case. It looks sloppy, but it works.

14 Double-check all your connections.

If you had to remove cables to install the expansion card, reconnect them now. Make sure the card and any cables are firmly connected. If the card requires any DIP switches on the motherboard to be set, do that now, before you put the lid back on.

15 Power up the PC and test the new configuration. Then put the lid back on. Be careful not to snag any cables and pull them loose.

You may have to run a setup program for some upgrades on AT-level systems. Some cards come with a diagnostic disk you can use to check the card and your installation.

Once everything is working, you need to set up the software side of the card (see the next section for detailed information). Some cards come with disks that contain configuration programs. You should run them to make sure the hardware is working properly. Add any software drivers to CONFIG.SYS as necessary. And try out your software that takes advantage of the new card to make sure the card works.

*A*dditional Setup

Aside from setting DIP switches on the motherboard or the card and working with a setup program, there are two other things you may have to deal with after you install an expansion card:

- Setting up software
- Solving card conflicts

Setting Up Software

The software setup varies with each card, so for memory cards, hard and floppy controllers, and video cards, refer to the individual chapters on these components for more detailed information.

There will probably be some software included with the card, even with memory and video cards. Memory cards may have drivers for RAM disks and print spoolers; EMS cards may have an EMS driver. Video cards may have sample graphic images and demo programs to show off the graphics, or they may contain device drivers for CONFIG.SYS or some of your applications.

Whatever the case style you have and whatever the card, there are usually three types of software that come with an expansion card:

- Configuration software
- Utilities
- Fun programs

Configuration software comes with some of the better-designed cards and all MCA cards. Remember, the MCA cards don't have DIP switches, so you need to run software to configure them. For other cards, the configuration software may also contain test programs. Most of the better memory cards have memory-testing utilities. You should run them all night to verify that the RAM on the card is up to snuff.

Utilities come with nearly all expansion cards. Multifunction and memory cards come with software drivers for RAM disks, print spoolers, and disk-caching programs. Mouse cards come with testing and calibration software, as well as tutorials to help you learn the mouse. And some utilities may come in the form of software drivers to let DOS and certain applications get the most from the new hardware.

Finally, some expansion cards come with fun software. Music cards come with sample sound files; mouse cards come with games and puzzles you can play.

To take advantage of a new hardware goodie, it always helps to let your software know. You should update CONFIG.SYS and AUTOEXEC.BAT, as well as all the applicable programs in your system, to get the most out of your new expansion card.

Solving Card Conflicts

The competition between two cards for the same turf is called *contention*. The ISA bus is not able to manage port conflicts—if there is a conflict, things just won't work.

For example, it's possible to configure two LPT1 printer ports in a PC. This configuration was common in earlier display adapters that had built-in LPT1 printer ports. When these cards were placed in a system that already had an LPT1 port built into the motherboard, the net result was "no printer port."

Similarly, memory cards must be told where their memory starts in RAM. It's possible to have overlapping memory using two memory expansion cards both mapped to the same area of RAM. If so, the result is "no memory."

The problem also happens with modems and COM ports, as well as with display adapters that conflict. Although you can have both a monochrome and color display in a PC, you cannot use both of them simultaneously. (You can use the MODE command in DOS to switch between them.)

The resolution to these conflicts lies in careful planning—by setting DIP switches and jumpers on a card properly. If you've added a printer port and suddenly you have none, then you're experiencing contention. You must reset the jumpers on one of the printer cards to make one port LPT1 and the other LPT2 (or some other number).

The problem is worse with serial ports. Under DOS 3.3, you can have up to four serial ports, COM1 through COM4. Some internal modems insist on being COM1. Some expansion cards insist that their serial port be COM1. In this case, you must switch the expansion card's serial port to COM2.

Another interesting serial communications problem happens when you have two serial ports on two different cards (aside from a modem card). For example, a dual serial-port card combined with a serial port on a multifunction card usually means no serial port at all. For some reason, dual serial-port cards insist upon being COM1 and COM2 in combination with no other card in the system. When this happens, you must disable the serial port on any other card in the system or on the motherboard.

◣ Summary

Expansion cards are the key to your PC's flexibility. They allow you to add a number of options to your computer system, giving you features that suit your needs.

Expansion cards come in a number of configurations. Commonly, there are PC/AT cards and XT cards, or 16- and 8-bit cards.

Expansion cards plug into the PC's bus. The bus is a direct line of communication between the microprocessor and the expansion cards. The most popular PC bus is the ISA. The MCA bus (found in some of IBM's PS/2 computers) and the EISA offer advanced features, but are out of the price range of most users.

Expansion cards are easy to install, but you have to configure them for your system by setting DIP switches on the card or by running software configuration programs. Some expansion cards come with software of their own, such as device drivers, configuration and testing programs, utilities, and fun applications.

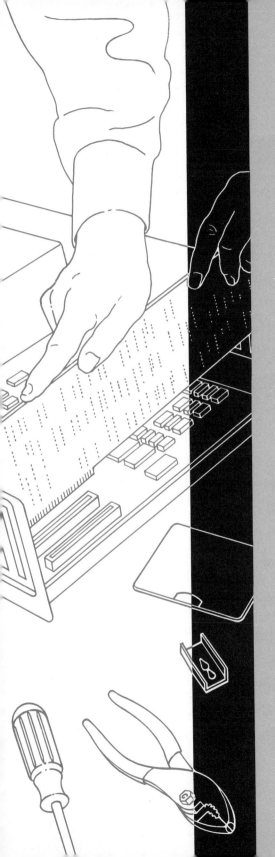

10

The Power
Supply

IF THE MICROPROCESSOR IS YOUR COMPUTER'S BRAIN, then the power supply is its heart: It is responsible for supplying electricity to all parts of your computer.

The power supply is an awkward-looking device hidden well out of sight in your computer. It's a reliable beast; unlike just about everything else in your computer, there is no software required to support it. However, occasionally things do go wrong, and it's always a good idea to make sure your PC has a power supply able to give it enough juice.

All About the Power Supply

This section contains some background information on power supplies. This isn't technical stuff, though some electronics terms are used. Don't worry—they're fully explained for you.

The Power Supply's Duties

The power supply has three distinct duties:

- It supplies the PC with power.
- It cools the system.
- It protects the internal components.

The power supply's first duty is to supply the PC with power. It converts the 120 volts of alternating current (at 60 hertz) coming out of your wall socket into plus or minus 5 volts or plus or minus 12 volts of direct current for use inside your PC.

The power supply also cools your system. It comes with a built-in fan, which is why PCs always make noise when you turn them on. The fan draws in air from the front of the PC through the slits in the lid and the disk drives. The air flows over the motherboard and between the expansion cards. It's then drawn in through the power supply and out the exhaust port behind your PC.

The cooling power of a power supply explains why most tower PCs have their power supplies on top. Heat rises, so to cool the system, the fan is placed on top of the system where it can continue to draw the rising hot air up away from the components and out of the system. If you're mounting a desktop PC on its side, remember to put the power-supply side up as well.

Finally, the power supply protects the PC. The PC won't start if there isn't enough juice coming through the wires, as happens during brownouts.

Also, the power supply is designed so that if it blows up it won't take the rest of the system with it. When the power supply dies, it pops. You may even see blue smoke rising from your PC and smell ozone. Replacing the power supply is usually all you have to do to fix the computer.

Location of the Power Supply

The power supply is located in the right rear of your system unit. It's up against the back and right walls of the PC. This allows you access to the On/Off switch (on the right side) and the power connectors (in the rear). Both of these components are actually part of the power supply, not the PC's case.

When you open a PC and look inside, you'll find that space is really tight in the rear of the system unit. No more than a quarter-inch separates the power supply from the back of the drives. And though the expansion cards aren't close to the power supply's left side, this area is usually filled with cables.

The power supply is anchored to the case in two ways: by four screws that hold it to the back of your PC (one screw for each corner of the power supply) and by two clips on the bottom of the case. There are two corresponding holes and slots on the bottom of the power supply. This keeps it secure and stable inside the PC.

Parts of the Power Supply

The power supply looks like a metal box—all the working parts are internal. (Never open up the power supply!) Refer to Figure 10.1 to find the components discussed in this section.

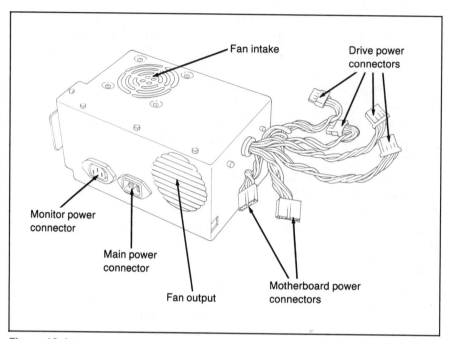

Figure 10.1: Parts of the power supply

The Top

The top of the power supply has two components:

- The fan intake
- A label

The *fan intake* (usually on the top, but it may be on the side) is a series of concentric air holes—the fan lies underneath. There may be one or two fans and intakes, depending on the strength of the power supply.

The label is important to read, not only because it warns you against taking the power supply apart, but because it lists the power supply's rating. The important thing to look for is the number of watts that the power supply gives to the PC. You'll read about why this is important in a moment.

The Right Side

The right side of the power supply has the On/Off switch. *On* is often labeled with a 1 and *Off* with a 0.

The Back

The back of the power supply has up to four components:

- The power connector
- The monitor's power connector
- The fan exhaust port
- A European power switch

The *power connector* is the three-pronged male connector, usually to the right (if you're looking at the back of the PC), into which you plug the power cable that goes to the wall socket.

The *monitor's power connector* is a three-pronged female connector. Some monitors have special power cables that plug into this connector. If yours does not, you can plug the monitor directly into the wall socket. (IBM's original monochrome monitor used this connector, and many monochrome monitors today use it.)

The *fan exhaust port* is the hole out of which the power supply blows all the hot air and dust it sucks through the PC. Some power supplies may have a *European power switch*. This is a small, usually red, slide switch that has *120V* printed on one side and *220V* on the other side. (In the United States, 120 volts at 60 hertz is the way utility companies deliver current. In Europe, 220 volts at 50 hertz is standard.) The switch allows you to use the power supply on either continent. Some power supplies, called *switchable*, don't need the manual switch. They automatically detect the change in voltage and cycles (hertz) and compensate for it.

The Left Side

On the left side of the power supply, there are six items: two 6-wire connectors and four 4-wire connectors. The 6-wire connectors are used to supply your motherboard with power. There are two of them, and they look alike.

The connector that goes toward the rear of the PC has three black wires, a yellow wire, and a white wire. The connector toward the front of the PC has two black wires, a blue wire, and three red wires. (The number of wires may be different in your PC.) The important motherboard connector is the one with the single white wire, the Power Good line, which supplies a signal to the motherboard indicating whether there is enough power to start up. That wire is the only white wire and, if you look carefully, you'll notice that there is no wire next to it, in the pin 2 position.

The 4-wire connectors are for your disk drives. They're all notched, so you can't plug them in wrong. You'll notice that two of them are longer than the others. These are for the drives in your right drive bay. Also, some of the older power supplies have only two 4-wire connectors. If you add any additional drives, you'll need a power-supply splitter, or Y, cable.

The Bottom

The bottom of the power supply has two recessed holes into which clips on the bottom of the PC's case slide. The clips, in addition to the screws on the back of the case, anchor the power supply to the PC's case.

Configuration of the Power Supply

Power-supply capacity is measured in *watts,* or work per unit time. Each electronic part in your computer requires a certain amount of electricity to do its job. That amount is measured in watts. A light bulb's brightness, for example, is measured in watts—the higher the wattage, the brighter the bulb.

The power supply is responsible for supplying a total amount of wattage, which is then used by each item in your computer. Since each item in the computer consumes a bit of the total wattage pie, you need to have a power supply that provides enough watts. If your power supply doesn't, then your computer may not be able to work at peak efficiency or may not work at all.

The original PC had a power supply rated at only 63.5 watts. But when you add 640K of RAM and a hard drive to that configuration, the power draw approaches 63.5 watts. In fact, many of the original PC power supplies blew when people started adding too many peripherals. Later, the PC/XT and PC/AT came with beefier power supplies.

Having enough wattage for everything in your computer is important. Today, a PC-style system should have at least a 135-watt power supply, preferably 150-watt. An AT-level system should have at least a 200-watt power supply.

Your computer probably came with a capable power supply. But if you're adding a lot of peripherals, a second hard drive, or a couple of megabytes of RAM, then the issue of power consumption gets critical—especially if you have a PC/XT with only a 135-watt power supply.

All About Electricity

Fear of electrocution bothers a lot of people. But learning some basic things about electricity will alleviate some of that fear and enable you to understand the power supply's role in your PC.

Some Basic Terms

There are only five terms you need to be familiar with when referring to electrical power in a PC:

- Alternating current
- Direct current
- Volts
- Amps
- Watts

Alternating Current and Direct Current

There are two main sources of electrical power: *alternating current* (AC) and *direct current* (DC).

The wall socket supplies alternating current. *Alternating* refers to the way the current reverses its direction at regular intervals. These changes, or *cycles,* are measured in *hertz.* (In the United States, AC current is 60Hz.)

Direct current is current that moves in one direction only (a battery supplies direct current). The components inside a PC use direct current, so one of the jobs of your power supply is to convert the alternating current from the wall socket to direct current for use in the PC.

Volts and Amps

Electricity itself is measured in *volts* and *amps,* or amperes.

A volt is the difference in electrical potential between two points. If you compare electricity to water, then the number of volts delivered by a power line is comparable to the amount of pressure in a water line.

The volume of electricity is measured in amps. Though amperage has nothing to do with the thickness (gauge) of a wire, it does tell you how much juice is being delivered.

Watts

A *watt* is a measure of work per unit of time. You calculate watts by multiplying volts by amps: Watts = Volts × Amps. This gives you the amount of work the electricity is capable of doing. As far as running a computer goes, you don't need to know any more than this, and you never need to calculate watts. Just remember that there is only so much wattage your power supply can provide.

Potential Power Problems

Power supplies are susceptible to the whims of the electric company and of natural conditions. Actually, in most locations electricity is relatively cheap and highly reliable. It's old Mother Nature that will occasionally zap you. A thunderstorm can toss a lightning bolt that suddenly ups the voltage coming through your wall socket by a few billion watts. This will usually make your motherboard look like a sheet full of burnt cookies.

Here are six potential power problems you need to be aware of:

- Blackouts
- Brownouts
- Dips
- Line noise
- Spikes
- Surges

Blackouts are caused by a complete loss of power. If you're working at your computer when one happens, it turns off. The result is the same as turning off the power switch or yanking the plug from the wall. There's no chance anything in the computer will be harmed. (If you haven't saved your work to disk, you will probably lose it).

Brownouts are like miniblackouts. Instead of the power disappearing, it merely drops to a lower voltage (the lights dim, making everything look brown.). During a brownout, the PC power supply's Power Good signal tells the computer that there isn't enough juice, and the PC may stop. If you try to turn on a computer during a brownout, it may not come on.

Dips are small drops in voltages. For example, when the refrigerator's condenser kicks in, you may notice that the TV gets dimmer for a moment. This usually only happens in older houses with poor wiring. If you have such a house, consider plugging your computer into a circuit that isn't shared with a device that may cause a dip (the refrigerator, a heater, etc.).

Line noise is electrical interference caused by an electric motor. Those fuzzy lines you see on the TV screen when the blender is on are caused by line noise. Noise from a computer's power supply may cause your system to do funny things: A program may crash, the system may reset, etc.

Spikes are the most deadly enemy of a computer's power supply. They are caused by a sudden increase in the amount of voltage in the line. Usually, you'll only get a spike when lightning strikes a power line (even one a few miles away), but mishaps at the power station may cause them as well. This is why it's a good idea to unplug the computer during an electrical storm.

Surges are the opposite of brownouts. They're periods of sustained high voltage that can do much more damage than spikes because they last longer. A surge happens when the electric company is supplying a lot of power and suddenly everyone turns off their air conditioners. The extra juice that keeps flowing through the system can damage your PC or power supply.

There are many ways to deal with the six enemies of your PC's power supply. You can get an uninterruptible power supply (UPS) to prevent damage caused by blackouts, brownouts, and dips. You can also get a power strip that provides protection against line noise, surges, and spikes. These devices are covered in the last part of the chapter.

Buying a New Power Supply

There are only two reasons for buying a new power supply:

- The one you have just died.
- You want one with more wattage.

Your power supply may blow up if you're drawing more watts from it than it can provide. Adding another hard drive, more RAM, or a tape backup unit can push the amount of watts consumed over the supply provided, blowing the power supply.

Power supplies are one of the simplest things to buy for a PC. Unlike RAM chips, which have different speeds and capacities, and hard drives, which have different capacities, controller cards, and whatnot, power supplies differ only in wattage and size.

Wattage is the primary thing to look at in a power supply. Though a PC/XT-level system can get by with a 135-watt power supply, a 150-watt one is better. You can find larger power supplies, some with more than one fan, and some with auto-cooling, which adjusts the fan's rate according to how hot your PC is (you'll pay more for this feature).

If you have an AT-level system, you'll want a power supply that gives you at least 200 watts. More is better, but don't go overboard.

Paying a lot for a big power supply when you don't need the extra wattage is a waste of money.

The second thing to look at in a power supply is its size. PC-style cases have only one configuration. No matter who makes the power supply, it will fit into the case. AT-style systems use a different power supply. Beware: Some XT-style systems are in AT-style cases. They can't use the AT's power supply. So get a power supply based on what type of system you have, not what the case looks like.

And then there are the oddballs. Not every computer is a perfect clone of the original PC or PC/AT. For example, the old Leading Edge computers came with a proprietary power supply. You had to order a new one from Leading Edge itself. IBM's PS/2s use a different-style power supply. And COMPAQ computers should only have COM-PAQ power supplies installed. This is one of the few areas of DOS computing where hardware incompatibilities exist, so check the requirements of your system before you buy a new power supply.

◣ *Replacing the Power Supply*

Removing an old power supply and installing a new one is per-haps the most involved upgrade procedure. You need to know how to remove disk drives and sometimes expansion cards to get at the power supply. Fortunately, it is an upgrade you will rarely have to do.

Procedure: Remove an old or a dead power supply and install a new one

Tools: Medium flathead screwdriver, medium Phillips screwdriver

1 Power down the PC.

2 Unplug everything.

3 Remove the lid.

4 Disconnect the power cables.

Remove the monitor's power supply from the back of the PC. The main power cable (which connects to the wall socket) should already be unplugged.

5 Locate the power supply, the shiny metal box in the right rear of the PC. Note how close it is to the disk drives.

6 Unscrew the four mounting screws and set them aside.

The power supply is anchored to the case by four mounting screws on the back of the system unit. They're smaller than the case's screws. Each screw is located in one of the four corners of the back of the power supply.

7 Slide the disk drives forward.

If you have an AT-style case with mounting rails, where the drives screw into the front of the case, just remove the angle brackets in front of each drive, and carefully slide the drives out about 3 or 4 inches. You don't need to totally remove them.

If you have a PC/XT-style case, unscrew the drives directly from the drive bays. For the right drive bay, that's no problem. But the left drive bay's screws may be obscured by some expansion cards—you may have to remove some of the longer cards to get at the screws.

8 Disconnect the white plastic power-supply connector from each of the drives.

9 Disconnect the power supply from the motherboard.

The power supply attaches to the motherboard via two 6-wire connectors, somewhat larger than the disk-drive connectors.

10 Remove the power supply.

Slide the power supply toward the front of the PC, then lift it straight out. You have to slide it forward because the power supply is attached to the bottom of the case by clips.

11 Lower the new power supply into the case, a few inches from the back of the system unit.

12 Slide the power supply toward the back so that the clips on the bottom of the case slide into the holes on the bottom of the power supply.

13 Reattach the 6-wire power connectors to the motherboard.

It may take some muscle to connect them. If you have problems, remove the power supply and attach the connectors first. Angle in the connector toward the motherboard and press. Then slide in the power supply.

14 Reattach the power connectors to each of your drives.

There should be four of the plastic connectors; they're notched, so you can't plug them in wrong. Note that two of the connectors on power supplies with four connectors are longer than the other two. They are for the drives in your right drive bay.

15 Double-check all your connections.

16 Slide the drives back into position, and reattach the mounting-rail angle brackets to the front of the case. (If you have a PC/XT-style system, screw the drives back into position.)

17 Replace any expansion cards you may have removed.

18 Screw in the power supply's four screws.

19 Power up the PC to make sure everything is OK.

20 Put the lid back on.

Under normal circumstances, everything should work just fine. But a few of the following problems may make your heart sink.

If nothing happens after you turn on your PC, you could be in a brownout, the PC might not be plugged in, or one of the motherboard connectors may be incorrectly installed. Also, the power supply itself could be dead. One way to check it is to plug in the power supply before you install it. Then flip the switch. If the fan comes on, then you know the power supply is OK.

If you hear a long, loud beep or a series of short beeps, then the problem is in the power supply. Recheck your connections. Also, you could be in a brownout. Try turning on the PC again later.

If the disk drive doesn't work, you probably neglected to re-attach its power connector. Also, check to see if any cables were pulled loose during the upgrade.

Preventing Power Mishaps

There are three devices you can use to prevent electrical damage to your PC:

- Power-protection strip
- Surge and spike protector
- Uninterruptible power supply

A *power-protection strip* is a long device full of sockets that plugs into a single wall socket. Some of them come with surge suppression and line-noise filtering built in. But beware: Not every power strip offers this protection. Some give you extra outlets and little else.

A *surge and spike protector* is specifically designed to protect the computer from surges and spikes, sacrificing itself instead of the power supply and other items in your PC. Buy one that offers RFI/EMI filtering. (RFI stands for *radio frequency interference* (line noise), and EMI stands for *electromagnetic interference*.) They cost more than simple power-protection strips, but the cost is worth it.

Incidentally, you should plug everything into these power strips: your monitor (unless it plugs into the PC), printer, modem, fax machine, and so on. Some even come as a flat unit you sandwich between your system unit and monitor. They have switches that specifically turn items in your PC on or off, plus a master switch. People like the master switch because it lets them turn on the entire PC system at once.

An *uninterruptible power supply,* or UPS, is basically a battery that automatically takes over in the event of a power outage or brownout. These are expensive. There are also backup power supplies, which run the PC off a battery that's constantly being recharged, and standby power supplies, which give you just enough electricity after a blackout or brownout to save your data and power down the system.

The UPS is ideal for companies with systems that they cannot afford to have affected by power problems. Hospitals use UPS systems, not only for their computers but for everything else that is electrical.

◣ Summary

The power supply supplies electricity to all your computer's components. It's generally a reliable device, but when it fails, you can replace it yourself. You may also want to install a power supply with more wattage.

The electrical power output of your PC's power supply is measured in watts. The amount of wattage used by the PC's components must be less than the amount supplied by the power supply. For XTs, a power supply from 135 to 150 watts will do the job, but most ATs require 200 watts or more.

A power supply is also susceptible to environmental conditions: Power surges and spikes can damage your power supply and possibly the computer itself. Although a dead power supply generally does not take the rest of the system with it, you might consider getting a surge and spike protector. For crucial business computing, an uninterruptible power supply (UPS) is also a good investment.

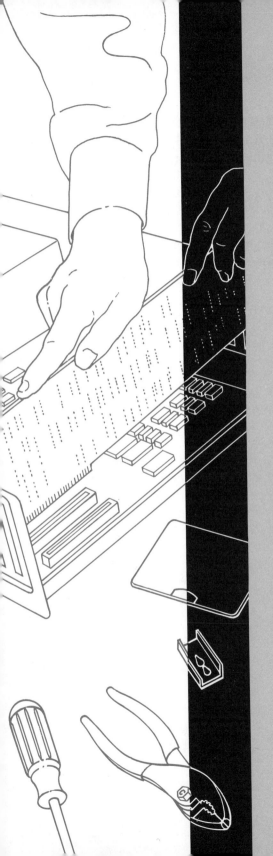

11

Monitors and Display Adapters

OF ALL THE COMPONENTS IN YOUR COMPUTER SYSTEM, the monitor is the most visible. But the monitor is only half of what graphics and video display are about in the PC. The other half is the *display adapter*—the electronic circuitry that controls the monitor. Since the majority of PCs have no built-in video, the display adapter is added as an option; you choose which one you want, based on your text and graphics needs.

Buying a monitor is much like buying a TV set; the display adapter is upgraded just like an expansion card.

 ## Types of Monitor Displays

PC graphics have come a long way. The first PC was introduced without graphics. Positioning its first microcomputer as a "business machine," IBM assumed color and graphics were not needed. Graphics were for the home game systems. So IBM offered color and graphics only as an afterthought, trying to grab that small, affluent section of the market that wanted to play games on the PC.

The next-generation operating system for the PC (whether it will be Microsoft Windows or OS/2 remains to be seen) will need color and graphics to be used to its full potential. And thanks to competition, equipping a PC with color and high-resolution graphics isn't as much of a financial burden as it was in the early days.

You have many options with PC graphics. There are lots of standards, lots of manufacturers, and many ways to put a system together. But when you take into account your software and your budget, your choices usually boil down to one or two.

There are two options for type of monitor display:

- Monochrome
- Color

Monochrome Display

Historically, monochrome video displayed nice-looking text and had no capability for graphics. IBM's Monochrome Display

Adapter (MDA) offered text-only displays. The characters were nicely formed, easy on the eyes, and the display was crisp. The ability to draw circles, boxes, shades, and other computer graphics was impossible on the MDA. The system was only built to handle text characters. The MDA was not built with an *all-points-addressable* mode, in which individual dots, or pixels, on the display could be manipulated to create graphic images.

The MDA also offered text attributes that made work in some applications easier. The text could be underlined, shown in inverse (black letters on a white background), highlighted, or shown flashing. Even today, monochrome text is the only kind of text display on the PC that offers natural underlining.

The Hercules Graphics Card

One way around monochrome's graphics limitations is to use the Hercules graphics card. Hercules developed an MDA ''clone'' card in the early '80s. The card did everything the original MDA did, but in addition it offered a high-resolution graphics mode.

Users with an MDA setup could simply replace their MDA card with a Hercules card to get graphics. (The monitor didn't need to be replaced.) Thanks to Lotus's 1-2-3 spreadsheet program, which offered direct support for Hercules graphics, the card took its place as the leader on the monochrome side of the PC graphics world. Eventually, MDA faded away.

Hercules is one of the few secondary (non-IBM) standards in the PC computing industry. Hercules clone cards are in nearly all monochrome PC clones.

To combat the clone cards, Hercules introduced the Graphics Card Plus in the mid-'80s. It offered a special mode known as RAM Font, in which the card could support multiple fonts and character sets. Some software, such as WordPerfect, took advantage of RAM Font, but as a standard it never took off like the original Hercules card.

Reasons for Using Monochrome

With the many inexpensive color/graphics cards on the market today, it seems rather odd that someone would want monochrome. Originally, the reason for choosing it was that it was inexpensive compared to color, but there are other reasons why you might consider buying a Monochrome Display Adapter.

If much of your work is with text, then monochrome is a good choice. It is also easier on the eyes. Even though color displays are much better than they used to be, monochrome is still the easiest on the eyes over a long period of time.

Color Display

The color display monitors for the PC have always been renowned for their fuzzy, hard-to-read text. This was especially true in the early days. You sacrificed a lot for color and graphics: your eyeballs, money, and availability of software that used color and graphics.

In the early days, there were fewer pixels per inch for a color, than for a monochrome, display. The result was fuzzy characters.

In graphics mode, the graphics adapter card (which controls the monitor) leaves its text character mode and switches to APA (all-points-addressable) mode—the adapter individually controls all the pixels on the display. A color display gives you the ability to draw lines, circles, and shades.

Recent advances in color-video hardware have made incredible things possible for PC color graphics. So in addition to better-looking text, more sophisticated graphics are possible. Because their price keeps dropping, color systems currently outnumber monochrome systems.

Some software packages look better in color. Certain word processors use color to denote different styles of text on the screen. And color is used in many software packages to identify special text and warning messages.

Also, more and more software requires color to be used to its full potential. Applications such as Windows, Excel, Corel Draw, and AutoCAD look better with color graphics.

 ## Text and Graphics Modes

In the text mode, text characters are displayed on the screen. This is the normal mode used by many applications. On a color system, the text is displayed in color; on a monochrome system, the text is displayed in green, amber, or white (depending on your monitor).

In the graphics mode, the PC can draw lines, circles, squares, and dots on the screen. What confuses people is that text can also be displayed in the graphics mode. The text is treated as a graphic, even though it looks like the text you see in the text mode.

The Text Mode

The text mode is offered by both color and monochrome systems. The standard PC screen displays 80 characters across by 25 characters down—that is, 80 columns by 25 rows. Each location on the text screen, the intersection of a specific row and column of text, can contain a character and its attributes.

On a monochrome system, the 80 × 25 setup is all you get. But that's really all you want. The Hercules card offers additional modes (for the display of more columns), which some spreadsheet applications support. Color displays have a variety of text modes. For example, all PC color displays support a 40-column mode. This mode was created in the early days of the PC, when IBM thought some people would be using TV sets as monitors.

The EGA and VGA graphics adapters have additional display modes as well. However, these modes alter the number of rows on the display, not the number of columns. Using these modes, you can have up to 50 rows of text displayed on the screen at once.

Some applications take advantage of the extended display modes of the EGA and VGA color adapters—but DOS doesn't. For example, if you run an EGA card in its 43-row mode and type CLS at the DOS prompt (to clear the screen), only the top 25 lines of the screen are cleared.

The Graphics Mode

The graphics mode is available on all color video systems and only on Hercules or Hercules-clone monochrome systems. Each point, or pixel, on the screen is individually controlled by the video controller card. On Hercules systems, a pixel can be turned on or off.

On color systems, a pixel's color is changed to the same color as the screen background when the pixel is turned off.

In graphics mode, the resolution is measured in pixels. The number of pixels across the screen is the horizontal resolution, and the number of pixels down the screen is the vertical resolution.

Color systems have thousands of different colors available. Each pixel on the screen can be displayed in one of those colors. The relationship between graphics resolution and the number of colors available is what constitutes a graphics *mode.* Different graphics adapters give you different graphics modes, each with a different resolution and number of colors.

The resolution and number of colors that a graphics card is capable of producing is dependent on the amount of video memory (RAM) on the card. Each color takes up a certain amount of memory. The more colors there are, the more memory is required (this is particularly an issue with EGA). But memory is also tied to the resolution that the card provides. The higher resolutions require more memory, so there's a trade-off: You get fewer colors.

A graphics mode with low resolution and lots of colors is usually best for playing games and showing pictures. Higher-resolution modes are best for drawing programs and applications (such as desktop publishing) where color isn't needed.

The total number of colors that a graphics card is capable of producing (its *palette*) is almost never what you can see on the screen at once; this is a limitation of video memory. You should keep this in mind when you shop for a monitor. For example, the first graphics adapter for the PC had a total of 16 colors available. But in graphics mode, you could only select from a few of those colors at a time.

Types of Color Display Adapters

There are three popular color graphics adapters for the PC:

- Color Graphics Adapter (CGA)
- Enhanced Graphics Adapter (EGA)
- Video Graphics Array (VGA)

CGA

The Color Graphics Adapter, or CGA, was the first text-and-graphics card available for the PC. The text quality was lousy, but the display was colorful. The graphics had low resolution and there were few colors, but it was all there was until 1985 when EGA came along.

For years the CGA was the color graphics standard on the PC. Even after the introduction of EGA, you could bet that all PC software supported it. But today it's seldom seen.

EGA

The Enhanced Graphics Adapter, or EGA, became the standard PC graphics adapter starting around 1986, a few years after the card was introduced. IBM originally offered EGA cards with the PC/AT, but the price was too high for most users. CGA cards were cheaper and more widely supported. And it took a few years for EGA software to appear. By then the EGA standard was supplanted by VGA.

The first EGA cards offered more colors and higher resolution than CGA, but they had some compatibility problems with earlier CGA systems. Eventually, developers cloned the EGA card and brought in CGA compatibility—there was a new PC graphics standard with software to support it. Unlike CGA, the EGA standard offers up to 64 colors and a variety of high-resolution graphics modes.

The EGA card also allows more characters to be displayed than the CGA card. EGA has support for downloadable character sets, allowing you to include foreign-language characters and other symbols in the standard 256-character set. A few word-processing applications took advantage of this, some of which even produced true underlining on an EGA system.

As with all standards in the PC industry, as soon as EGA started to take hold, and EGA graphics card clones became cheap and available, IBM introduced the PS/2 computers and yet another graphics standard, VGA.

VGA

The Video Graphics Array, or VGA, is the graphics adapter with high resolution and lots of colors built into IBM's line of PS/2 computers, introduced in 1987. It has a lot of features and flexibility. In fact, a VGA adapter is *the* choice for anyone considering a color adapter for their system.

VGA cards are widely cloned and cheap, and the clones offer features that IBM's VGA lacks. For example, clone VGA cards include some of the more common MCGA modes. (MCGA, or Memory Controller Gate Array, is another graphics standard that is on some PS/2 systems.) MCGA offers more colors at a lower resolution than traditional VGA, and most VGA clone cards offer it as well.

Some VGA cards even offer Hercules graphics emulation and can be used with a monochrome or multiscanning monitor. VGA has its own monochrome mode as well.

The VGA standard was improved upon by several of the clone makers, who dubbed the new standard Extended VGA or Super VGA. This graphics standard offers additional resolutions beyond the upper limit of standard VGA. But note that only a few software packages support Super VGA—more might in the future, which is why buying Super VGA is a good insurance policy against being left behind with an outdated graphics adapter.

 ## *All About Monitors*

To see the data you input and the PC's output, two parts are required: a display adapter and a matching monitor. Only the proper combination of both will give you the video system you want.

When buying a monitor, you should think about the type you want, the manufacturer, and the price. Certain types of monitors are designed to go with certain cards. You must be careful to find the perfect match. Why? Because if you don't, you may severely damage your monitor, or the monitor may not work at all. This is one area in PC upgrading where you can't afford to be cheap.

The monochrome category includes all MDA, Hercules, and Hercules-clone cards. You can usually choose between amber, green, or white for the monitor's display color.

VGA and Super VGA cards require an analog monitor. This is quite different from the digital RGB monitor used by the CGA and EGA cards. If you have a VGA card, you need a VGA monitor. Not all

VGA monitors are in color; some are paper-white. The paper-white monitors display the VGA colors in shades of gray—up to 256 of them. So monochrome VGA monitors provide an inexpensive way to get VGA graphics (an analog color monitor costs a lot more than the VGA card).

Types of Monitors

There are several terms used to describe the various video displays you can hook up to a PC. Though your choice of monitor is narrowed by which display adapter you've selected, you should be familiar with some of the ways monitors can be categorized.

Analog vs. Digital Monitors

Analog and *digital* describe the monitor's input signals. An analog monitor receives analog signals, and a digital monitor receives digital signals. An analog monitor is actually an improvement over a digital monitor (which sounds backward when you consider that digital sound recordings are considered superior to analog recordings). The reason is that more colors are possible on an analog monitor.

When talking about analog and digital, it helps to think of a clock. A standard dial clock is analog, measuring time with constantly moving hands. A digital clock displays numbers, giving you an absolute time measured by certain increments. In computers, digital and analog are used the same way. Everything inside the PC is digital, with bits and bytes representing discrete values. The real world is analog, so an A-to-D (analog-to-digital) converter is used to convert analog data for use by the computer. The best example of this is your PC's joystick or mouse, both of which produce fluid movements (analog) that are translated into digital information.

An analog monitor is capable of producing more colors than a digital monitor because it has a smooth range from dim to bright for each colored pixel. A digital monitor can change the brightness of each pixel only in given increments. (TTL, or direct-drive, monitors, which are compatible with Hercules, CGA, and EGA cards, are digital.) A VGA card should be paired with an analog monitor. Not doing so will severely damage the monitor. So if you're shopping, make sure your monitor is VGA-compatible.

Composite vs. RGB Monitors

RGB was the first type of color monitor, popular for use with CGA systems. It's a digital monitor, so using one with an EGA limits the EGA's performance, and using one with a VGA adapter can seriously damage the monitor.

RGB stands for red, green, and blue, which are the colors produced by three electron guns in the back of the monitor. Each gun produces a colored dot on the monitor's screen. You can compare this with the standard TV set, which uses only one electron gun that fires differently colored dots at the TV screen. With an RGB monitor, you get crisply displayed colors.

Still, RGB has its faults. Because it is digital, it doesn't offer as many colors. Its popularity on CGA systems has faded.

Composite (or single-color) monitors were developed as cheaper alternatives to expensive RGB monitor systems for the CGA cards. A composite monitor converts the three colors produced by an RGB display into shades of either green or amber. The results are less than spectacular.

Be careful not to confuse a composite monitor with a monochrome monitor. They're not the same. For today's PC graphics, composite monitors are not desirable.

Multiscanning Monitors

A multiscanning monitor is capable of changing its video frequency to match different display modes. Some multiscanning monitors can even switch from digital to analog, allowing you to use the same monitor with a CGA, EGA, or VGA system. A multiscanning monitor may also be called a variable frequency monitor or a MultiSync (which is actually a brand name).

Parts of the Monitor

The inside of a monitor is not something you have to concern yourself with. The monitor is riveted shut (like the power supply), so you should never open it. The high voltage could kill you.

On the outside of the monitor are the casing and the display. The display is what faces you when you use the computer. The computer, through the video adapter card, uses the display to display data.

Some monitors have antiglare screens, sometimes in the form of a nylon mesh over the display. The screen cuts down on reflections. You can buy an antiglare screen separately and attach it to a monitor that does not have one.

The typical monitor has various knobs for making adjustments, similar to the knobs on your TV. They may be on the front, on the sides, underneath, or on the back of the monitor, or hidden behind a panel.

The adjustment knobs allow you to change the brightness and contrast of the image. Additional knobs control the size and position of the image on the screen, the vertical and horizontal sync, and the color saturation or hue.

People have different opinions about how brightness and contrast should be set. The settings vary depending on how the monitor is designed and how well it's using electricity. For example, if your PC has a built-in monitor (as some portables do), and you have the brightness turned up all the way, then the monitor isn't getting enough power.

For most monitors, the best way to set brightness and contrast is to position the monitor under your normal working light, then turn up the brightness until you see diagonal lines on the display. These are the scan lines made by the electron gun(s) as they create the image on the display. After you turn up the brightness, adjust the contrast to your liking. It's best if the screen has both highlighted and normal text so you can adjust the contrast between them. When the contrast is set, turn down the brightness until the scan lines disappear.

Monitor Technical Terms

Monitors are often described by baffling technical terms. This section explains some of the more popular terms, telling you why they're important. The most common terms are the following:

- Bandwidth
- Dot pitch
- Interlacing
- Resolution

- Scan rate
- Picture tube size

Bandwidth

The speed at which information is sent from the computer to the monitor is known as the *bandwidth*. It's measured in megahertz (MHz); the higher the value, the better the image.

Dot Pitch

The distance between each dot (pixel) on the screen is the *dot pitch*. It's measured in tenths of millimeters from the center of two neighboring dots. The closer the dots and the smaller the dot pitch value, the finer the resolution of the monitor.

Interlacing

Information on a monitor is displayed by an electron gun scanning the phosphor on the inside front of your display. The gun scans from top to bottom and from left to right, with each scan displaying a *frame*.

To prevent a flickering image, some display adapters force the monitor to create an *interlaced* image. Instead of scanning from top to bottom in a continuous manner, the electron gun skips every other line. On the second pass, it hits the lines it missed the first time, creating the full image in two scans instead of one. This interlaced display provides a flicker-free image and allows for higher vertical resolution.

Resolution

A monitor's *resolution* is the number of distinct pixels the monitor is capable of displaying. The value is given in horizontal and vertical pixels. For example, a monitor with a resolution of 640 horizontal pixels by 480 vertical pixels is capable of handling most, if not all, VGA modes, whereas a monitor with lower resolution is not.

Scan Rate

The *scan rate* is the speed at which the monitor's electron gun passes over the inside surface of the display. It's measured in kilohertz (kHz) for both horizontal and vertical scanning (the values will be different). As with the bandwidth, the higher the scan rate values are, the finer and crisper the monitor's image is.

Picture Tube Size

A monitor is also described in terms of the size of its picture tube, measured diagonally in inches. Typical sizes for a monitor are from 10 to 14 inches, though some huge monitors are available, as well as nonstandard page-size and so-called landscape monitors. If you go with an unusual size, make sure your software can support it.

There are also flat-screen monitors, which some users prefer because they display an undistorted image. Some monitors offer darker glass, which is preferable in brightly lit offices.

A General Strategy for Upgrading Video Display

There are only two times when you'll be making a decision about a display adapter or a monitor:

- When you first buy a PC
- When you decide to upgrade one or the other

For example, you may have started out with a monochrome system (they're cheaper and faster) but now have a pressing need for color. You can upgrade either the monitor or the display adapter, as long as they're compatible.

There are three steps you should follow to equip your PC with a new or better video system:

- Find out what your software requires.
- Pick a graphics adapter and monitor.
- Shop around for the best-priced equipment and buy it.

Your software dictates the needs of your hardware. If you work a lot with graphics, you should buy a color monitor, especially if you work with high-power graphics applications: anything that runs under Microsoft Windows, graphic-design applications, CAD, desktop publishing, and games. But if you're only doing data entry or word processing, then a monochrome system is ideal (and will save you money).

If you want color, go with VGA. If your needs are more specific, check your software for additional graphics-adapters that it may support. Some of them may give you higher resolutions and better results than VGA. If you want monochrome, go with Hercules if it's in your budget, or some generic Hercules clone if it's not.

After you figure out your software needs, go graphics-adapter hunting. Since the adapter determines what monitor you need, look for the adapter first. Find one that offers you high resolution and lots of colors, plus any other options you may need, then match the adapter with a monitor. Aside from studying the technical information about a monitor, sit down and *look* at it. Is the image easy on your eyes? Is the image crisp enough for you?

You may be hesitant about buying a monitor/graphics card combination because of new standards. But don't let that hold you back. Graphics standards take two or three years to catch up with software. And VGA is fine for most people's needs today.

If price is holding you back, remember that you have the option of upgrading only the monitor or only the display adapter. You don't have to do everything at once. For example, buy the VGA card first and use it with your monochrome monitor (if your current monochrome monitor works with VGA). Later on, when you can afford it, buy a decent analog color monitor.

 ## Buying a Color Display Adapter

When you buy a color display adapter, look at the following:

Resolution   How high is the resolution? Is it VGA or Super VGA?

Colors   How many colors does the adapter offer? VGA supports a full 262,144, but only 256 can be displayed on the screen at once.

Compatibility   Are all IBM's VGA resolutions and colors supported? Does the VGA card offer MCGA compatibility? Hercules compatibility? Will the store update your card's ROM if future incompatibilities are discovered?

Price There is a whole range of prices for VGA cards, which may make you wonder why some are more expensive. How much video RAM does the card have? How many compatible modes does it share? Does it come with any software drivers to make it work with major applications?

Buying a Monitor

When you buy a monitor, look at the following:

Compatibility The issue here isn't compatibility with IBM, but compatibility with the adapter card you've chosen. Is the bandwidth properly supported? Are the horizontal and vertical scan rates compatible? Is it an analog, a digital, or a multiscanning monitor?

Dot Pitch The dot pitch tells you the crispness of the image, coupled with the monitor's potential resolution. The figure, however, should be used for comparison purposes only. It's hard to see differences in dot pitch with the naked eye (unless the differences are very dramatic).

Price Compare prices and consider a monitor's warranty. Some monitors have typical TV picture tube warranties of two years, but a few have warranties up to five years.

Upgrading a Display Adapter Card

You have to upgrade a video adapter if you're moving up to a VGA system from monochrome, going the other way (which does happen), or adding video to a new PC. The steps are similar to upgrading an expansion card, with a few additional details to double-check.

Procedure: Removing a display adapter card and installing a new one

Tools: Medium and tiny flathead screwdrivers

1 Power down the PC.

2 Unplug everything.

3 Remove the lid.

   If you're adding a card to a new system (not removing one as well), then go to step 9.

4 Locate the old video adapter.
   The adapter is the one connected to your monitor. It may have MDA, Hercules, CGA, EGA, or VGA stenciled on it.

5 Unscrew the monitor cable from the back of the card.
   You may need a tiny flathead screwdriver, or the cable may have thumb tighteners on it. If a printer cable is attached, remove it.

6 Unscrew the adapter's mounting bracket from the PC's case.
   It's usually held by a small, flathead screw, though some PCs may use Phillips screws. Remember to save the screw.

7 Lift the card up and out.

8 Put the card into a static-free bag, preferably the original one it came in, or use the new card's bag.

9 Set any jumpers or DIP switches on the new card. (Remember to ground yourself.)

10 Slide the card into the PC.
   If you're adding a card in a previously unused slot, you have to remove the expansion slot's mounting bracket. This is discussed in Chapter 9. If you're replacing a card, install it in the same slot from which you removed the old card—unless the old slot is 8-bit and the new card is 16-bit. In that case, put the card into a 16-bit slot.

11 Tighten the mounting bracket screw.

12 Check all your connections.

13 Reattach the monitor cable. (In some cases, this may not be possible due to the short length of the monitor's cable. If so, save this step for last.)

14 If there is a printer port on the card, attach the printer cable. If there isn't a printer port, and you need to attach your printer to something, move the cable over to another printer port in the system. Change that port's setting to LPT1 or to whatever the old port's value was.

15 Set any DIP switches inside the PC.
   If you have a PC/XT-level system, set the DIP switches on the motherboard to reflect the new video configuration. If you have EGA or VGA, you must tell a PC/XT that it has *no* video display installed. If you have an AT system, you have to run the setup program if there's an error when you power up.

16 Test the PC's new configuration and put the lid back on.

◣ *Upgrading a Monitor*

Adding a monitor to your system is easy; you don't need to take your PC apart. Just make sure that the monitor and display adapter card match.

Procedure: Adding a monitor

Tools: Tiny flathead screwdriver (optional)

1 Power down the PC. (Never plug anything into a computer with its power running.)

2 Unplug everything.

<u>3</u> Remove the old monitor.

Unhook the monitor's cables from the back of the PC (where they attach to the display adapter card). Lift up the monitor and put it away somewhere, preferably in its original packing.

<u>4</u> Put the new monitor on top of or by the side of your PC.

<u>5</u> Attach the monitor's cable to the display adapter card.

The connector is a D-shell connector and can only go on one way. Tighten the thumb twists or use a small screwdriver to anchor the cable in position. If the cable is not long enough, you can buy a monitor extension cable.

<u>6</u> Plug in the monitor. (Don't plug an EGA or a VGA monitor into the back of your PC; use a wall socket or power-strip socket instead.)

<u>7</u> Power up the PC.

You may get a POST error if the monitor and display adapter types don't match what your computer already knows about. This can happen if you don't set a DIP switch properly on a PC/XT system. If you have an AT system, run the setup program to remedy the situation.

If you don't see anything on your screen, make sure the monitor is plugged in and turned on. (Most monitors have their own power switches.) Check to make sure the brightness isn't turned all the way down. Recheck all your connections.

 ## *Running Two Monitors on a PC*

Since the days of the first IBM PC, all PCs have had the ability to support two monitors at the same time. Some software is friendly to this setup, using the color monitor to display graphics and the monochrome monitor to display text, user options, and menus.

If you decide to run two monitors on your system, you must tell the PC, adapter cards, and software about the change.

Tell the PC

Some PC/XT- and AT-level systems have a DIP switch or Setup option that specifically states *dual monitors.* If you have a color monitor and a monochrome monitor, flip the switches or run the setup program to tell the PC about it. Check your machine's documentation for the proper settings.

Tell the Adapter Cards

The biggest problem with running two display adapters and monitors is memory contention—that is, two segments of RAM battling it out for control over one area in the PC's memory.

You can run a standard MDA and CGA setup together just fine. The memory in these systems doesn't conflict. But if you have a Hercules monitor in a dual-monitor setup, you must configure the card to its *HALF* setting. When you load the Hercules driver in your AUTOEXEC.BAT file, the HALF switch should be specified as follows:

HGC HALF

Technically, this prevents the Hercules graphics card from using the upper part of memory segment C, where the CGA uses memory.

If you're using an EGA or a VGA driver, you must configure the card's DIP switches or jumpers so that the card won't interfere with the monochrome adapter. VGA cards have special flexibility in this area. But note that it will shut you out of some of the Extended VGA graphics modes.

Tell the Software

Not all software can support two monitors. From DOS, you can change between them by using the MODE command. To activate the monochrome monitor, type:

MODE MONO

To activate the color monitor, type:

MODE co80

Your software will probably run on whichever monitor is active as dictated by DOS. However, some applications may commandeer one monitor or the other, depending on how well designed the software is.

Remember that some software packages will pick up on your dual-monitor setup and display information on both. But other software, including some popular packages, will lock up and die when faced with two monitors.

 ## Software Considerations

All hardware upgrades require some attention to software, and upgrading your PC's video display is no exception. A few years ago this wasn't the case. But with inexpensive, high-quality graphics available to everyone, setting up software to work with the right video display has become a necessary step.

Using Companion Disks

In the old days, you were lucky if you got an instruction booklet with your CGA card. Today, you may get a disk full of READ.ME files, documentation, software drivers, and demonstration programs. Graphics have come a long way.

Companion disks that come with most graphics adapters contain four or more types of programs, including

- Diagnostics
- Utilities
- Driver software
- Sample programs and demos

The diagnostics and utilities are good to know about. You should run the diagnostics right after installing the card and monitor. The utilities come in handy to adjust the monitor, to automatically dim the monitor after periods of inactivity, or to get extra graphics modes under DOS.

Driver software is provided to interface the new video standard with some popular programs. For example, to get a 132-column by

43-row spreadsheet in Lotus 1-2-3, you can run a driver program that comes with your VGA card. Unfortunately, drivers usually only come with the most popular programs, and they aren't always compatible.

Sample programs and demos help you show off your new graphics abilities. Some adapters even come with sample program files to assist programmers in implementing new graphics modes.

Changing Your Software

The second half of the software side is updating the software that is already in your system. If you're moving from monochrome to color, you may find you have to reinstall some packages, execute setup programs to set the color and graphics modes, and reconfigure applications.

Having a color display definitely makes you choosy. In the monochrome world, you have no choices for text appearance. In the color world, with sixteen foreground and eight background colors, you can spend hours selecting the proper combinations for your screen.

Summary

The world of video on a PC is divided into two halves: monochrome and color. Both modes are capable of displaying text; you need a color video system to take full advantage of graphics software on a PC. The Hercules graphics standard allows you to use graphics on a monochrome monitor.

Your monitor and display adapter card work together to provide your PC with video display; the two must be compatible. Currently, the standards for monochrome are the Hercules and Hercules-clone cards, and the standards for color are the VGA and Super VGA cards. Monitors come in many different types, including TTL, analog, and multiscanning.

When you upgrade your PC's video system, in addition to setting any DIP switches, remember to reconfigure your applications to take full advantage of your new video setup.

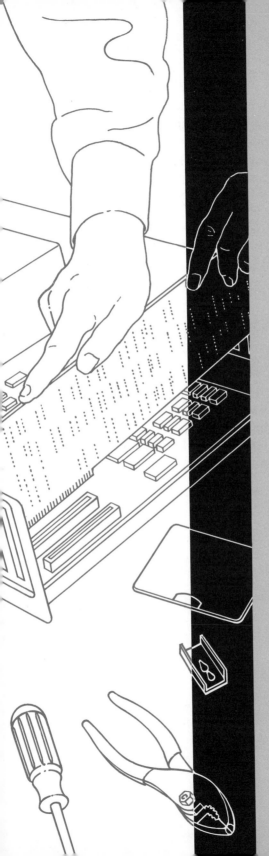

12

Printers

THERE ARE HUNDREDS OF DIFFERENT PRINTERS AVAILABLE for the PC family of computers. (At last count, the WordPerfect word processor offered direct support for over 700 different printers.) Because of this, most books on upgrading your PC skip printers altogether; there are just too many of them and there are few official standards. Though IBM makes printers, there's nothing special about them that you can't find in a model by Panasonic, Hewlett-Packard, Epson, or Canon.

Rather than talk about nuts and bolts, this chapter discusses printers in general to help you buy your first printer or upgrade to a better one.

 ## *Printer Components*

Next to monitors, printers are the most common computer peripheral. Today, nearly every computer sold goes home with a companion printer. But there are few printer standards.

Printers come in different sizes and shapes. There is no generic printer, but the following components are found on most printers:

- Cables
- Front panel switches
- DIP switches
- A ribbon or cartridge

You should be able to locate all these items on your own printer.

Cables

Every printer has at least two cables: a power cable and a printer data cable.

The *power cable* goes from the printer to the wall socket or power-protection strip. The printer has its own power switch and operates independently from the PC (though the printer won't work if it's plugged into the PC and the computer isn't turned on).

The *printer cable* extends from the printer to the computer. It's the line through which the PC and printer communicate.

Printers themselves can plug into either a dedicated printer port or a serial port.

Front Panel Switches

Nearly every printer has a set of switches or buttons on its front panel. The three most common buttons are the online, line-feed, and form-feed buttons. (Laser printers do not have a line-feed button.)

Some printers have a slew of buttons, knobs, and dials. Some laser printers even have small digital displays.

The switches on the front panel give you limited control over the printer. The online button is used to make the printer available for printing. When the printer is offline, it won't print. (The button is sometimes called Select/Deselect.)

When the printer is offline, the line-feed and form-feed buttons can be used to adjust the paper in the printer. Line feed advances one line at a time through the printer; form feed advances an entire page at a time.

The buttons serve other purposes as well. Sometimes, pressing two or more in combination will change the selected font or print a text pattern.

DIP Switches

In addition to front panel switches, nearly every type of printer (except for laser printers) has a row of DIP switches somewhere. Dot-matrix printers have DIP switches on the inside or on the back of the case.

DIP switches on a printer are used to set the following:

- The printer's compatibility mode
- A parallel (printer) or serial interface
- Communication speeds for a serial interface
- Line feeds

- Character spacing and style
- Page length

Printer compatibility is crucial. If your software doesn't support your particular brand of printer, you can make your printer emulate another printer by setting the proper DIP switches.

A printer's serial interface, unlike a parallel (standard printer) interface, must be set to communicate with the PC at a specific speed and format. You tell the printer that by setting DIP switches.

Ribbons and Cartridges

Printers need ink to make an image on paper. The ink is stored in the printer either in the form of a ribbon (as on a typewriter) or a cartridge. Some cartridges contain ribbons.

Laser printer cartridges contain the toner that the laser printer fuses to the paper to create an image. They last longer than standard printer ribbons, but they're more expensive.

Finally, some specialty printers use reservoirs of ink and spray it directly on the page. These so-called ink jet printers aren't as messy as they sound, and they are the quietest of all computer printers.

Printer Types

All printers do the same job, but there are different types of printers that give you different degrees of quality and performance. The two major categories of PC printers are dot-matrix printers and laser printers.

Dot-Matrix Printers

Dot-matrix printers are the traditional type of computer printer, and they've come a long way in the past decade. (A generic dot-matrix printer is shown in Figure 12.1.) A dot-matrix printer works by firing a series of metal pins, arranged vertically in a column. These pins press down the printer's ribbon, which then forms a dot on the

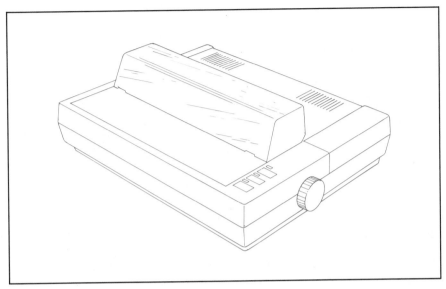

Figure 12.1: A dot-matrix printer

paper. As the print head (the device that contains the pins) moves back and forth across the page, the pins create a pattern—a matrix of dots—in which characters are formed.

These dots are the telltale sign of a computer printout. For years, you could easily spot material printed on a dot-matrix printer. The quality wasn't the best. But around 1985 or so, manufacturers upped the number of pins in the print head from 9 to 24. Essentially, they gave you two rows of smaller pins (12 to a row) instead of one row of fatter pins. The results were impressive.

A 24-pin dot-matrix printer is capable of producing what the industry calls NLQ, or near letter quality, text. Letter-quality text refers to the quality of characters produced by a typewriter.

Today, dot-matrix printers are still the most popular type of computer printer. Their prices vary, depending on print quality, speed, and the printer's carriage width.

*L*aser Printers

The laser printer is the most versatile printer you can hook up to a PC. (A generic laser printer is shown in Figure 12.2.) It is also the

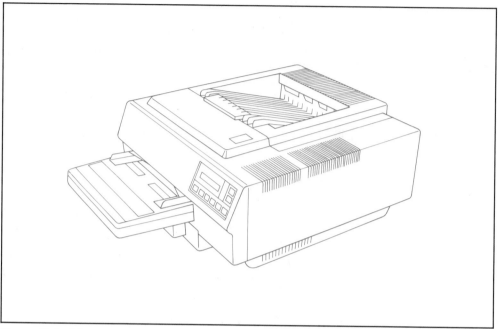

Figure 12.2: A laser printer

most expensive. However, since 1989, some laser printers have been discounted to under $1000, making them an affordable option for most small businesses and some home use.

In a laser printer, the image is created by a laser beam. Sophisticated electronics control the beam, positioning it in very tiny increments. The beam paints an image on a drum inside the laser printer. An electrical charge is created where the beam touches the drum.

The drum rolls under a toner cartridge, collecting toner on the part of the drum that's electrically charged. When the drum comes in contact with the paper, the toner image is transferred to the paper. Heat is used to fuse the toner to the paper.

It's a complex process, but the results are spectacular. Although laser printers are more expensive than dot-matrix printers, they're faster. The output can be near typeset quality.

Some laser printers come with sophisticated electronics, their own microprocessor, and megabytes of RAM. These components are used to save processing time in the PC. The better the printer's processing power and the more RAM it has, the faster it prints.

The advantages of a laser printer over a dot-matrix or any other type of PC printer are great. It's the ideal printer if you want top-quality text, even allowing you to print on your business letterhead, and produces great graphics. Although dot-matrix printers can create low-quality graphics, the process is slow and noisy when compared to the efficiency and high quality of a laser printer. The ability to couple text and graphics on the same page makes the laser printer the ideal output device for desktop publishing. Any other type of printer is second-rate.

Specialty Printers

Aside from dot-matrix and laser printers, which have a lot of variety in price and performance, there are other types of printers you can hook up to your PC, including color and ink jet printers, plotters, thermal printers, and daisy-wheel/impact printers. You can still find these printers around. But if you don't need their special features, you'll probably find a better dot-matrix or laser printer for the same price.

Printer Characteristics

The quality and performance of a printer is judged in terms of its type quality, its speed, and the fonts that it has. You can use these characteristics to compare individual printers to help you decide which one to buy.

Type Quality

Type quality is judged by how good the characters look on paper, which is dependent on how the printer produced the image.

For example, dot-matrix printers come in both 9- and 24-pin varieties. A 24-pin dot-matrix printer is capable of producing some very well formed characters. The type quality is said to be near letter quality (NLQ), or roughly equivalent to what you get on a typewriter. Some 9-pin dot-matrix printers are also tagged as NLQ. They achieve it by printing the same line three times.

With laser printers, type quality is judged in terms of the dots-per-inch (dpi) measurement. The typical laser printer slaps down 300 dots on one inch of paper. This resolution is far better than a dot-matrix printer's resolution.

The type quality on a laser printer is said to be near typeset quality. A typesetter, such as the one used to produce this book, can produce type of 1240 dpi or greater. That's very fine resolution, but too expensive to achieve with a personal computer and a laser printer.

There are option boards that you can add to many laser printers to boost their resolution. Improvements of 400 to 600 dots per inch are possible, but at a high price. There are also some high-end laser printers that can produce type of 600 to 800 dots per inch.

Printer Speed

Another characteristic of a printer is its speed. The old daisy-wheel printers were judged by the number of characters per second (cps) they could produce. A daisy-wheel printer that could print at 40 cps was considered a top-speed model, even though it took a few minutes to print just one page of text.

A good dot-matrix printer may chug along at 80 cps. Faster printers can manage 160 cps or even 240 cps in draft mode, which is fairly fast. But the quality drops at these higher speeds.

Laser printers are the fastest printers of all. Their speed is measured in pages per minute (ppm). The first laser printers could print four pages per minute. Today's models can manage up to 8 ppm or more. But these figures are highly optimized—real-life usage only rarely produces the maximum speed.

The values for cps and ppm are usually attained in the laboratory under ideal conditions. For example, to get a high cps value, dot-matrix printer manufacturers print only one long line of text. The amount of time taken for line feeds and form feeds is never factored in, so your actual speed will be less.

For laser printers, the high 8-ppm figure is attained only when printing the same page a number of times. When each page differs— and especially when there are graphics and different fonts—printing is slower. When you shop for a printer, use the cps and ppm values for comparison purposes only.

Printer Fonts

The term *font* comes from typesetting and design. A font is the complete assortment of type of one size and face. For example, the text in this book is typeset in the 11-point Garamond font. There are dozens of popular fonts, each giving a different look to the text. (There are many books available on using and choosing fonts for your desktop publishing and word processing tasks.)

Font Attributes

Fonts have certain attributes, including style and size. *Style* refers to whether the font is bold, italic, underlined, outlined, and so on. In traditional typesetting, a bold or italic style is simply another font. You have Times Roman, Times Roman Bold, and Times Roman Italic—three different fonts. But with computers, bold and italic are styles of one font.

The size of a font is measured using the typesetting term *points*. There are 72 points to an inch. A 72-point font has 1-inch-tall letters. Newspaper text is usually 10-point.

Be careful not to confuse point size with *pitch*. On a typewriter, pitch is used to refer to the number of characters you can fit on a line. Ten-pitch characters are called *pica,* and you can fit eighty of them on a line (ten to the inch). Twelve-pitch characters are called *elite,* and you can fit ninety-six of them on a line (twelve to the inch).

Font Technology

To produce different fonts, printers use various techniques. Dot-matrix printers usually have a limited font set built-in or none at all. Only a laser printer can give you decent font output. Fonts in a laser printer can either be built into the printer (in the printer's ROM), added to the printer by means of an expansion slot or a font cartridge, or *downloaded* to the printer by using software.

Built-in fonts are best. They're either encoded in the laser printer's ROM or added via a font cartridge. Since the fonts are on chips and are already a part of the printer's circuitry, printing them is fast and quick, and they don't gobble up the printer's processing time or RAM.

Downloadable fonts are fonts the printer can't produce by itself. They're supplied by software you load into the PC. When it comes time to print, the information necessary to produce the fonts is sent to the printer. The printer calculates the look of each font and creates the image on the page.

Downloadable fonts chew up your PC's processing time. They definitely use up printer RAM, which slows down printing. Managing downloadable fonts on a PC is a real chore, but sometimes using them is the only way you can get different fonts for your printer.

PostScript and Outline Fonts

Two special types of fonts are PostScript and outline fonts. These fonts are also referred to as *scalable.* You can change the size of the font to just about any height or width.

Scalable fonts always give you the best printed results, in contrast with fixed fonts, which are created at specific point sizes and can only print (or only print well) at these sizes.

For your own printer, note which fonts are available and whether or not your word processor can access them. Your printer may have lots of fonts, but if your software doesn't know about them, they're of little use.

Miscellaneous Characteristics

There are other characteristics you can look at to compare printers. They're not as crucial as type quality, printer speed, and font availability, but still worth considering.

Hardware Compatibility

As we've seen, PCs lack a hardware standard for printers. But there are two types of hardware compatibility you have to consider when buying a printer: whether it is HP-compatible and whether it is PostScript-compatible.

Hewlett-Packard (HP) pioneered the PC laser printer with the HP LaserJet. The LaserJet and its descendents use a printer control language called PCL. It's a good sign if your printer offers PCL or provides any compatibility with the LaserJet.

Of course, if LaserJet compatibility concerns you, you should buy a LaserJet. However, there are LaserJet emulators in software that you can purchase.

PostScript is a page description language offered by Adobe. PostScript fonts and graphics are a standard in the PC industry. So if your laser printer supports them, you have access to a wealth of fonts and graphic programs that support PostScript.

But PostScript is expensive. Apple's LaserWriter printers all incorporate PostScript and can use PostScript's scalable fonts. But this feature adds about $2000 to the price of Apple's PostScript-compatible printers. (You can hook one up to a PC if you so desire.)

Remember that compatibility is determined by your software. Although your printer may support PCL or PostScript, if your software cannot take advantage of it, it will be of no use to you.

Carriage Width

Carriage width is a consideration only with dot-matrix printers. It's a measure of how wide the paper is that you can use with your printer.

Standard dot-matrix printers have a letter-size carriage width. They can only accept paper in standard 8½″ × 11″ format, though some printers allow you to insert the paper sideways. The wider-size format allows for 14-inch-long paper to be inserted. This paper is ideal for printing wide spreadsheets. In fact, the ability to print out spreadsheets or wide invoices is usually the only reason for getting a wide-carriage dot-matrix printer. They also cost more.

The paper that a laser printer uses is usually of either legal or letter size. However, using software, the laser printer can print sideways on the page. This orientation is referred to as *landscape.* The standard orientation (up and down) is called *portrait.*

Paper-Feed Mechanism

Paper for a laser printer is supplied manually, one sheet at a time, or automatically through a paper tray. The paper tray holds letter- or legal-size paper and feeds it to the printer one sheet at a time, just like a copy machine.

Dot-matrix printers can have one of three types of paper-feed mechanisms. Sometimes these are built into the printer, but often they're options. If the latter, remember to buy one when you buy the printer.

The three types of feeding mechanisms are

- Platen, or friction, feed

- Pin feed

- Tractor feed

Platen feed advances the paper the same way a typewriter does. You insert the paper in the printer, roll the knob forward, and position the paper just under the top of the print head. This method is best for printing one sheet at a time or printing envelopes.

Both pin- and tractor-feed mechanisms are used to feed long, continuous sheets of paper into the printer. This is the kind of paper that comes with holes on the side. The holes match up with pins in the printer that are used to move the paper through the printer.

A printer's design includes either a pin- or tractor-feed mechanism, so you don't have a choice between them. (You do have a choice between a feed mechanism or a platen.) Tractor feed works better—pin-feed mechanisms sometimes jam because they push the paper into the printer.

The PC–Printer Interface

Printers are independent. A PC can use just about any printer, so your computer, software, and DOS all have to be flexible enough to deal with a variety of printers.

The *printer port* is the means by which your PC accesses the printer; you can't use a printer without a printer port of some type. Your software has to communicate with the printer if you ever expect to see any output, or hard copy. DOS also deals with the printer, but only on a simple level. In fact, most software avoids DOS when using the printer, preferring to access the printer port directly.

*T*he Printer Port

Your PC communicates with the printer through a cable, commonly called the *printer cable.* One end plugs into your printer; the other end plugs into the printer port on the computer.

A port is a device that provides for communications. Your PC talks to a printer, mouse, or external modem through a port.

Serial and Parallel Ports

There are parallel, or Centronics, ports, and serial ports. Only old-timers call a printer port a Centronics port. Centronics is the name of the company that set the standards for printer cables and hooking up computers and printers.

Parallel refers to how information travels between the computer and printer. Each byte you send to the printer, which eventually forms a printed character on the page, is composed of eight bits. In a parallel port, these eight bits are sent through the cable side by side, as if they were walking eight abreast in a parade.

A parallel port is a one-way communications line in a PC. Information is only sent *to* the printer. Although the printer may send a few messages back to the PC (such as ''I'm out of paper'' or ''I'm not ready''), it doesn't send any bytes of data back.

A printer can also be hooked up to a serial port. In that instance, you can still call the port a printer port (because it's hooked up to the printer), but it's really a serial port.

Serial ports communicate with a variety of different devices. They're much more versatile than parallel ports because they offer two-way communications—for example, information sent to and received from a modem.

Serial refers to how information is sent through the port. Unlike a parallel port, where the bytes are transmitted in rows of eight, a serial port transmits all the bits in a byte through one wire, one after the other. They travel in a straight line, as opposed to eight abreast.

The standard PC printer has a parallel interface, so most printers are hooked up to a parallel printer port. But a few printers are serial, including most of the older daisy-wheel printers (some support both ports). The early laser printers were all serial, but today laser printers support parallel as well.

Serial is better than parallel over longer distances. A serial port's signal can travel quite a few yards before it begins to fade. Parallel is faster, but its signal fades after about 20 feet or so. Keep in mind that parallel is the standard printer port for all PC printers, and you can hook up just about any printer to it. It's always a good idea to have both a parallel and a serial port in your computer.

How to Locate Ports

Unfortunately, there are no labeling standards for PC printer ports. Some computers (high-end models mostly) label their built-in serial and parallel ports, but finding a parallel port on the back of a typical PC can be frustrating.

The printer port's connector is a D-shell 25-pin, but there are a number of these connectors on the typical PC, one of which is probably a serial port. If you plug in the printer and it doesn't work, you've probably plugged it into a serial port or into a secondary printer port.

Starting in about 1985, serial ports came with only nine pins in a D-shell connector. If you have a newer system, especially an AT-level system, it probably has a 9-pin serial port, which means only the parallel ports will have 25-pin D-shell connectors. The only hassle is trying to find out which port is which number, if you have more than one.

Printer Drivers

Imagine a world where you have a PC and a printer and software that understands them both. Erase the term *printer driver* from your mind, forget about incompatibilities, forget about output looking one way on your home computer's printer and another way altogether at the office. Imagine . . .

What you're imagining is a style of computing only possible on the Macintosh. But on the PC side, there are difficulties.

Earlier in this book, I said that the PC is a collection of off-the-shelf parts. This architecture gives you a tremendous advantage as far as configuring a flexible system is concerned. There is lots of competition among hardware component manufacturers, so you have a lot of choices and the opportunity to buy parts at bargain prices. But because of this variety (especially in printers), your software can easily become confused.

Most software packages don't have any trouble dealing with memory and different video standards. Monitors and display adapters have variety, but they're still standards more or less defined by IBM. Printers are altogether different.

If you're using an application that relies on good-looking output (like Corel Draw or Harvard Graphics), it has to know how to control your printer. If you want graphics or different type styles or sizes, your software must know precisely which printer you have. Only then can it speak to the printer in the printer's own language and get the printer to do what you want it to do. This is made possible by a software device known as a *printer driver*. (Printer drivers aren't the same as device drivers loaded in CONFIG.SYS. Device drivers are for DOS—which really couldn't care less about which printer you have.)

A printer driver is a custom part of an application, or a separate program, that provides for direct communication with a particular printer. For example, the commands to print italic text are different for the HP LaserJet, Epson LQ 1500, and Panasonic 1080i printers. But by using a driver for each printer, an application can simply say "print in italics." The driver then translates that instruction into the printer's code for producing italic text.

You have to know whether drivers are available for your printer. There are hundreds of printers in the marketplace and some software applications only support a limited range. If your printer is not supported, there may be a similar printer that has a driver available that you can use. Information on supported printers is usually listed on the side of the software box. To get the driver, you usually have to call up the developer's support line.

If your printer isn't supported, it may be possible to create your own driver. Some applications have utility programs that allow you to construct (or modify) a driver from the ground up. To do this, you need your printer's manual or a list of printer codes for your printer.

Writing your own printer driver is a real hassle. I've written several, including some that had to be programmed in assembly language. If you're into programming, it's an interesting challenge. Some printer drivers are quite easy for the nonprogrammer to create.

Boosting Printer Performance

Printers are reliable peripherals, so you don't need to know a lot about their operation. But there are ways to supercharge a printer by using both software and hardware, giving you better performance. Because of advances in the design of laser printers and the boom in desktop publishing, there is more reason than ever to improve the quality of your output.

The Software Side

There are a couple of things you can use on the software side to boost printer performance:

- Printer spoolers
- Emulation software

Printer Spoolers

A *printer spooler* is a software program in your computer (as opposed to a printer buffer, which is hardware). The spooler monitors and intercepts all printer activity. It either saves data to disk as a file or keeps it in spooler memory. Then, every so often, the spooler dishes out a handful of characters to the printer while you're doing other work on the computer. Printing is done "in the background," so your time is not wasted waiting for the printer to print. The spooler's *queue* is the list of files that are waiting to be printed by the spooler.

Some sophisticated printer spoolers save the information to be printed to a file on disk. The files are kept in a special spooler subdirectory to keep them separate from other files. Each file is fed to the queue while you're doing something else. This type of spooler allows you to delete certain jobs before they are printed. Most spoolers even let you print documents at given times or redirect printing to another printer.

Emulation Software

The issue of printer compatibility crops up when you try to interface your particular printer with software that doesn't support it. Though your printer may have a nationally known name, you may have software that doesn't recognize it. Also, some printers are too new for older applications to recognize them and support all their features. When this happens, you can do one of three things:

- Use your printer in the dumb mode.
- Select a compatible printer.
- Buy emulation software.

In *dumb* mode, the printer prints just simple text and no fancy fonts, italics, or graphics. Even though your printer may support these features, if your software doesn't know how to make the printer work, you have to run the printer in dumb mode.

A compatible printer may be the same model as yours but manufactured under a different brand name. The old NEC 8023 printer was the same model that C. Itoh manufactured, as well as that sold by Apple as the ProWriter. If an application supported any of these printers, your own model was compatible.

If your printer isn't compatible, and it doesn't have any DIP switches that you can set to make it compatible with anything else, and you don't want to waste time writing a printer driver, your only choice is to buy emulation software.

Top-notch software developers try to support every printer on the market, but it's an impossible task. Some printers even come with disks containing printer drivers for various applications. But when your luck runs out, emulation software is the only way to go.

One of the hottest printer emulation packages is LaserTwin, available from Metro Software. It allows practically any laser or dot-matrix printer to emulate a Hewlett-Packard LaserJet printer.

The Hardware Side

On the hardware side, software developers are constantly looking for new ways to boost printer performance. But unlike software techniques, these methods are often expensive, specific solutions for high-volume printer problems. It would be nice if there were a $29.95 gadget that you could plug into a printer to get more out of it. But sadly, that's not the case.

There are four ways you can boost your printer performance by using hardware:

- Add printer RAM.

- Use a printer buffer.

- Buy font cartridges.

- Buy a laser-printer assistant card.

Adding Printer RAM

As with the computer itself, a good way to get more performance from a printer is to add more RAM.

Dot-matrix printers use RAM simply as a buffer to store incoming characters. If you add RAM to a dot-matrix printer, you don't have to wait as long for the printer to print. But unlike adding RAM to the computer, you have to buy a special printer RAM board for each printer. These boards are usually expensive.

Laser printers use RAM as well, usually to store information that you send to the printer. But because some laser printers are like computers (they have their own microprocessor and RAM), they use the RAM to make calculations and to prepare images for printing. This takes up much more RAM than the simple character storage for which RAM is used on a dot-matrix printer. PostScript printers in particular require lots of RAM to create their images, 1.5Mb and up.

You can add RAM to just about any printer, but usually it's in the form of some proprietary (and expensive) upgrade option available only from the printer's manufacturer. Some PC add-on boards come with extra RAM for the printer.

Using a Printer Buffer

A *printer buffer* works like a printer spooler. But instead of using the PC's RAM, the buffer holds its own RAM. This gives you more memory to run DOS programs, and it eliminates the mess sometimes caused by memory-resident printer spoolers.

A printer buffer is one of those famous black boxes that you hook up to your PC. It plugs into the printer cable between your PC and the printer and is packed full of RAM. All characters sent to the printer are first stored in the buffer's RAM space. The buffer contains electronic circuitry that monitors the printer, sending characters when the printer is able to print them.

A printer buffer saves you printing time, but that's about all it does. (In fact, using a buffer is simply a way to add more RAM to a printer without buying a proprietary RAM board.) Printer buffers are limited in how much control they give you over what's printed. Usually, the only way to stop a buffer is to unplug it, which erases the information stored in the buffer.

Using Font Cartridges

Another way to boost the performance of your printer is to buy *font cartridges.* A font cartridge is a ROM chip on a special, user-installable expansion card. The card plugs into a custom slot on the printer and gives your printer and software access to the fonts encoded in ROM. There are even font cartridges available for dot-matrix printers.

The problem with font cartridges is that they're expensive. Typically, you'll pay from $150 to $450 for a cartridge of different fonts. This is more expensive than the downloadable software fonts you can buy. The advantage of a font cartridge is that the fonts take up no extra RAM or megabytes of disk space in your PC.

Using a Laser-Printer Assistant Card

To give your laser printer more power, you can add a *laser-printer assistant card* to your PC. It's an expansion card that boosts the printer's power or assists the printer's circuitry in some way—for example, by boosting the printer's resolution.

Most laser printers print at a resolution of 300 dots per inch. That's an impressive figure (and apparently an acceptable one to the masses because few laser-printer manufacturers have bothered to improve upon it). Although it is possible to buy a printer with higher resolution, these printers are expensive and best suited for professional environments, such as professional publishing and graphics arts houses.

One of the jobs of a laser-printer assistant card is to boost the performance of a laser printer's controller. You install the card in your PC and connect the laser printer to the card. The card then takes over the job of controlling the printer's laser beam, increasing its resolution to 600 dots per inch or more. These cards, however, are very expensive.

In addition to boosting the laser printer's resolution, the laser card can also add its own RAM to the printer's RAM, add fonts, or give the printer PostScript or PostScript-like scalable fonts and graphics. But the negative side is that the laser card may also use up a lot of your PC's RAM and processor time to do the job. For high-capacity printing though, nothing can beat this upgrade.

 # Summary

Printers are very useful devices that you can hook up to your PC, but due to a lack of standardization, dealing with them can be bewildering.

There are two basic printer types for the PC: dot-matrix printers and laser printers. Dot-matrix printers represent the low end. Laser printers are the workhorses of PC printing. They produce both top-quality text and graphics output. They're quiet, fast, but fairly expensive.

The biggest problem with printers isn't the devices themselves but how PC software interacts with them. Since there are few accepted standards, it's up to you to figure out how to interface your software with your computer. If you're lucky enough to own a popular printer, then this isn't much of a problem. If you're not, there are printer drivers and emulation software packages available that will make your printer work like other printers.

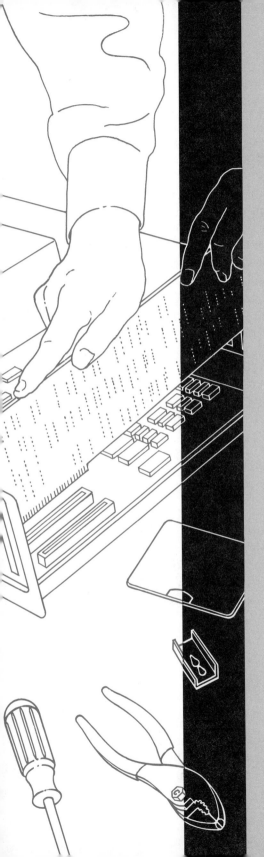

13

**Making
Your PC
Faster and
More Efficient**

YOU CAN UPGRADE YOUR PC FOR ANY NUMBER OF reasons: to keep your PC state of the art, to give yourself more RAM or disk storage, or to keep your hardware compatible with your software. But one of the best reasons to upgrade your PC is to make it faster.

As software becomes increasingly more powerful, it continues to require more and more of your PC's processor time, RAM, and hard-disk storage. By making your computer run faster, you will be better able to take advantage of what software has to offer you. This chapter takes a general approach to the subject of speeding up your PC, from both a hardware and software perspective. There is some overlap with previous chapters, but there are also some new topics not previously covered.

The hardware techniques use hardware items you can add to make your PC more powerful. Although the effect of software changes isn't as noticeable as the effect of hardware changes, software is something you can add to your PC without lifting a screwdriver or paying the steep price of some hardware parts.

Hardware Solutions

A common question I'm asked is, "How can I make my computer work faster?" The speed of a computer is directly proportional to how much work it can do for you. Although you can enter information only so fast, a fast PC can manipulate that information very quickly. Fast results are what most computer owners want.

You have two choices if you want a faster computer:

- Buy a new one that's faster.
- Upgrade the one you have.

The decision is based on price. What can you afford?

A newer, faster computer is the best solution but costs more. Upgrading an older PC piecemeal is less expensive. But once you start on the upgrade path, you'll find that the sum of the individual parts you add can be greater than the cost of a new PC. So before you set out to make a faster PC, consider buying a new computer.

For most situations, one or more of the following will make your PC run faster:

- A faster hard drive
- More memory
- A math coprocessor
- An accelerator card
- A CPU upgrade

The upgrading option that will produce the greatest increase in speed depends on what kind of hardware you have and what kinds of applications you typically run.

Adding a Faster Hard Drive

It is possible to increase the speed of your computer without seeing any noticeable difference in the speed at which your software runs. A good example of this is running a database application, such as dBASE. The huge amount of information stored on disk isn't affected by the speed of the microprocessor, the amount of RAM in the computer, or the typing speed of the operator. The crucial element is the speed of the disk drive. (If you already have a fast hard drive, you may need to defragment the files on your disk if your work seems to have noticeably slowed.)

Of all the hardware speed upgrades, a faster hard drive is mentioned here first because most people don't give adequate consideration to the size of the hard drive when buying a PC. If you run a business, not only will your database files of customers and inventory get bigger and bigger, but PC applications swell in size. So whether you need a new hard drive for increased speed or higher capacity, it's generally one of the first upgrades you should consider doing.

Benefits of a Faster Drive

A faster disk drive can work miracles for disk-intensive PC operations. Everything from spell-checking a word processor document to sorting a database and from working with large documents and drawings to doing CAD illustrations can be sped up by adding a faster hard drive. The more applications you use that require the benefits of a hard drive, the more you will notice the advantages of a faster drive.

Though your database program and all its manuals may weigh more than the computer, the program itself is a relatively light load on the microprocessor. Traditionally, databases keep all their information stored on disk. All the records and the information in the records are in a disk file. As your customer database (or record collection, recipe files, or Christmas-card list) grows, the file on disk gets bigger and bigger and your PC gets slower and slower. What works against speed is the rate at which the disk drive can write and read that information to and from the disk.

Adding a faster hard drive also decreases the time it takes to load and run programs and their data files.

What to Look For

The speed of a hard disk is measured in milliseconds, abbreviated *ms*. The capacity is measured in megabytes. Because both of these are linked to the type of controller your PC has, adding a hard drive may require an upgrade of your hard-disk controller as well.

You can buy a new hard drive without buying a new controller. Search for the fastest hard drive with the largest capacity as governed by your controller (as well as your budget).

You can also buy a new hard drive *and* a new controller. Here the limiting factor is your PC. Some of the older systems can't support a superfast hard drive.

Making the Move

If you decide to improve your PC's speed by upgrading the hard drive, you should first perform a full backup of your hard drive to protect your data.

When you get the new drive, install it and initialize it according to the instructions in Chapter 8 or any instructions provided with the drive. Once the drive is initialized, restore your backup.

Adding a faster hard drive is a uncomplicated upgrade. There's no need to reconfigure software or worry about new incompatibilities. And the nicest part is that you'll notice the speed increase almost immediately.

Adding More Memory

All computers can use more RAM, but PCs have a unique problem. Though we can add megabytes of memory to our computers, DOS can still only run applications in the basic 640K. But DOS applications have been written that can cheat the 640K barrier, so a RAM upgrade is always of benefit.

Your first step in a RAM upgrade is to fill out all your PC's conventional RAM—all memory from location 0 up to 640K. There's no point in even mentioning the advanced memory tricks until you have supplied the full 640K of RAM. One of the best ways to get that memory is to buy an EMS memory card that provides for memory backfill.

Expanded Memory

Under DOS, the memory you'll want to add to your PC is expanded memory. From Chapter 5, remember that expanded memory is merely a memory pool—a storage area for data. You cannot run applications in expanded memory; it's for storage only.

To make expanded memory accessible on your system, you need an expanded memory card (hardware) and an EMS (Expanded Memory Specification) driver (software). (Remember that 386 systems have LIM 4.0 abilities built in.) The best types to get are an LIM 4.0-compatible EMS memory card and an LIM 4.0-compatible software driver.

An LIM 4.0 memory board can provide backfill memory to bring your basic RAM up to 640K. When LIM 4.0 EMS memory becomes part of your Conventional DOS memory, the memory control software can do many things with it.

If you have a 386 system, however, you should load the system with extended memory and convert that memory into expanded memory for use by DOS.

Extended Memory

The 286 and 386 microprocessors can address more memory than 8086 DOS was designed for. That extra memory is referred to as extended memory, and it cannot be used directly by DOS. Why? Because DOS can only see the first megabyte of RAM. Any memory beyond that—extended memory on a 286 or 386—doesn't exist as far as DOS is concerned.

To make extended memory useful under DOS, a software driver can be used to convert the memory into expanded memory. On a 286 system, extended memory is first provided by an EMS board. The EMS software driver converts it into expanded memory.

A 386 microprocessor requires only software to convert its extended memory into expanded memory. The 386 already contains built-in hardware for memory management, giving it power equal to and surpassing that of LIM 4.0 EMS boards. Once the EMS software is installed on a 386, the software will emulate expanded memory.

In addition to converting extended memory into expanded memory for use by DOS, you can make extended memory available to some DOS programs that use it directly. These applications are called DOS extenders. Although they are compatible with DOS and run under DOS, they actually operate in the 286 or 386's protected mode. In that mode, they have access to all the advanced features and power these microprocessors have to offer. But when they need to use DOS, they switch back into the DOS mode (called the *real mode*).

To make all this happen and to keep extended memory, expanded memory, and DOS extender software from bringing down the system like a house of cards in an earthquake, certain standards were developed. The most important of these is the VCPI, covered later in the chapter.

Advantages of Extra Memory

Extra memory in a PC is only of use to you if you have programs that need it. If all you're using is a simple 40K word processor on your laptop, you probably don't need 6Mb of expanded memory. But more and more applications are recognizing and using expanded memory. And when DOS extenders become popular, they'll need extra memory as well.

There's really no direct way to increase the speed of your PC by adding memory. The benefits come from applications that use the memory, such as print spoolers, RAM disks and disk caches, and memory management programs that let you get more work done when you have extra memory. These are all covered later in the chapter.

Adding a Math Coprocessor

A math coprocessor is an assistant chip—it works like a calculator for your microprocessor. It helps the microprocessor by performing complex mathematical calculations. When the microprocessor encounters a mathematical problem, it simply passes it off to the coprocessor. In the end, the PC works faster because the microprocessor doesn't get bogged down doing math problems.

But there's a catch: The speed improvement that a math coprocessor offers is only apparent when you are running applications that support it—usually programs that require lots of math, such as spreadsheets and CAD applications.

All About Math Coprocessors

A math coprocessor is a chip, like your microprocessor, but it's a special support chip. It's entirely possible to run a PC without one, which is why PCs are sold with a math chip as an option. The microprocessor is perfectly capable of doing math by itself. But when you add a math chip, math calculations are speeded up by almost 300 percent.

The number on the coprocessor chip is exactly the same as the one on your CPU, except for the last digit. The last digit in the typical microprocessor chip number is a 6—the math coprocessor has a 7. The math coprocessor for a 80286 microprocessor, for example, has the number *80287*.

As with memory chips, there is a second number associated with math coprocessors, which refers to the speed of the chip. The math coprocessor always runs at the same speed as the microprocessor. If you pair a 16MHz 80387 coprocessor (labeled 80387-16) with a 20MHz 80386 microprocessor, you'll burn out the coprocessor.

One reason why every PC doesn't come with a math coprocessor is that it would add anywhere from $100 to $800 to the price of the computer. Not every application requires a math coprocessor, so don't buy one unless you need it for high-end graphics, animation, or number crunching.

Installing a Math Coprocessor

Installing a math coprocessor is as easy as plugging in a RAM chip, albeit a very expensive RAM chip. You must be very careful when handling one.

Procedure: Adding a math coprocessor

Tools: None

<u>1</u> Power down your PC.

<u>2</u> Unplug everything.

<u>3</u> Remove the lid.

<u>4</u> Locate the coprocessor's socket on the motherboard.

<u>5</u> Orient the chip properly, and press down firmly (see Figure 13.1).

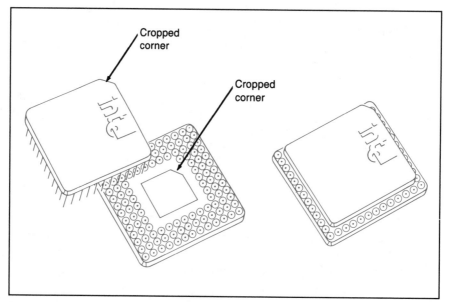

Figure 13.1: Inserting a math coprocessor

Figure 13.1 shows the correct way to orient one of the large, square coprocessor chips. Some of these chips may sit in the middle of a socket that contains far more holes than there are pins in the chip. Note the location of the cropped corner. Like the dot or notch in a RAM chip, it should match the crop on the coprocessor's socket.

If you have a PC/XT-level machine, remember to set the DIP switch that tells the computer it now has a math coprocessor. Test your new configuration and close up the PC. If you have an AT-level system, the system detects the presence of the coprocessor automatically. However, you should check your setup program to make sure that it found the coprocessor. If it didn't, check your PC's troubleshooting guide, or recheck your installation.

Finally, you have to let your software know that you added a coprocessor. Some software, such as some spreadsheets, may immediately detect the coprocessor's presence. You'll notice a marked increase in speed right away. But other programs must be set up or reinstalled to take advantage of the math coprocessor. Check your software manual.

Replacing the Microprocessor

A drastic method of increasing the speed of your PC is to perform a complete brain transplant by installing a new microprocessor. Since PCs provide such a basic snap-and-plug approach to upgrading hardware, it's often thought that you can boost the power of your microprocessor by simply plugging in a faster chip. Alas, it's not that easy.

Not only are microprocessors shaped and sized differently, but the circuitry of your PC is designed to work with a microprocessor running at a specific speed (or set of speeds if you have a dual-speed, or turbo, CPU).

Depending on which microprocessor you have in your PC, you can upgrade to something more powerful by doing one of these upgrades:

- The 8088/8086 to V20/V30 upgrade
- The 286 to 386SX upgrade

The 8088/86 to V20/30 Upgrade

If you have an old PC/XT, there is a simple microprocessor upgrade you can do. The NEC V-series of chips was designed to replace the 8088 and 8086 microprocessors by using a pin-for-pin compatible replacement. The V20 chip replaces the 8088, and the V30 replaces the 8086.

The V-series chips run faster than the original 8088/86, but not really fast enough for the increase to be noticeable. At best, maybe a 5 percent improvement in speed can be achieved by replacing your microprocessor with a V-series chip. But 5 percent adds up to several minutes of time saved by the end of the day.

The best part about the V-series chips is that they are plug-in compatible with the 8088 and 8086. The price isn't that steep, and they're still available.

The 286 to 386SX Upgrade

The 80386 is the microprocessor worth upgrading to. It has long been called the "platform of the future." It is fast, efficient, and works well with many advanced applications. (The 80486 is basically a better-designed 386. But for upgrading purposes, the 386 is more economical and gives you more choices.)

The 80386 runs in full 32-bit mode. A little brother to the full 80386 is the 80386SX, or 386SX. It's about the same size as the typical 80286 chip, and it only runs in 16-bit mode, as opposed to the full 32-bit mode of the regular 386. But it's still a 386 microprocessor with all the abilities of the 386 chip.

Because a 386SX looks like a 286 chip, a lot of industry pundits were led to believe that you could simply drop a 386SX chip into your 286 system to give you 386 power. Alas, you cannot do this. However, adapter modules are available that enable you to plug a 386SX chip into your 286 system's CPU socket. One of these is the Cumulus 386SX.

The Cumulus 386SX is a tiny expansion card. To install it, you pull the 286 chip from your AT's motherboard and plug the Cumulus card into the 286's socket. The Cumulus 386SX card comes with a 386SX chip, plus circuitry to make it work with your AT system.

After you do the upgrade, all the software that runs under the 386 system is available to your computer. For the price, it's possibly the best CPU upgrade you can do.

Some other options are SOTA Technology's SOTA POP and ALL Computer's ALL ChargeCard, which are both plug-in adapters for 286 systems. Unlike the Cumulus card, they don't contain a 386SX chip. Instead, they contain circuitry that gives the 286 chip some of the 386's memory management abilities.

When you plug a SOTA POP or ALL ChargeCard into your 286 system, you immediately get memory compatible with LIM 4.0 EMS memory in your 286 system. You also get some of the advanced 386 memory management abilities. Although you still only have a 16-bit 80286 microprocessor, it's capable of performing some memory management feats that only a 386 can perform.

Both of these options are cheaper than the Cumulus 386 upgrade, primarily because they cut out the need for a 386 chip. If you want to increase the speed of your CPU with a minimum of system modification, they offer an economical solution.

Adding an Accelerator Card

The traditional approach to making a faster computer is to buy an accelerator card. It is actually a complete microprocessor on a card that takes control from the microprocessor on your motherboard. Adding an accelerator card is not as elegant a solution as replacing the microprocessor, but there are more options available.

An accelerator works by giving your PC an entirely new microprocessor, plus circuitry to support it. The new microprocessor comes on an expansion card that you install in one of your PC's expansion slots. You usually have to remove the motherboard's CPU and replace it with a cable to the accelerator card. To preserve compatibility, you can put the old microprocessor on the accelerator card. When you fire up the PC, the new microprocessor and its support circuitry take over.

In addition to support circuitry, some cards offer other options. The most important is the amount of memory. A good accelerator card should come with at least 1Mb of RAM for the new microprocessor to use. Any additional support circuitry is beneficial, because the major disadvantage of adding only an accelerator card is that the rest of the PC's circuitry remains unchanged. The expansion slots, memory, hard drives, and so on are all geared to work with a slower CPU. To get the most from a new microprocessor, you should probably upgrade the entire motherboard as well.

Two accelerator cards worth looking into are Intel's InBoard and Orchid Technology's Tiny Turbo. Each of these offers different options and different price ranges for a variety of microprocessor upgrade situations. It's best to get an accelerator that offers a 386 microprocessor with as much 32-bit RAM on the card as possible.

Swapping Motherboards

The most drastic option for upgrading your microprocessor is to buy a new motherboard. Unlike the other options covered so far, if you install a brand-new 386 motherboard in your PC's case, you get the following:

- A real 386 microprocessor
- Circuitry to support the microprocessor
- 32-bit memory
- 16-bit expansion slots
- A 32-bit proprietary memory expansion slot

Only by completely replacing the motherboard will you get all these goodies. The other solutions only go halfway. But the drawback here is price. A new 386 motherboard costs a lot (it may even cost more than a complete, new 386 system at a local discount outlet). If you're also adding a new hard drive, a 1.2Mb floppy drive, and a beefier power supply, you might as well just buy a new computer.

This subject brings up the often-asked question, "What about building my own computer?" A lot of people rightly come to see that adding a new motherboard, a new power supply, and new disk drives is just one step short of building the entire computer from the ground up. Using all the information covered in this book, you *can* build your own PC. Some dealers used to offer do-it-yourself kits, but they stopped. Why?

It turns out that building your own PC, although an exciting project, just costs too much. Buying all the parts separately costs about 10 percent more than buying a fully assembled PC, plus you don't get the store's warranty.

Local dealers stopped providing do-it-yourself kits because there was too much support involved. A good 50 percent of the systems sold were eventually returned to the shop for proper assembly. It proved to be too much of a hassle to continue offering the kits.

 ## Software Solutions

You can use some interesting software tricks to speed up your PC (a lot of these have already been covered in this book). Nearly all of them affect your PC's memory, so if you want to get the most from your PC through software, first consider a good EMS memory upgrade. Then look into one or more of the following:

- RAM disks
- Disk caches
- Printer spoolers
- Memory managers

Ram Disks

A *RAM disk* is an area of memory controlled by a device driver. The device driver fools DOS into thinking that the memory is actually a disk drive, so DOS formats it and assigns it a drive letter. The advantage is that the disk drive in memory is the fastest drive in your system. The disadvantage is that when you turn off the PC, all the information in the RAM disk is erased.

Setting Up a RAM Disk

In the old days, RAM disks were used out of necessity. Some PCs had only one disk drive. If you had a 256K PC system, to get another drive, you could create a 128K RAM disk. That still left you enough

RAM to work with, but gave you an additional, faster, electronic disk drive for storing additional files.

As the PC's memory situation got worse and worse, people started abandoning the RAM disk. Having memory for applications was more important than using part of your 640K for a RAM disk. But with extended or expanded memory, there is often enough room to spare for a good-size RAM disk.

Several utilities are available to create EMS RAM disks. A common one is VDISK, a RAM-disk device-driver that comes with DOS. To install it in your CONFIG.SYS file, type

DEVICE = C:\DOS\VDISK.SYS

Note that you should replace C:\DOS\ with the subdirectory (drive and path) in your system that has the VDISK.SYS program.

VDISK has up to four options that set the size and location of the RAM drive. The full format of the command is

VDISK.SYS *bytes sectors files* [/E:m ¦ /X:m]

Bytes specifies the size of the RAM disk in K. You can enter values from 1K (for a 1K RAM disk) up to the total amount of RAM you have. If you don't specify a value for *bytes,* a 64K RAM drive is created. If the size you specify leaves less than 64K of available memory, VDISK adjusts the RAM disk size downward.

Sectors sets the size of the sectors used on the RAM disk. Floppy and hard drives use 512-byte sectors, but for a RAM drive under VDISK you can specify a 128-, 256-, or 512-byte sector size. The default is 128 bytes.

Files tells VDISK how big to make the RAM drive's root directory. Values can range from 2 to 512; 64 is the default. (The root directory on any drive is limited in the number of files it can hold. Subdirectories, however, can hold as many files as will fit on the drive.)

The */E:m* and */X:m* options are used with DOS 4.0 to place the RAM disk in extended and expanded memory, respectively. (DOS 3.3 has only the /E switch.) The *m* option specifies the number of sectors VDISK will transfer at a time from the RAM drive to Conventional DOS memory. Values for *m* range from 1 to 8; 8 is the default.

The drive letter assigned to the RAM drive is dependent on the highest drive available in your system. For example, if the highest drive you have is drive C, then the RAM drive is drive D.

After entering the proper VDISK.SYS line in your CONFIG.SYS file, all you have to do is reboot the computer. For example, if you enter C:\DOS\VDISK.SYS, a 64K RAM drive is set up, with 128-byte sectors and room for 64 files in the root directory (VDISK's defaults).

This RAM drive occupies Conventional DOS memory. If you have memory to spare, that's fine. Otherwise, you can create a 1Mb RAM drive in expanded memory by entering the following:

DEVICE = C:\DOS\VDISK 1024 512 128 /X

If you have a 286 or 386 with extended memory, enter the following to create a 1Mb RAM disk in extended memory:

DEVICE = C:\DOS\VDISK 1024 512 128 /E

When you reboot, you'll see a message similar to the following:

VDISK Version 3.30 virtual disk F:
Buffer size:	1024 KB
Sector size:	512
Directory entries:	128
Transfer size:	8

This example was produced on a 386 system with extended memory and a hard drive partitioned to logical drives C, D, and E. The 1Mb RAM drive was given the letter F.

A 1Mb RAM drive is fine, providing you have extended or expanded memory to spare. If you have more than enough memory, consider creating a larger drive.

Using a RAM Disk

Most books tell you how to set up a RAM drive, but they don't tell you how to exploit the drive to get the most from your system. The best way to get the full benefit from a RAM drive is to place commonly accessed files there. If, for example, you're going to be sorting a database that has 10,000 records, copy it to the RAM drive first, then do your sort. Since the RAM drive is not an actual physical drive, it can be accessed very quickly and does not suffer the wear and tear that a hard drive does. When you're done, remember to copy the sorted records back to the hard drive.

Any application that accesses information from disk can benefit from a RAM drive. A word processor's spelling checker is a prime example. As part of your AUTOEXEC.BAT file, you can copy your word processor's spelling dictionary files to the RAM drive, or you can copy the files in any batch file that runs your word processor. Then set up your word processor so that it knows to look for these files on the RAM drive. The speed of the spelling checker will be greatly increased.

The secret to boosting speed with a RAM drive is to copy into it the application files that you access most often. As long as you're only copying data files and not saving any new information to the RAM drive, you won't be in danger of losing information if there is a power loss.

Disk Caches

Disk caches are buffers—storage places in memory—for all information read from disk. The program that controls the cache also monitors all disk activity. If any information to be read from disk is already stored in the cache memory, then it's read from the cache instead. This greatly speeds up all disk operations (about 60 percent of all disk activity is the repetitive reading of information). A disk cache has few disadvantages other than taking up memory. Unlike the RAM disk, since the cache only stores information already on disk, nothing is lost when the power goes out.

Printer Spoolers

The *printer spooler* is used to speed up the slowest part of your PC system—the printer. The spooler's job is to intercept all characters that are normally sent to the printer. It stores the characters in memory or on a file on disk. Then, every so often, the spooler sends a few characters to the printer. It does this while you're using the computer for something else so that printing doesn't slow you down. The advantage is that your computer doesn't have to wait for the printer.

There are few disadvantages, but the lack of decent spooling software keeps most people from using a spooler. (Refer to Chapter 12 for more information.)

Memory Control Programs

After you install extra memory in your PC, the best way to put it to work is by using a memory control program. These programs make the best use of your PC's memory, allocating memory in such a way that you'll have the maximum available RAM for running your applications.

Before going into the details, note that memory control programs work best when both the following conditions are met:

- Your PC has lots of EMS memory available.
- Your EMS memory is LIM 4.0-compatible.

Memory control programs are true miracle workers. What they do can be summarized as follows:

- They fill out your Conventional DOS memory.
- They fill in High DOS memory.
- They move device drivers and TSRs (Terminate and Stay Resident programs) to High DOS memory.
- They allow for program switching and multitasking.
- They control all memory in the PC.

These may seem like alien concepts to you. But they've become slowly accepted as ways of boosting DOS's performance and skirting the 640K memory barrier. By using these memory management tools, you can give DOS the power and abilities of advanced (and expensive) operating systems of the future.

Using High DOS Memory

High DOS memory is memory between the 640K DOS limit and the top of DOS memory, 1024K. It includes video memory, video

ROM, hard-disk ROM, and your PC's ROM (the BIOS). But there are also lots of little "holes" in this area.

If you look at a PC's true memory-usage map (see Chapter 5), you'll find a lot of unused space in High DOS memory. This space can be addressed as RAM, but normally no RAM is put there. Why? Because DOS has no way to access it.

Memory control programs allow you to access High DOS memory as RAM. Because LIM 4.0 memory can be mapped to any location in the PC—and in any size—it's possible to remap High DOS memory and fill in the nooks and crannies with usable RAM. The RAM is monitored, used, and controlled by the memory control software.

Once you have usable RAM in High DOS memory, what can you do with it? A 4K sliver of RAM between your VGA ROM and hard-disk controller's ROM isn't going to do you any good. Or will it?

Memory control programs can load certain types of programs and drivers into High DOS memory. A device driver can really go anywhere in DOS's 1Mb of address space. Normally, CONFIG.SYS loads drivers into low areas of memory as you boot your PC. But memory control programs load these device drivers into areas of High DOS memory. For example, your ANSI.SYS, MOUSE.SYS, or network device driver can probably fit somewhere in High DOS memory. You don't need to worry about the exact location—the memory control software figures that out for you.

For example, consider the following entries in the CONFIG-.SYS file:

```
DEVICE = C:\SYSTEM\DV\QEMM.SYS RAM EXTMEM = 1024
BUFFERS = 20
FILES = 30
DEVICE = C:\SYSTEM\DV\LOADHI.SYS C:\SYSTEM\DOS\ANSI.SYS
DEVICE = C:\SYSTEM\DV\LOADHI.SYS C:\SYSTEM\MOUSE\MOUSE.SYS
DEVICE = C:\SYSTEM\DV\LOADHI.SYS C:\SYSTEM\DOS\VDISK.SYS 1024 /E
```

The first line loads Quarterdeck's QEMM, a 386 memory management program. QEMM powerfully manages and controls the 386's memory, turning extended memory into LIM 4.0-compatible expanded memory and offering VCPI control. (VCPI is covered later.)

One of QEMM's optional switches, RAM, causes the 386 to fill High DOS memory with RAM so that device drivers can be relocated there. Another switch, EXTMEM = 1024, sets aside 1Mb of 386 memory as extended memory (for VDISK). The rest of RAM is converted to expanded memory by QEMM.

The LOADHI.SYS programs (the final three lines in CONFIG.SYS) are used to relocate device drivers in High DOS memory. The format specifies the LOADHI.SYS DOS device after CONFIG.SYS's DEVICE command. In the example, three device drivers—ANSI.SYS, the mouse driver, and VDISK for a RAM disk—are located in High DOS memory. This configuration saves some 40K of Conventional DOS memory and opens the door for other applications to use the freed-up memory.

Whether a device driver is in High DOS memory or Conventional DOS memory, it still works the same way. But the benefit of relocating a device driver in High DOS memory is that it leaves you more of the basic 640K to run your applications.

Memory control programs can also relocate DOS's FILES and BUFFERS, as well as memory-resident and TSR programs (such as SideKick). All of these can be placed in unused portions of High DOS memory—even in expanded memory if they're compatible. By using these programs, you'll have much more of the basic 640K of RAM available for running applications.

Multitasking and Program Swapping

Multitasking and program swapping allow you to use more than one program at a time on your PC. This may sound kind of dumb. After all, you only have one head and one set of hands. So why would you want to run more than one program at a time?

The answer is that quite a few programs require little direct input to do their work. When you're backing up files, downloading information from an online network, printing long documents, or sorting a list in a database, you're just sitting there. The program doesn't require your attention. At times like these, you could be working on a second program, *concurrently* with the operation of the first.

Multitasking is the ability of a computer to do more than one thing at a time. Two or more things aren't actually being done by the PC at once. After all, like you, the computer only has one brain (the microprocessor). But the computer is able to switch quickly between two or more activities, giving the illusion that it's doing more than one thing at a time.

Program switching (or swapping) works similarly to multitasking. The difference is that programs you're not currently working on don't continue to run. In a multitasking situation, when you switch from one application to another, the first application continues to run in the background. When you use a program switcher, the operation of the first application is suspended, and only the program on which you're currently working continues to run.

There is PC software available for both multitasking and program switching: DESQview, Windows, Software Carousel, and Switch-It, to name just a few. But to really make these applications hum, you need a good memory control program. (Some multitaskers and program switchers come with their own memory control program.)

The memory control programs quickly swap programs in and out of Conventional DOS memory. Remember, programs can only run in Conventional DOS memory. So when a program isn't running, it's swapped out to EMS memory. Since LIM 4.0 allows for large chunks of memory to be swapped, this makes fast program switching and multitasking possible.

The VCPI Specification

In addition to its high speed and outstanding memory-management abilities, the 80836 microprocessor has the ability to emulate an 8086, the original microprocessor around which the first IBM PC was built. The 80286 has the same ability, which is why we can run DOS on both those systems. But the 8086 mode is not the native operating mode for either chip. When a 286 or 386 works like an 8086, it's said to be running in the *real* mode. The native mode of either chip is the *protected* mode, where extended memory is used.

In addition to having real mode like the 286, the 386 also has a virtual 86, or V86, mode. In that mode it operates just like an 8086 computer. But there's a bonus: The 386 runs dozens of V86 modes. With the proper software, you can have the equivalent of dozens of V86 machines inside a single 386 computer. It's like having several PC/XTs all running at the same time inside a single 80386.

To take advantage of the 386's V86 mode, you need memory control software, plus V86 control software. The V86 software manages all the V86 modes inside a 386, converts extended memory into expanded memory for use by DOS, and does all the memory management tricks covered so far in this chapter.

To organize memory management in the 386 PC, a standard was adopted: The Virtual Control Program Interface (VCPI). It was co-developed by Phar Lap Software and Quarterdeck Office Systems. VCPI lays down rules and regulations for the use of extended memory in a 386, management of the V86 modes, and control of how the computer operates. It specifies how DOS extenders, memory managers, and operating systems communicate. Fortunately, the VCPI is widely accepted and provides a way to prevent 386 memory management chaos.

A VCPI-compatible program can run in a 386 PC without crashing the system. For example, an extended DOS application can use extended memory and the 386's protected mode under DOS. While it's doing that, another program can run in V86 mode. Still another program can manage memory, device drivers, and TSRs under DOS. As long as all these applications adhere to the VCPI specification, your computer will run efficiently, and you'll be able to get a lot of work done.

Remember that VCPI isn't a program you can buy; it's a standard for memory management inside the 386 computer. Though it's not something you can look for on the side of a software box, you should know that it exists. If possible, try to request VCPI-compatible software to keep your 386 system running at top speed and efficiency.

Buying Memory Control Software

Memory control software is a relatively new development in DOS computing. If you have a PC/XT or 286 system, you can try Quarterdeck's QRAM (pronounced "cram") or Qualitas's MOVE'EM. If you have a 386 system, try Quarterdeck's QEMM or Qualitas's 386MAX.

These packages are also discussed in Chapter 5. Note that both QEMM and 386MAX are VCPI-compatible control programs for 386

PCs. All four applications give you basic memory management, freeing up more of your basic 640K for DOS programs. If memory in your PC is tight, you should definitely check them out.

Summary

Computer users care about how fast they get their work done. There are ways to speed up a computer's operation on both the hardware and software sides.

On the hardware side, there are many things you can do to make your PC faster and more efficient. First, you can buy a faster, larger-capacity hard drive. Faster hard drives are a boon to disk-intensive operations, especially managing databases. Second, you can add more memory to your PC. Third, you can install a math coprocessor. Though a coprocessor won't speed up everything, it will make those programs that support it work faster. Finally, you can add an accelerator card or replace your PC's microprocessor with a faster or next-generation chip.

On the software side, the way to squeeze more power from your system is to exploit what you already have. You can use memory management software to relocate device drivers and memory-resident programs in High DOS memory, and use disk caches, RAM disks, and printer spoolers.

All these techniques help give you a faster, more powerful PC. In fact, some of the memory management techniques enable you to do things under DOS on your PC that are only possible on some of the advanced, high-priced operating systems.

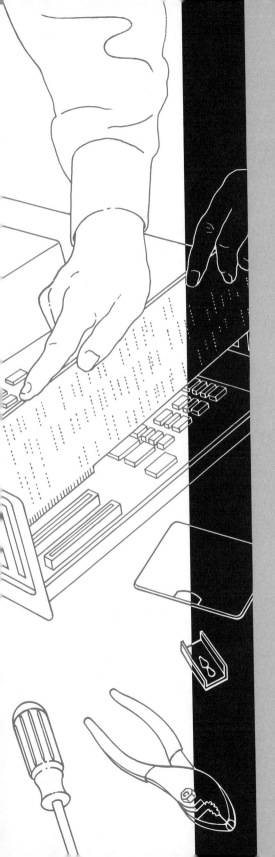

14

**Troubleshooting
and Maintaining
Your PC**

EVERYTHING'S GOING ALONG JUST FINE WHEN ALL OF A sudden—poof! Something's gone wrong. That's the way trouble happens in a PC. The last time you turned the system off it was working just fine. Then something happened while the PC was asleep. Now it doesn't work the same. What could it be? Gremlins? The phase of the moon? Little kids with peanut butter?

Keeping a PC in top-notch condition requires some effort on your part. It requires being able to recognize what causes problems and knowing how to fix them. A lot of that knowledge comes from performing upgrades and getting a feel for the inside of the machine. As you've discovered while reading this book and doing the various upgrades, no two PCs are alike—not even the generic varieties. Being able to troubleshoot your own system depends greatly on your familiarity with it.

But more important than troubleshooting is preventing the problems before they surface. On a PC this involves fairly routine operations. Unfortunately, not everything that can go wrong with a computer can be explained in a few sentences. But any problem can be narrowed down and evaluated, which helps you to find a solution.

This chapter focuses on testing out equipment after you buy it, identifying the sources of problems and possible solutions, and maintaining your PC. Additional information on each specific area of the computer can be found in the chapter relating to that area.

 ## Testing Equipment

One of the best troubleshooting techniques is to use the equipment you have upgraded at a level above and beyond normal, routine usage. The object is to break in the new equipment.

Electronic parts are very reliable and will last for years if you treat them right. But occasionally a lemon will surface. Not every RAM chip will be good off the assembly line. You want to find the bad part quickly, before it fails later on down the road when you really need it.

All PCs and PC components come with a warranty. The warranty usually states that if anything goes wrong within a given duration after the date of purchase, the developer (or dealer) will fix or replace the part for free or for a nominal charge.

Some warranties are more liberal than others. The typical warranty on a PC is 90 days. Some national brands give a one-year warranty. When IBM announced the PS/2, they were going to offer an unprecedented five-year warranty. The reason was that the parts were just that much better in a PS/2. But IBM failed to push their five-year warranty through the dealers, because dealers make a lot of money on service contracts.

A service contract is an extension of the basic warranty. It's also a rip-off (not just from IBM, either), unless you have a lot of PCs. Sure, you may feel better paying up to $500 a year to have your dealer come out and repair the computer—whether or not it breaks. But PCs just don't break that often after the warranty period. If one does break, chances are that the part that needs replacing costs less than the service contract.

Buying a service contract or an extended warranty is really up to you. But if you test the warranty as part of your basic maintenance, you probably will never need to waste your money on a service contract.

To test the warranty, you try to make the PC fail during its first two weeks of use. The odds are fairly good that any defective part inside the computer will fail within the first two weeks of activity.

Most national-brand PCs come with diagnostic disks. These contain programs that evaluate your system and report back to you on its condition. No-name clones and some national brands don't come with a diagnostic disk, but you can order the disks from third-party sources, which often provide better testing and results than the national brands.

When you first buy a computer, or when you upgrade it, run your diagnostics. If there are overnight tests, run them. (Some tests destroy data, such as information stored on a hard drive or on a RAM disk, so be careful.) Always run these tests before you begin serious use of the PC or the upgraded part.

Even if you're not using your computer that often, leave it turned on to keep the juice flowing through all the circuits. Once a day, turn the system off and then on again to check the power supply. At night, turn off the monitor—or better still, invest in a screen-dimming program.

After two weeks, stop torturing the computer. If it was going to fail, it will probably have done so by now. A flaky RAM chip or suspect hard drive will have already shown signs of stress under the two-week torture test. Odds are fairly good that you'll see anything questionable by the second day.

After two weeks, use the computer as you normally would. The parts inside are reliable and will probably last you through the warranty period and beyond.

Not all PC warranties cover items you can upgrade yourself. Although the new item you've purchased may be covered, installing it in your PC does not include it in the PC's service contract. In fact, a do-it-yourself upgrade may void a warranty or service contract. (In the old days, TRS-80 owners sat out the full 90 days of the warranty before they began modifying their computers.) In these situations, it's best to ask. Of course, if you have a service contract, you probably don't want to do your own upgrade anyway. Let the dealer do it instead—you're paying for it.

Using the POST to Diagnose Problems

That boring memory test, the pause your PC makes each time it boots, is important. It's the POST, your computer's Power-On Self-Test. An error message from the POST is one of the first clues you'll have that something is amiss in the PC. (See Appendix A for a complete list of POST error codes and their meanings.)

The POST isn't the be-all and end-all in error-checking diagnostics. Although this book does provide a list of error codes, not every PC follows them. Some PCs are quite verbose, giving error messages in English that tell you exactly what's wrong. Other PCs just sound a few beeps. Whichever is the case, the POST will be your first clue that something isn't working right inside your PC.

How you evaluate POST error messages depends on your PC. Some POST errors can be expected; when you upgrade RAM, you'll get a POST error telling you to run the setup program to adjust the total RAM amount. (If you have a PC/XT-level system, you'll get a POST error if you set your DIP switches incorrectly.) It's the unexpected POST errors that throw you.

After you get a POST error, write it down. If you've just upgraded something, then either recheck the upgrade or check your system's setup program (which is probably what needs to be done anyway). Once that's done, power down the system and turn it on again. If you get the error message again, you should go over the checklist in the next section to make sure everything in the PC is working properly.

Sometimes the failure of unrelated items will throw you—for example, the failure of your AT's battery at the same time that you do a RAM upgrade. Or you may have unplugged your video adapter to install a hard drive and then forgotten to reinstall it before you powered on the PC. These are common mistakes.

A Troubleshooting Checklist

When you get a POST error or something doesn't work as it should, remind yourself that whatever error occurred isn't your fault. Then check through the items listed in the next two sections. (Some of these problems do not lead to POST errors.)

External Components

If nothing happens when you turn on your PC or a part is not functioning properly, check the following external items on your PC:

The Power Cable

Is the computer plugged in? Is the cord plugged into both the wall and the PC? It's funny how many people will remember to plug the cord into the wall socket or power strip, but forget to stick the other end into the PC.

The Power Switch

Is the power switch turned on? Some people run their PCs from power strips or devices that have master switches. If you were extra careful and turned off the master switch in addition to the PC's power switch, recheck the PC's power switch.

Missing Pieces

Always check for missing components, such as cables. (A POST error code will help you identify the missing piece.)

The Monitor

Monitors are often a source of problems, but the solutions are usually quite simple. The biggest problem is a blank screen. There are three items you can check to make sure your monitor is working properly.

Cables　Is the monitor plugged in? Is it turned on? Are all the cables properly connected? Note that there may be several port-size monitor connectors on the back of your PC. Make sure you've connected the proper one.

Screen Brightness　Turning down the brightness on a monitor is a good way to save the picture tube from the effects of phosphor burn-in (in which an image is permanently etched on the screen). Check the brightness before you assume the monitor is broken. (Sometimes a screen-saving program takes over and dims the monitor—usually a tap on one of the keys brings the image back.)

DIP Switches and the Setup Program　Check to make sure your system's DIP switches (on the display adapter card as well) or setup program is properly configured for your type of monitor. Some older PC/XT systems have to be set for "no monitor" if you're using an EGA or a VGA display.

If you're lucky you can hear the monitor and tell if it's working. A monitor makes a high-pitched humming sound.

Internal Components

After your external inspection, look over the following items found inside your PC:

DIP Switches and Jumpers

Did you set DIP switches and jumpers properly? Were any accidentally set or reset? Refer to the installation manual to make sure all the switches are set properly for your PC's configuration. (A POST error code may alert you to the problem.)

Cables and Connectors

Sometimes cables get pulled from drives or expansion cards when you replace the PC's lid. Sometimes you'll forget to reattach a cable after an upgrade (this is very common). Check all the computer's cables and connectors, even if they're nowhere near the item you upgraded.

Floppy Drives

Floppy drives fail because they have moving parts. They can also get knocked out of alignment through everyday use. Since the front of the floppy drive is open, it's used as a vent by the power supply's fan to suck in air—which contains dust and debris that can accumulate inside a floppy drive and gum up the read/write heads.

A floppy-drive failure isn't the end of the world. If a drive is out of alignment, you'll know because it will not be able to read disks formatted on another drive, such as a new program, a disk formatted at the office, or a disk from your second drive. It will, however, probably be able to read disks that were formatted by that drive.

To fix an alignment problem, you should take the PC to a professional. A tiny screw has to be adjusted inside the floppy drive, and an oscilloscope test has to be run to make sure the drive is properly aligned.

For any other kind of floppy failure, the best remedy is usually replacement. This enables you to buy a new drive that has a higher capacity than your old one. The cost of a new floppy drive is way below the cost of a service contract. Note that if your only floppy drive breaks, you'll have no way to back up the hard drive before you replace the floppy drive.

If all your disks cause disk errors, then the problem is probably in the drive you upgraded. Some disks, when formatted to an unusual capacity, will produce errors on some drives. To fix the problem, bulk-erase the disk.

Don't forget that disks only live for so long. Blaming a drive when you have a bad disk is a common mistake.

If you use a disk every day, then you should constantly back it up. Use DOS's DISKCOPY command to make an exact duplicate of that disk. A disk used every day will last about three months. I've fielded questions on radio talk shows from callers who wonder why the same disk they've been using for three years doesn't work anymore. (Many utility packages can rehabilitate bad floppy disks by marking questionable sectors as bad and relocating data to healthy areas of the disk.)

Also, buying a box of low-capacity disks and formatting them in a high-capacity drive is asking for errors, unless you use the FORMAT command to format the disks at low capacity.

Hard Drives

Hard drives fail after several years of use. Over time, the bearings wear out (the drive will make noise as it spins), and sometimes they just stop working altogether. When that happens, you have to replace the drive. (And you'd better have a recent backup of the drive's contents handy.)

Sometimes, all you need to do to "repair" a bad hard drive is to reformat it, because suspect sectors and read/write and seek errors accumulate on some drives. Follow these steps (or refer to the instructions in Chapter 8):

1. Back up the hard drive (if possible).

2. Use your drive's low-level formatting routine (or use DEBUG).

3. FDISK the drive.

4. Reboot the computer.

5. Perform a high-level format by using DOS's FORMAT command on each of the drive's partitions.

You should also check the drive's interleave factor.

Some hard-disk-analyzing software claims to magically fix all these problems. The best way to cure some problems is to perform a low-level format of the drive, which is precisely what this kind of software does.

Before you do a low-level format, back up the hard drive and follow the instructions for low-level formatting that came with the drive (or refer to Chapter 8).

If low-level formatting doesn't work, you can send your drive to a national outfit that fixes drives. I can't recommend any offhand, but they usually advertise in the more popular computer magazines.

Chips

Chips often wiggle out of their sockets. If you see a loose chip, ground yourself, then press down gently on the chip using your thumb or forefingers. (This is called *reseating* the chip.) Never reseat a chip when the power is turned on.

ROM

After you do an upgrade, your PC may suddenly become incompatible. It may not recognize VGA graphics. Your new hard drive may not boot. Or you may have gotten a deal on an old, original IBM PC, but find out it can only have 576K of RAM in it. To solve these problems, upgrade your ROM.

Most PCs are sold with fully compatible PC ROM that should work for the rest of DOS's lifetime. Some manufacturers make updates and improvements available.

The Battery

The battery that keeps the clock alive in a PC/XT and backs up the CMOS RAM in an AT system only lasts so long—usually, about four years. Before it fails, you may get a low-battery message (if your PC is smart enough). If you don't get the message, one day you'll turn on your computer, and it will say that you don't have a hard drive. (When the battery-backed-up RAM is gone, the hard-drive definition is lost.)

When the battery goes, you should replace it with the same model or one of the same size and type. The best source for batteries is the dealer from whom you bought the computer. Some mail-order houses also offer battery replacements.

The Power Supply

Power supplies die because there's a drain on the system, sometimes caused by surges or spikes.

If your power supply dies after you add 16Mb of RAM, two hard drives, and a tape backup unit, then you need a new power supply that puts out more watts. If the power supply dies because of power-line evils, you can replace it with a beefier model, but a better investment is a surge and spike protector.

If You're Still Having Problems

If you've checked all the system's components and need help, ask yourself the following questions before you contact the experts. You might find that going over these questions will help you narrow down the problem's location even further.

Is the Problem Consistent?

When does the problem happen? Can you repeat the error? For example, does your hard drive only come online after the PC has warmed up for five minutes, or is the behavior more erratic? Does the modem always go offline when someone else in the house picks up the phone? Does the error occur only after running a specific piece of software?

Has the Problem Only Occurred Since You Upgraded?

Did you start getting odd-looking characters on the screen after you installed a mouse card? Did the printer stop working after you installed a new video card?

Is the Problem Related to Hardware or Software?

Remember that the upgrading of hardware requires a change in your software. If some program no longer works after an upgrade, you might want to reinstall it. Or maybe you need to install a device driver in CONFIG.SYS to make the new hardware work. Sometimes when you're in a rush to play with some new toy, you forget to do these kinds of things.

Have You Traced All Your Steps?

You should trace all the steps up to the point you encountered the failure. This will help you immensely in narrowing down the problem.

First, start with the power supply, then the motherboard and the disk drives. Next, think about external components: the keyboard, monitor, and printer. Finally, consider your software.

If the glitch happens between the keyboard and the computer, then the problem may be with the keyboard. They do fail and can easily be replaced. (It may be unplugged.)

 ## Troubleshooting Your Printer

Troubleshooting a printer can get quite involved. But most of the major problems are covered in the following sections.

Port Conflicts

Port conflicts occur when you have two or more printers hooked up to a PC, each of which you've assigned to the same printer port. A PC can have up to three printer ports, LPT1 through LPT3. Each time you install another printer port, you must make sure it doesn't conflict with an existing port. If there is a conflict—say you have two LPT1s in your computer—then the end result is no LPT1. Since DOS can't arbitrarily decide which is the real printer, it gives you no printer.

To prevent port conflicts, keep track of your PC's printer ports. Most people only use one printer, which they hook up to LPT1. A second printer—for example, a printer for printing labels, envelopes, or checks—could be an LPT2. Most applications allow you to install a printer as a device other than LPT1.

Printer Diagnostics

Every printer has built-in diagnostics. On a primitive level, these will print characters in succession until you turn off the printer's power. More advanced diagnostics will print complex graphics and ''dump'' their character sets. For example, some laser printers will cough up a sheet detailing their graphics prowess as well as their full complement of fonts. Check your printer's documentation to see how you run the diagnostics.

What you should look for in the diagnostics are completely formed characters (having a good ribbon helps). If you notice that a row of dots is missing, a pin is missing from the print head. Sometimes this pin is one of the crucial lower pins that print the descenders on characters. (Any letter that dips below the baseline of text is a descender; *Egypt* has three descenders: g, y, and p.)

Unwanted Double Spacing and Paper Travel

The problem of unwanted double spacing seems to happen a lot on some dot-matrix printers. The source of the problem is the setting of a single DIP switch that determines whether the printer supplies the line-feed character or whether the character is sent from the computer.

When the switch is set incorrectly, you'll either see all text printed on the same line or all text double-spaced. Dust off the printer manual, find out which DIP switch controls line feeds, then change the setting.

A similar but unrelated problem is paper travel. Sometimes the paper in your printer will shift to the right or left—you might notice that each page has text printed slightly lower than the page before. It means the paper isn't going through your printer properly.

To stop paper travel, you should buy a tractor- or pin-feed mechanism for the printer and use standard, fanfold printer paper. There is also a paper pressure bar inside the printer, usually next to the platen on the left side. Some bars are marked with a tiny plus and minus. Adjust the bar to the plus side, which increases the platen's pressure on the paper.

Pc Maintenance Tips

There are many things you can do to keep your computer running well; most of them are common sense. The first rule of PC maintenance is to keep food, drinks, and smoke away from the PC.

Drinking and computing don't mix. Spilling a coke into a keyboard is a common mistake. If you turn off the PC right away, the keyboard will probably dry up and continue to work. But it will be sticky. If you want to clean it out, pop off the key caps and apply some cleaning solution to the keyboard by using a cotton swab.

Using Head-Cleaning Disks

Magnetic oxide can rub off a floppy disk and build up on your drive's read/write head. Dust, and especially cigarette smoke, can also accumulate there. A quick and easy way to remove the buildup is to use a head-cleaning disk. Sometimes this brings a dead drive back to life.

Some say, however, that only professionals should clean disk drives. After all, floppy drives are delicate mechanisms. An abrasive scrubbing by a head-cleaning disk can sometimes do more damage than good.

The danger comes when people treat the disks as if they were magical: "My drive is acting flaky—I think I'll use the head-cleaning disk." This is a bad approach. If you feel you must use a cleaning disk, then do it once a year at most. Otherwise, always have your floppy drives professionally serviced.

Checking for Cracked Solder

A major cause of component failure in a computer is cracked solder. This is due to the heat changes in a PC. If you start a PC on a cold morning and run it all day, it gets hot. When you turn it off, it cools. Doing the same thing five days a week causes the solder to crack over time, which causes whatever the solder is holding to fail.

There's nothing you can do about cracked solder, unless you're a pro with a soldering iron. My advice is to back up the hard drive and take the computer into the shop to have a professional deal with it. Be sure to tell them where the cracked solder is located.

Cleaning the Keyboard

To clean the keyboard, you can pop off all the key caps (be careful not to break the mechanism underneath) and then blow the dirt out of the keyboard with a can of compressed air. You can also buy one of those tiny, expensive keyboard vacuums. A better solution is to use your standard vacuum with the upholstery-cleaning end fitted to the tube. Tape a drinking straw around the end with duct tape. Then you can clean the keyboard using your vacuum cleaner and the straw.

Ventilating Your Computer

One of the PC's worst enemies is heat buildup. That's why the power supply has a built-in fan—one of its jobs is to circulate air through the PC. You can help by positioning the PC in an open area. Don't obstruct the vents on the front of the system unit, and keep the back of the PC's exhaust fan a good five inches away from the wall.

Moving Your Computer

Before you move your computer (across the room or across the country), you should take these precautions:

1. Back up the hard drive (if possible).

2. Park the hard drive (see Chapter 8).

3. Insert cardboard floppies or old disks in the floppy drives.

Parking the hard drive prevents damage if you drop or bump the computer in transit. Inserting cardboard or old disks in floppy drives keeps their heads from banging together.

Maintaining Your Printer

The kinds of maintenance you'll need to perform on your printer are dependent on what kind of printer you have. Consult your printer manual for specific tips.

Replacing the Ribbon

The only routine maintenance you'll need to perform on your printer is the replacement of the ribbon (if it has one). This sounds trivial, but too many people let the ribbon deteriorate for no good reason. Ribbons are too cheap ($10 at most) not to have a fresh one on hand.

Printers with 24 pins require a ribbon that contains a special lubricant for the print head. Without that type of ribbon, you could be causing excess wear on the print head.

Dot-matrix printers need all the help they can get. A fresh ribbon in a dot-matrix printer really does a lot for the output. As the ribbon gets older, the characters regain their "dottiness."

Recharging Toner

A toner cartridge is a black box you insert in your laser printer that contains the toner that's used to create the image on paper. The toner is transferred to a drum, depending on how the printer's laser beam has charged the drum. The toner is then transferred to the sheet of paper.

Toner cartridges run out after a few thousand sheets of paper. If you print a lot of graphics, especially dark graphics, the toner won't last as long. Fortunately, most laser printers are smart enough to recognize when they are low on toner and alert you.

When the toner gets low, you can remove the toner cartridge and rock it from side to side (shortways, not from end to end). This gives you about 20 more sheets before the "Toner Low" warning light comes on again. Then you need to either replace the toner cartridge or recharge it.

Toner recharging is a popular business, thanks to the low prices, high quality, and popularity of laser printers. An outfit will take your old cartridge and repack it with fresh toner. Included in the price is the cost of lubrication and maintenance of the toner cartridge. The cost (about $50) is less than half that of a new cartridge.

You can only recharge a toner cartridge so often—maybe once or twice, but that's it. The better recharging outfits tag older cartridges so you won't make the mistake of resubmitting one too often.

Keep in mind that recharging your toner cartridge tends to shorten the life of your laser printer.

Cleaning Your Printer

Since printers use ink and toner, they get grungy before anything else in your PC. Even your fingers will get inky after you change a ribbon. To prevent this, you can wear plastic gloves while changing ribbons.

Paper particles and dust accumulate in a printer very rapidly. You can pick up some of the dust with a keyboard vacuum and blow away the rest of it with a can of compressed air.

The worst mess happens when people attempt to put gummy labels through a printer. Most of the time, the labels advance and are printed on just like paper. But sometimes they peel off. This wouldn't be a problem, except that people try to wind the labels back through the printer. This peels the labels off the paper and onto either the platen or some dark crevasse inside the printer.

To remove gummy labels from the printer, you have to remove the platen. To do this, unplug the printer, unscrew its case, and remove the printer's lid. (You may have to detach the platen knob first.)

The platen is usually removed by releasing clips on either side. It should just pop right out. (Consult your printer's manual if you have any difficulty.) You can then get at the labels with your fingers, needle-nose pliers, or tweezers.

While the platen is free, you can clean it. Some typewriter stores sell cleaning solution to rub on the platen, but I usually use rubbing alcohol. Put it on a paper towel, and clean off the surface of the platen. Then reassemble the printer, and you're ready to go.

 Software and Maintaining Your PC

Why is it when something goes wrong on a computer, people always blame themselves. And the problem may not be in the hardware but in the software. No one stops to think that the software may not be working because it just can't do the job.

Not all computer software is perfect. Some commands are described one way in the manual and behave differently on the screen. Sometimes keys that you think would function logically aren't "hooked up" internally in the software. And some software will crash and burn if it's not tested properly.

If you have problems with your software, you have a number of choices. The first is to call the developer's support line. You paid for the support when you bought the software, so you might as well use it. Don't let the developer shuffle you off to the dealer—return the software and get your money back. Buy something else that works.

Support is also offered by local organizations known as computer user groups. They usually have meetings where computer owners can get together and offer each other advice. Listings of user groups are often provided by local computer dealers, computer magazines, and newspapers.

Summary

There are several things you can do to keep your PC happy, healthy, and running. The first is to test any new equipment during the warranty period. This is most important, especially if it's something you may not use that often. Faulty electronic equipment generally breaks quite early in its life cycle.

To keep your PC in working order, you have to be able to identify problems when they occur. This means checking POST errors, running diagnostic tests, and tracking down problems by following the PC's boot-up steps.

Finally, to keep your PC free of trouble, there are various things you can do as far as maintenance is concerned. Keep food, drinks, and smoke away from the computer, vacuum your keyboard and printer every once in a while, and use disk head cleaners sparingly, if at all.

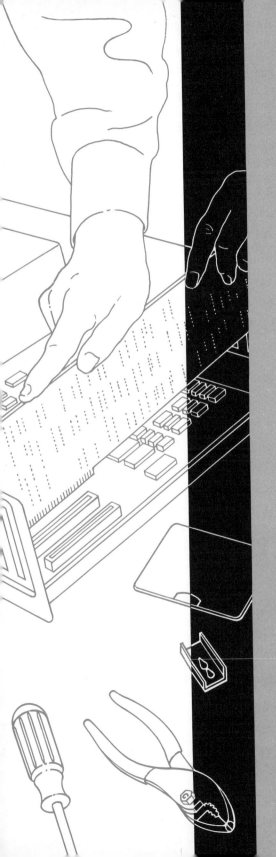

A

POST Error Codes

THE FOLLOWING LIST OF DIAGNOSTIC ERROR CODES HAS been compiled from a number of sources. There is no indication as to which types of PCs produce these errors or whether your own computer will produce them at all. Most are standard Power-On Self-Test errors on the PC/XT, PC/AT, and PS/2 systems. (Refer to Chapter 14 if you need further assistance in tracking down a problem.) The POST does not always report on these errors in such detail. To get some of these error numbers, you may have to run the tests that come on a diagnostic disk.

Code	Description
101	Main system board failure
102	PC/XT ROM BIOS checksum error
103	PC/XT BASIC ROM checksum error
104	PC/XT interrupt controller error
105	PC/XT timer error
106	Main system board error
107	Main system board, math coprocessor, or adapter card error
108	Main system board error
109	Direct Memory Access (DMA) test error
121	Unexpected hardware interrupts occurred
131	IBM PC-1 cassette wrap test failed
151	Battery-backed-up RAM or clock error
152	Main system board error
161	Battery/CMOS power error
162	Battery-backed-up RAM checksum error
163	Invalid date and time
164	Memory size incorrect (after adding extended memory)
165	PS/2 system options not set

166	MicroChannel adapter timeout
199	User-indicated configuration incorrect
201	Memory test failed
202	Memory error (address lines 0 to 15)
203	Memory error (address lines 16 to 23)
301	Keyboard software reset failure or stuck key
302	User-indicated error from the keyboard test
303	Keyboard error
304	Keyboard error
305	PS/2 keyboard fuse
365	Bad keyboard
366	Bad keyboard cable
367	Enhancement card or cable bad
401	Monochrome memory test, horizontal sync frequency test, or video test failed
408	User-indicated display attribute failure
416	User-indicated character set failure
424	User-indicated 80 × 25 display mode failure
432	Parallel port test failed
501	Color memory test, horizontal sync frequency test, or video test failed
508	User-indicated display attribute failure
516	User-indicated character set failure
524	User-indicated 80 × 25 display mode failure
532	User-indicated 40 × 25 display mode failure
540	User-indicated 320 × 200 graphics mode failure
548	User-indicated 640 × 200 graphics mode failure
556	Light-pen test failure

564	Screen-paging test failure
601	Disk power-on diagnostics test failed
602	Disk test failed
603	Disk size error
606	Disk verify function failed
607	Write-protected disk error
608	Bad command—disk status returned
610	Disk initialization failed
611	Timeout—disk status returned
612	Bad adapter card—disk status returned
613	Bad Direct Memory Access (DMA)—disk status returned
614	DMA boundary error
621	Bad seek—disk status returned
622	Bad CRC (Cyclic Redundancy Check)—disk status returned
623	Record not found—disk status returned
624	Bad address mark—disk status returned
625	Bad adapter seek—disk status returned
626	Disk data-comparison error
627	Disk change-line error
628	Disk removed
701	Math coprocessor failure
901	Parallel printer adapter test failed
1001	Alternate printer adapter failure
1101	Asynchronous communications (ASC) adapter test failed
1110– 1157	Individual errors within the ASC adapter, as reported by the diagnostic disk

1201	Alternate ASC adapter test failed
1210–1257	Individual errors within the alternate ASC adapter
1301	Game control adapter test failed
1302	Joystick test failed
1401	Color printer test failed
1501	Synchronous data link control (SDLC) test failed
1510–1549	Individual errors within the SDLC, as reported by the diagnostic disk
1604	Display station emulation adapter (DSEA) or network error
1608	DSEA or network error
1624	DSEA test failed
1634	DSEA test failed
1644	DSEA test failed
1652	DSEA test failed
1654	DSEA test failed
1658	DSEA test failed
1662	Defective DSEA, or switches set wrong
1664	DSEA test failed
1668	Defective DSEA, or switches set wrong
1669	Older diagnostic disk error
1674	Older diagnostic disk error
1684	Invalid feature, switches set wrong, or DSEA error
1688	Invalid feature, switches set wrong, or DSEA error
1701	Hard drive not ready or adapter test failure
1702	Hard-drive timeout

1703	Hard-drive error
1704	Hard-drive controller error
1705	No record found
1706	Write fault
1707	Track 0 error
1708	Head select error
1709	Bad error checking and correction
1710	Read buffer overrun
1711	Bad address mark
1712	Bad address mark or undetermined error
1713	Data comparison error
1714	Drive not ready
1730	Hard-disk adapter failure
1731	Hard-disk adapter failure
1732	Hard-disk adapter failure
1780	Drive 0 fatal error
1781	Drive 1 fatal error
1782	Drive controller failure
1790	Drive 0 nonfatal error
1791	Drive 1 nonfatal error
1799	Time to buy a Macintosh
1801	Expansion unit failure
1810	Enable/Disable failure
1811	Extender-card wrap test failed (disabled)
1812	High-order address lines failure (disabled)
1813	Wait-state failure (disabled)
1814	Enable/Disable could not be set
1815	Wait-state failure (enabled)

1816	Extender-card wrap test failed (enabled)
1817	High-order address lines failure (enabled)
1818	Disable not functioning
1819	Wait request switch set incorrectly
1820	Receiver-card wrap test failure
1821	Receiver high-order address lines failure
2001	Bisynchronous communications (BSC) adapter failure
2010	8255 port A failure
2011	8255 port B failure
2012	8255 port C failure
2013	8253 timer 1 did not reach terminal count
2014	8253 timer 1 stuck on
2016	8253 timer 2 did not reach terminal count, or timer 2 stuck on
2017	8251 Data Set Ready failed to come on
2018	8251 Clear to Send not sensed
2019	8251 Data Set Ready stuck on
2020	8251 Clear to Send stuck on
2021	8251 hardware reset failed
2022	8251 software reset failed
2023	8251 software "error reset" failed
2024	8251 Transmit Ready did not come on
2025	8251 Receive Ready did not come on
2026	8251 could not force "overrun" error status
2027	Interrupt failure—no timer interrupt
2028	Interrupt failure—transmit, replace card or planar
2029	Interrupt failure—transmit, replace card

2030	Interrupt failure—receive, replace card or planar
2031	Interrupt failure—receive, replace card
2033	Ring Indicate stuck on
2034	Receive Clock stuck on
2035	Transmit Clock stuck on
2036	Test Indicate stuck on
2037	Ring Indicate stuck on
2038	Receive Clock not on
2039	Transmit Clock not on
2040	Test Indicate not on
2041	Data Set Ready not on
2042	Carrier Detect not on
2043	Clear to Send not on
2044	Data Set Ready stuck on
2045	Carrier Detect stuck on
2046	Clear to Send stuck on
2047	Unexpected transmit interrupt
2048	Unexpected receive interrupt
2049	Transmit data did not equal receive data
2050	8251 detected overrun error
2051	Lost Data Set Ready during data wrap
2052	Receive timeout during data wrap
2101	Alternate BSC adapter failure
2110–2152	Alternate BSC errors (same as 2010–2052)
2201	Cluster adapter failure
2401	Enhanced Graphics Adapter (EGA) error
2408	User-indicated display attribute failure

2416	User-indicated character set failure
2424	User-indicated 80 × 25 display mode failure
2432	User-indicated 40 × 25 display mode failure
2440	User-indicated 320 × 200 graphics mode failure
2448	User-indicated 460 × 200 graphics mode failure
2456	Light pen failure
2464	User-indicated screen-paging test failure
2501	Alternate Enhanced Graphics Adapter (EGA) test failure
2801	Emulation adapter failure
2901	Color/graphics printer test failure
3001	Local Area Network (LAN) adapter failure
3101	Alternate LAN adapter failure
3301	IBM compact printer test failure
3601	IEEE 488 adapter test failure
3602–3698	Various failures for the IEEE 488 adapter
3801	Data acquisition adapter failed
3810–3844	Various failures for the data acquisition adapter
3901	Professional Graphics Adapter (PGA) test failure
3902–3995	Various failures for the PGA
4801	Internal modem failure
4901	Alternate internal modem failure
7101	Voice communications adapter failure
7301	Disk-drive/adapter-test failure

7306	Change line error
7307	Drive error (disk is write-protected)
7308	Bad command
7310	Track 0 error
7311	Timeout; drive error
7312	Bad drive controller
7313	Bad Direct Memory Access (DMA)
7314	DMA boundary error
7315	Bad index
7316	Speed error
7321	Bad seek
7322	Bad Cyclic Redundancy Check (CRC)
7323	Record not found
7324	Bad address mark
7325	Bad controller seek
7401	Video Graphics Array (VGA) test failure
8501	Expanded memory adapter failure
8601	PS/2 mouse error
8602	PS/2 mouse error
8603	PS/2 mouse error/system board error
8901	Music feature card failure
10001	PS/2 multiprotocol adapter failure
10002–10056	Various diagnostic errors for the PS/2 multiprotocol adapter
10480	ESDI hard-drive 0 failure
10481	ESDI hard-drive 1 failure
10482	ESDI hard-drive controller failure

10483	ESDI hard-drive controller failure
10490	ESDI hard-drive 0 error
10491	ESDI hard-drive 1 error

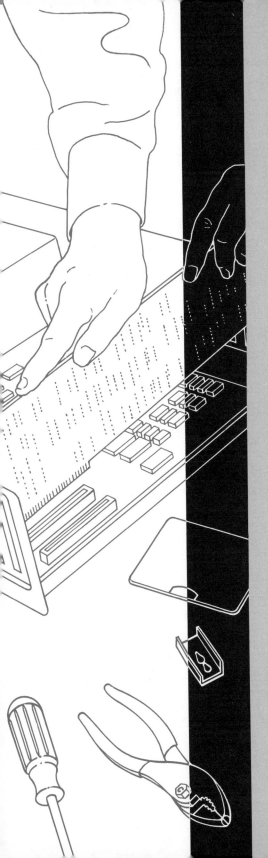

B

**Drive
Types**

AFTER INSTALLING A NEW HARD DRIVE IN AN AT-LEVEL system, you have to tell the computer's battery-backed-up RAM which type of hard drive it is. You have to identify the *drive type* and enter that value in your AT's setup program.

The drive type may be listed in the installation manual or on the drive itself. Some computer manufacturers supply their own lists of drive types. You can use the following table to select a drive type based on your drive's description.

Drive Type	Cylinders	Heads	Write Precomp	Landing Zone	Sectors	Mb
1	306	4	128	305	17	10
2	615	4	300	615	17	20
3	615	6	300	615	17	30
4	940	8	512	940	17	62
5	940	6	512	940	17	46
6	615	4	-1	615	17	20
7	462	8	256	511	17	30
8	733	5	-1	733	17	30
9	900	15	-1	901	17	112
10	820	3	-1	820	17	20
11	855	5	-1	855	17	35
12	855	7	-1	855	17	49
13	306	8	128	319	17	20
14	733	7	-1	733	17	42
15	---	-	---	---	--	--
16	612	4	0	663	17	20
17	977	5	300	977	17	40
18	977	7	-1	977	17	56
19	1024	7	512	1023	17	59
20	733	5	300	732	17	30
21	733	7	300	732	17	42
22	733	5	300	733	17	30

Drive Type	Cylinders	Heads	Write Precomp	Landing Zone	Sectors	Mb
23	306	4	0	336	17	10
24	830	10	-1	830	17	68
25	1024	9	-1	1024	17	76
26	918	7	-1	918	17	53
27	1024	8	-1	1024	17	68
28	918	7	-1	918	17	0
29	1024	4	-1	1024	17	34
30	820	6	-1	820	17	40
31	969	9	-1	969	34	144
32	615	8	-1	615	17	40
33	1024	5	-1	1024	17	42
34	1024	15	-1	1024	17	127
35	1024	15	-1	1024	26	195
36	1024	8	-1	1024	26	104
37	697	5	128	696	17	28
38	980	5	128	980	17	40
39	966	16	-1	966	17	128
40	809	6	128	852	17	40
41	1024	4	-1	1024	34	68
42	966	5	-1	966	34	80
43	966	9	-1	966	34	144
44	776	8	-1	776	33	100
45	925	9	-1	926	17	69
46	---	-	---	---	--	--
47	1024	5	-1	1024	35	87

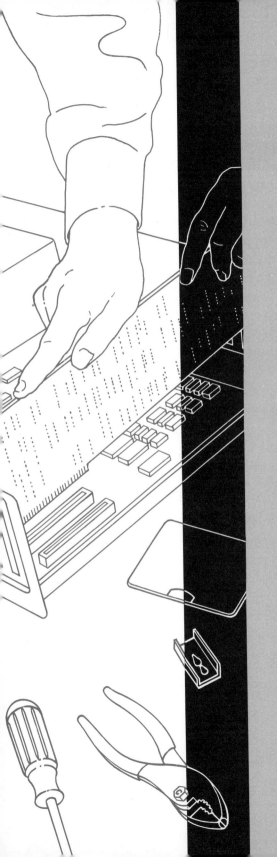

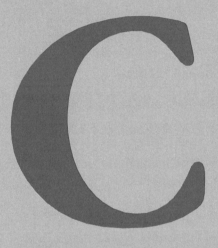

C

Product
Manufacturers

Above Software, Inc.
3 Hutton Centre, Suite 950
Santa Ana, CA 92707
(714) 545-1181

Above DISC memory manager

ALL Computers, Inc.
21 St. Clair Avenue East, #203
Toronto, Ontario M4T 1L9
Canada
(416) 960-0111

ALL ChargeCard memory manager

ATI Technologies, Inc.
3761 Victoria Park Avenue
Scarborough, Ontario M1W 3S2
Canada
(416) 756-0718

VGA Wonder video display adapter

Central Point Software, Inc.
15220 NW Greenbrier Parkway, #200
Beaverton, OR 97006
(503) 690-8090

COPY II PC option board

Cumulus Corporation
23500 Mercantile Road
Cleveland, OH 44122
(216) 464-2211

386SX expansion card

Merrill-Bryan Enterprises, Inc.
9770 Carroll Center Road, Suite C
San Diego, CA 92126
(619) 689-8611

Turbo EMS memory manager

Multisoft Corporation
15100 SW Koll Parkway, Suite L
Beaverton, OR 97006
(800) 283-6858
Super PC-Kwik disk-caching program

Orchid Technology
45365 Northport Loop West
Fremont, CA 94538
(415) 683-0300
Tiny Turbo accelerator card

Qualitas
7101 Wisconsin Avenue, Suite 1386
Bethesda, MD 20814
(301) 907-6700
MOVE'EM memory manager, 386MAX memory manager

Quarterdeck Office Systems
150 Pico Boulevard
Santa Monica, CA 90405
(213) 392-9851
QRAM memory optimizer, QEMM memory manager, DESQview
multitasker

SOTA Technology, Inc.
559 Weddell Drive
Sunnyvale, CA 94089
(408) 745-1111
SOTA POP memory manager

Index

Selections from
The SYBEX Library

HARDWARE

From Chips to Systems: An Introduction to Microcomputers (Second Edition)
Rodnay Zaks
Alexander Wolfe
580pp. Ref. 377-5

The best-selling introduction to microcomputer hardware—now fully updated, revised, and illustrated. Such recent advances as 32-bit processors and RISC architecture are introduced and explained for the first time in a beginning text.

Microprocessor Interfacing Techniques (Third Edition)
Austin Lesea
Rodnay Zaks
456pp. Ref. 029-6

This handbook is for engineers and hobbyists alike, covering every aspect of interfacing microprocessors with peripheral devices. Topics include assembling a CPU, basic I/O, analog circuitry, and bus standards.

The RS-232 Solution (Second Edition)
Joe Campbell
193pp. Ref. 488-7

For anyone wanting to use their computer's serial port, this complete how-to guide is updated and expanded for trouble-free RS-232-C interfacing from scratch. Solution shows you how to connect a variety of computers, printers, and modems, and it includes details for IBM PC AT, PS/2, and Macintosh.

NETWORKS

The ABC's of Local Area Networks
Michael Dortch
212pp. Ref. 664-2

This jargon-free introduction to LANs is fur current and prospective users who see general information, comparative options, a look at the future, and tips for effective LANs use today. With comparisons of Token-Ring, PC Network, Novell, and others.

The ABC's of Novell Netware
Jeff Woodward
282pp. Ref. 614-6

For users who are new to PC's or networks, this entry-level tutorial outlines each basic element and operation of Novell. The ABC's introduces computer hardware and software, DOS, network organization and security, and printing and communicating over the netware system.

Mastering Novell Netware
Cheryl C. Currid
Craig A. Gillett
500pp. Ref. 630-8

This book is a thorough guide for System Administrators to installing and operating a microcomputer network using Novell Netware. Mastering covers actually setting up a network from start to finish, design, administration, maintenance, and troubleshooting.

TO JOIN THE SYBEX MAILING LIST OR ORDER BOOKS
PLEASE COMPLETE THIS FORM

NAME _____ COMPANY _____

STREET _____ CITY _____

STATE _____ ZIP _____

☐ PLEASE MAIL ME MORE INFORMATION ABOUT **SYBEX** TITLES

ORDER FORM (There is no obligation to order)

PLEASE SEND ME THE FOLLOWING:

TITLE	QTY	PRICE
_____	____	____
_____	____	____
_____	____	____
_____	____	____

TOTAL BOOK ORDER ____ $____

CUSTOMER SIGNATURE _____

SHIPPING AND HANDLING PLEASE ADD $2.00
PER BOOK VIA UPS _____

FOR OVERSEAS SURFACE ADD $5.25 PER
BOOK PLUS $4.40 REGISTRATION FEE _____

FOR OVERSEAS AIRMAIL ADD $18.25 PER
BOOK PLUS $4.40 REGISTRATION FEE _____

CALIFORNIA RESIDENTS PLEASE ADD
APPLICABLE SALES TAX _____

TOTAL AMOUNT PAYABLE _____

☐ CHECK ENCLOSED   ☐ VISA
☐ MASTERCARD   ☐ AMERICAN EXPRESS

ACCOUNT NUMBER _____

EXPIR. DATE _____ DAYTIME PHONE _____

CHECK AREA OF COMPUTER INTEREST:

☐ BUSINESS SOFTWARE

☐ TECHNICAL PROGRAMMING

☐ OTHER: _____

THE FACTOR THAT WAS MOST IMPORTANT IN YOUR SELECTION:

☐ THE SYBEX NAME

☐ QUALITY

☐ PRICE

☐ EXTRA FEATURES

☐ COMPREHENSIVENESS

☐ CLEAR WRITING

☐ OTHER _____

OTHER COMPUTER TITLES YOU WOULD LIKE TO SEE IN PRINT:

_____

_____

OCCUPATION

☐ PROGRAMMER   ☐ TEACHER

☐ SENIOR EXECUTIVE   ☐ HOMEMAKER

☐ COMPUTER CONSULTANT ☐ RETIRED

☐ SUPERVISOR   ☐ STUDENT

☐ MIDDLE MANAGEMENT   ☐ OTHER:

☐ ENGINEER/TECHNICAL   _____

☐ CLERICAL/SERVICE

☐ BUSINESS OWNER/SELF EMPLOYED

CHECK YOUR LEVEL OF COMPUTER USE

☐ NEW TO COMPUTERS

☐ INFREQUENT COMPUTER USER

☐ FREQUENT USER OF ONE SOFTWARE

  PACKAGE:

  NAME _____

☐ FREQUENT USER OF MANY SOFTWARE

  PACKAGES

☐ PROFESSIONAL PROGRAMMER

OTHER COMMENTS:

_____

_____

_____

_____

_____

_____

_____

_____

PLEASE FOLD, SEAL, AND MAIL TO SYBEX

SYBEX, INC.

2021 CHALLENGER DR. #100

ALAMEDA, CALIFORNIA USA

              94501

General POST Error Codes

Code	Device That Failed the POST
02x	Power supply
1xx	Motherboard
2xx	Memory (specific location also listed)
3xx	Keyboard (specific key may also be listed)
4xx	Monochrome video
5xx	Color Graphics Adapter (CGA) video
6xx	Floppy drive
7xx	Math coprocessor
9xx	Printer adapter card
10xx	Secondary printer adapter card
11xx	Serial (RS-232) adapter card
12xx	Secondary serial adapter card
13xx	Game, A/D, controller card
14xx	IBM graphics printer
15xx	Synchronous Data Link Control (SDLC) communications
17xx	Hard drive
18xx	Expansion unit
20xx	Binary Synchronous Communications (BSC) adapter
21xx	Alternate BSC adapter
22xx	Cluster adapter
24xx	Enhanced Graphics Adapter (EGA) video
25xx	Secondary EGA video
28xx	PC/XT 3278/79 emulation adapter
29xx	IBM color graphics printer
30xx	Network adapter
31xx	Secondary network adapter
33xx	IBM compact printer
36xx	IEEE 488 adapter
38xx	Data acquisition adapter
39xx	Professional Graphics Adapter (PGA) video
48xx	Internal modem
49xx	Alternate internal modem
71xx	Voice communications
73xx	3 1/2-inch external drive
74xx	Video Graphics Array (VGA) video
85xx	IBM expanded memory adapter
86xx	PS/2 mouse or pointing device
100xx	PS/2 multiprotocol adapter
104xx	PS/2 ESDI hard drive